Ingredients of this picture:
Camera and film
Tripod
Sunrise time and azimuth data (Ditto moonrise – see Sec 9)
Reliable four-wheel drive off-roader positioned at 24°30'N, 04°15'E

The third edition of *Off-roader driving*, revised, re-titled

Published by Desert Winds

Four-by-four driving

Tom Sheppard

Published by

Desert Winds Publishing, 44 Salusbury Lane, Hertfordshire SG5 3EG, England
Written, designed and produced by Tom Sheppard, MBE
Copyright Tom Sheppard 2006

First published as *Off-roader driving* 1999, Edn 1.2 2005. This book September 2006

10 digit :	ISBN 0-9532324-3-3
13 digit with effect from Jan 2007:	ISBN 978-0-9532324-3-7

Photography

Grateful thanks and acknowledgement for corporate PR, or purchased, photography on the Section pages indicated:
Land Rover: 0.6, 0.8, 0.18, 1.9, 2.5, 2.9, 4.12, 4.39, 4.40(2), 4.41, 4.43, 5.13, 6.11, 7.12, 7.19. Jeep: 0.6, 0.13, 1.6, 2.7, 2.8(2), 2.20, 2.23, 4.21, 4.36, 7.26. Nissan: 0.7, 0.14, 1.11, 2.5, 2.13, 3.3, 3.9, 3.10, 8.2. Toyota: 0.9, 1.3, 1.9, 4.31, 7.16. Mitsubishi: 0.16, 8.2, 4.39. Honda: 0.5, 2.3. Kia: 4.8, 4.42. Mercedes-Benz: 0.12, 2.17. Suzuki: 0.8, 1.3. Daihatsu: 0.8. Hummer: 0.10. Subaru: 0.11. Vauxhall: 0.9. VW: 2.3. Michelin: 8.9(6). First Need: 7.33. Toby Savage: 8.4(2). Simon Herd: 7.10.

And courtesy photographs kindly supplied by: Autocar: 3.9. Roger Crathorne: 4.25. Mike Hallett: 5.11.

Remaining 189 photographs by Tom Sheppard.

Author's acknowledgments

This book has evolved from the first two editions of *The Land Rover Experience* with some influence from the three years' work on *Vehicle-dependent Expedition Guide.* And two editions of *Off-roader driving.* For their invaluable assistance with those books – and with bits of this one – I would like to express grateful thanks to:
Chrysler-Jeep UK (Steve Rose, Barry Stallard), BP-Castrol (Elspeth Barley), ExxonMobil (Dr Mike Wharton and Robin Gregory), Fortune Promoseven, Dubai (Matt Jones and family), Fresh Tracks (Daniel Collins), Ib Kidde-Hansen, Michelin Tyres (Alan Baxter, Jeremy Wheeler), John Nowell (Dubai), Paul O'Connor, Geoff Renner, Superwinch (Terry Mason).
At Land Rover: John Carter, Bob Dillon, Neil Doswell, Colin Hill, Phil Jones, Tony Northway (Dubai). And of course, Roger Crathorne.
The pre-distillation analysis for Sec 4.1 (On-road towing) was particularly demanding and special thanks go to Brian Bevan (The Motor Industry Research Association and IMechE paper C132/83), Professor Robin Sharp (Cranfield University), and Malcolm Burgess (Land Rover) for their help.

It's hard to know who to thank for the inspiration and breathtaking beauty of the remote regions of Algeria, Botswana, Libya, Mali, Namibia, Oman, South Africa, the United Arab Emirates and Zimbabwe portrayed here photographically.
.
And there would be no book at all without the design engineers of the best 4x4s plus the typically unsung wizards at Canon Cameras and digital technorati at Apple Computer, QuarkXpress, Adobe (Photoshop and Illustrator) software. Heroes all; may they prosper, sup wine and peel grapes to a contented old age.

Contents:

READ ME FIRST

SECTION 1. THE INGREDIENTS

SECTION 2. FOUR-WHEEL DRIVE SYSTEMS

Contents

SECTION 5. RECOVERY

SECTION 6. ADVANCED DRIVING

Contents

SECTION 7. EXPEDITION BASICS

SECTION 8. LOADING, TYRES

SECTION 9. REFERENCE

This book ...

First-timers, macho men, busy mums. This book is aimed at first-time four-by-four drivers and fleet users alike – a wide span of folk who have a surprising amount in common. Whether you are tip-toeing into the water or working hard at the deep end, it helps in both cases to know, or be reminded of, the principles of swimming. Since the standard licence test doesn't cover much cross-country driving, there's quite a bit on that here but the book also has much to make on-roaders nod and smile and feel enlightened.

Know what you are buying. The aim of the book is to distil the essence of what makes 'four-by-fours' different from normal cars and how to take best advantage of it – there's more to it than just the height and weight of the vehicle. With the Catherine-wheel of fancy trade names, bloated styling, mock bull-bars, side-rails, extravagant wheels and electronic tinsel, those restless marketing people have to maintain the illusion of something new – and, naturally, more complicated. This book keeps a steady eye on the fundamentals all the time and points out in the friendliest way what isn't particularly new, tries to explain what it is really all about and distinguishes between essentials and confectionery.

Wide, blurred market. The 4x4 market now covers a wide span of application. Increasingly manufacturers recognise the benefits of sharing the power between all four wheels, even on small, decidedly on-road cars. Nor, despite the band-wagonners pointing accusing fingers at 'non-politically correct 4x4s', does it take much to differentiate between what is needlessly heavy and thirsty for the job it does and a modest, fuel-efficient vehicle that just happens to benefit from four-wheel drive. But there are, of course, people who do need a highly capable off-road performer for which four-wheel drive is just the first weapon in the armoury.

4x4 systems. Is your 4x4 actually in four-wheel drive all the time? If not, why not and how is it engaged? (Yes, it does help to know even if you just go to the supermarket.) Can you use 4x4 anywhere? Do you actually need it on the highway? What about the 'little gear lever' or the twisty knob? Amazingly, many magazine 'road tests' ignore these points – as do some manufacturers' presentations; comment about the plastics, the cup holders, the glove box light or the stitching on the upholstery often leave no space for the fundamentals.

But I never go off-road ... ! Does the 4x4 system actually matter? Do I need to know? Yes; it really does help. Despite all the fancy trade names like Supa-Tork or Megga-Grip and nonsense about 'directing the torque to the wheel that most needs it ... ' there are only three basic types of 4x4 and, as Sec 2.1 shows, the concepts are very simple.

... and I do (go off-road)! The off-road techniques outlined in this book will help you realise the fullest potential of your off-roader. They'll make your driving as safe and relaxed as possible, ensure that in difficult conditions you get stuck as infrequently as possible, hazard your vehicle as little as possible and that you damage it not at all.

Using the book. You will not carry all of this book in your head. Reading it, you will not only get to know the strengths and limitations of your vehicle but you will learn how to read the ground and apply the variations of technique you will encounter. Soon it will be instinctive; you will have written your own book.

This book ...

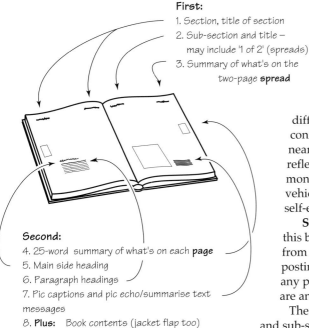

First:
1. Section, title of section
2. Sub-section and title – may include '1 of 2' (spreads)
3. Summary of what's on the two-page **spread**

Second:
4. 25-word summary of what's on each **page**
5. Main side heading
6. Paragraph headings
7. Pic captions and pic echo/summarise text messages
8. **Plus:** Book contents (jacket flap too)
   Section contents
   Index

Manual and automatic transmission. Because manual transmissions require more detailed description, the emphasis in this book should not be interpreted as favouring that technology. Automatic transmission has considerable advantages; used on- or off-road, it is very driver- and vehicle-friendly. A well-matched engine and gearbox driveline is a dream to use, especially off-road.

Additive experience. Many readers will already have experience in off-road operation and have developed their own techniques of doing things differing slightly from advice here. In the preparation of this book it was found that such inputs were usually suited to subtly different conditions, and were not conflicts of method. Experience was nearly always additive rather than reflecting opposite views. Given common aims of safety and care of the vehicle the best course was usually self-evident.

Signposting. Not many will read this book from cover to cover; or even from the front. So easy access and signposting has been one of the aims. Open any page and you will know where you are and what is under discussion.

The book is broken down into Sections and sub-sections. Coverage of the section – eg Sec 2.3 – is also summarised on the title page of that section.

The diagram (left) summarises the signposting. Some terms used in the book may be new to you and a glossary (Sec 9.1) gives some insight into how things work.

And the new title? If you knew the previous books titled *Off-roader driving* you may be wondering about the new name on the cover. As you go through the book you will see why. There was a time when 4x4 and 'off-roader' were interchangeable terms but as mentioned opposite there's been a lot of blurring. Some 4x4s today are built like the Forth Bridge, others sensibly have four-wheel drive but, just as sensibly, would not stray off the road. Just take a look at these two ...
.

Fundamentals

The environment

Opposite extremes. Pared-down off-road functionality and a luxury carriage that won't get too bogged down on a beach.

Philosophy

The hard stuff

On/off-road vehicles are here to stay. Industry, civil engineering, the emergency services, the overseas relief agencies, agriculture and the defence Services would be severely handicapped and in some cases totally incapacitated without them. In many overseas regions such vehicles are often the only means of maintaining point-to-point

land communications and transport.

New usage

And in the developed countries they have, in addition, found a niche in the automotive marketplace among those warming to their capabilities as being the most practical of family hold-alls and maids of all work – the kind of vehicle that can tow a canoe-trailer to a mountain lake or do the school run and return with four children, a wet dog, a lawn mower and four sacks of compost picked up en route. As a bonus, these vehicles are also enormous fun to drive.

Special responsibilities

But the very popularity and versatility of the larger, off-road-capable vehicles confers on us, as operators, users, and owners, a special responsibility towards the environment in which we live and they, newly, can

operate. The engineers and legislators continue their work in the pursuit of clean air; the latest diesels and catalyst-equipped petrol engines minimise atmospheric pollution.

Pity the legislators

The legislators, particularly, have a hard time and do a difficult and unpopular job. To cries of horror from industry they must assess what is achievable and level the playing field so that all manufacturers meet the same standards and we all benefit.

Tread lightly

More locally and within our own sphere of influence as users, we must also be certain not lastingly to damage

'Be certain not to damage the ground we drive on – especially vulnerable when wet.'

the ground we drive on when off-road – especially vulnerable when wet. In so far as many of them will be new to the capabilities of their vehicles, recreational users must be especially aware of their responsibilities. There are currently many miles of off-highway road open to the public around the world. In recent years ever-growing numbers of off-road enthusiasts have increased the potential for damage to vegetation, soil, water, wildlife and the solitude afforded by these areas.

All users of vehicles with an off-road capability will wish to familiarise themselves with environmental principles.

The Americans, who have a way with words, coined the

Idyllic setting for off-roader use. Well-drained chalk track and dry grass obviate any environmental damage here. One of a select group of 4x4s that, like the Range Rover, Discovery and Land Cruiser, combine comfort with ultimate functionality, Nissan's formidable Patrol adds simplicity of operation to its credentials.

phrase 'Tread lightly' to encapsulate the sensitive approach to the use of off-roaders on fragile landscapes that are prone to damage or erosion.

Torque gently

'Torque gently', more specifically, conveys both an exhortation to drive with a gentle right foot on the throttle (or brake) – as well as the implied suggestion also to 'talk gently' and not indulge in inappropriately 'macho' antics in our powerful machines.

Following the dual meaning will preserve both our vehicles and our environment for the future enjoyment of ourselves and others. Few, if any – deep down – could disagree with such a philosophy.

Practicalities

And few, applying little more than common sense and good manners, would not come up with the following list of practical points to remember when operating away from tarmac roads:

People and wildlife

• Allow wildlife priority over your own progress.
• Domestic animals too, especially horses and ponies, may be unused to the presence of vehicles in remote areas. Accommodate their nervousness; switch off and wait if necessary.
• Sheep that have strayed onto a track often run ahead of a vehicle rather than leaving the roadway. Be patient. Stop and let them disperse or pull over to let them by.
• Gamebirds and other wildlife often soak up the warmth of tarmac by sitting in the middle of country lanes or other clearings. Your vehicle may panic them into running across your path rather

than away from you – their rationale is to return to where they were before the danger appeared. Be prepared for this – and for the last minute appearance of a second or third bird from the hedgerow.

• Animals are often dazzled by headlights and may be unable to get away from the danger. Be aware of this; drive with extra care on unfenced lanes or open tracks. And that really does mean driving slowly.

• Be especially courteous and considerate towards walkers or riders – especially in remote areas. Like it or not, you have an ambassadorial role to play and inevitably, arriving in a comfortable off-road vehicle whilst others are progressing 'the hard way', you will, to a degree, be perceived in the idle villain's role!

• Always respect the privacy of other people; not always easy to assess, but many go to remote areas to savour the peace and solitude.

> **'Caring for the environment is far more important than the current fashion it may seem.'**

Access

• It is essential to be certain of your right of access to tracks and wild areas. At the time of writing new legislation is being promoted to limit even further the rights of access of motorised vehicles to 'green lanes'. (The good news is the growth of off-road driving schools and recreational practise areas.)

• A road marked on a map does not automatically confer a right of way. If in any doubt at all, ask or refer to a highly detailed map such as, in the UK, one of the OS 1:25,000 series.

• Access rights to land for vehicles varies from country to country. Make

There's a growth in off-road practise and fun courses to make up for restrictions in off road use around UK. Discerning structural engineers will be pleased to know this bridge is not reliant on the rope to prevent collapse – but it does lend atmosphere.

yourself aware of the appropriate regulations for the country in which you are driving. Developed, highly populated or densely legislated countries usually have complex regulations. See Sec 7.1 for an overview of UK access rights.

• Observe the Country Code – an encapsulation of common sense – whatever country you are in. Close gates you have opened.

Erosion

Four-wheel drive vehicles can contribute enormously to erosion when carelessly used off-road. Guidelines to minimise damage:

• New ruts form rain channels which cause erosion – especially where surface vegetation such as grass has been

Ideal for the parachutes, parkas and packed lunches, Mitsubishi's L200 has always taken a large slice of the UK pick-up market. Probably running higher tyre pressures than the Beaver, neither will damage the firm landing ground.

'Litter ... wherever you are, leave *nothing.'*

scraped away by spinning wheels. So keep off soft ground if possible – sinkage causes ruts.

• Do not spin your wheels on grass.

• Where a track exists, stick to it. Your wheel tracks away from it can tempt others to do the same and a another swathe of land can be spoiled.

• When travelling over open meadows with two or more vehicles, do not follow in each others' tracks. This precludes the forming of damaging ruts.

• Be doubly cautious when using mud tyres. Ideally they should be used only when deep mud is envisaged; they can quickly damage other ground.

• Use designated areas for training.

Litter

• Never leave litter under any circumstances – matchsticks, teabags, food wrapping, tins, bottles, anything plastic. Wherever you are, leave *nothing.*

• Take back what you brought with you.

Polishing your halo

Observing all the recommendations above will seem impossibly onerous the first time you read them. The second time you read them you will see just how much common sense and simple courtesy is involved. The third time (and this may be a little later), you will start realising that this is what you actually do and will feel good about it.

Caring for the environment is far more important than the current fashion it may seem. We all share humankind's newly realised responsibility. Enjoy your driving!

Tourist litter. It won't go away. Wherever you are, leave nothing.

Section 1

The ingredients

1.1 The appeal

Why buy – the appeal

The chicken and the egg. This sub-section could be – if you already have your 4x4 – preaching to the converted. Or it could be providing a welcome rationale for one of those heart versus the head situations that plague you when trying to decide on or justify a purchase that you want to make anyway. Why do people buy 4x4s? The American flair for the neat phrase has dubbed them SUVs – sport-utility vehicles – which sums up their appeal and uses very well. It may be, however, that you are trying to take a cool look at the reasons people buy these vehicles that everyone seems to want and, possibly a different list, also look at what they do actually offer.

The appeal. Part of it undoubtedly is the 'Tonka-toy syndrome'. Driving a big truck, flying a large aircraft, driving a 4x4 – if you have been to your dealership and just driven round the block you will recognise the instant subjective appeal of even a small 4x4. To this you can add further, more practical, advantages to come up with your initial, day-to-day benefits list that starts to look like this:

- High-up, 'command' driving position.
- View over all other traffic.
- Feeling of security and strength.
- At last the ability to take all the kids on the school run *and* their bags *and* the shopping, *and* the wet dog *and* leave the mower at the place who'll fix it.

There's more – a lot more. The list above is what you could use every day, be it a four-wheel drive or a large two-wheel drive estate. But in most off-roaders there is more than this. The 'four-wheel drive-ness' of the vehicle – putting power through all four wheels instead of just two – has benefits on-

Buy-appeal lies in high-up driving position, the feeling of security and carry-all capability. This would apply in two-wheel drive. In 4x4 there's a lot more.

road and, together with other attributes we'll examine later, irreplaceable benefits off-road. An incidental benefit of the high-up driving position is that it is usually associated with a low waist-line so the feeling of spaciousness is enhanced too.

'Soft roaders' – blurring the edges. But there is a burgeoning sub-class of 4x4s now, one that is maturing and addresses those with few, if any, off-road aspirations in giant all-terrain capability vehicles. These buyers, often of medium or small 4x4s – a class of vehicle sitting in the same territory as a modest estate or medium sized MPV – are seeking a capacious, taller vehicle with easy access, a good-visibility driving position and, above all, the ability of a 4x4 to cope with traction-hungry surfaces like snow, ice or wet grass. These are the 'soft roaders', usually without low range gears (see p 1.11) and technically far more sophisticated than before.

On-road

What you get with 4x4. You get some of the points mentioned on the left – the feeling of security and huge carrying capacity – with some large estate cars and other vehicles. But putting the engine power through all four wheels – either:

- all the time,
- when selected, or
- 'automatically' (ie when sensors decide you need it) –

will also give you grip when you wouldn't otherwise have it. (The different generic types of four-wheel drive are dealt with a few pages on in Section 2.1 – it does help to know what they are.)

Getting a grip. Subliminally you already know what the next list is going to contain – those situations that take you a little by surprise and make you uneasy at the wheel regarding road grip. You'll nod seeing:

- Wet, 'greasy' corners.
- Wet autumn leaves on corners.
- Tree-shaded, north-facing corners where the frost hangs on.
- Country corners to which a blind gate has just discharged a muddy tractor.

All sizes. Compact 5-door Grand Vitara (upper left) still has full off-road capability. Colorado offers more space and elevation. Double-cab 4x4 pick-ups are practical workers: hay, oil drums, people ; hugely popular in South Africa for bush camping.

And of course:
• Packed snow.
• Snow or ice in the gutters or verges that allow one wheel to spin.
Having all four wheels handling the power in these situations – and wheel-spin inhibited too – is going to make things that little bit easier and safer.

Off-road

No contest. In the context of off-road operations the rationale for 4x4 provides its own answer and opens huge vistas of capability, and enjoyment, for professional and recreational use. The needs of public utilities, armed forces, farmers, civil engineers and in recent years the sheer enjoyment that off-roaders' capabilities bring, ensures the widest application of designers' ingenuity in achieving off-road performance.

Horses for courses. However, as with most other commodities, you will find vehicles built for specific sectors of the market – built down to a price, up to a capability target, to this or that level of comfort and interior luxury. Know about this. Look beyond the shallow technophobic brochures lovingly depicting the bottle-holders and upholstery pattern; look at the basics of the concept and what a vehicle is really designed to be capable of. And you'll know of the irrational, paradoxical specifications where the ultimate in luxury has been combined with the ultimate in off-road performance. It sells but it may not be for you.

Within the limits. Because you may need most guidance on this, utilising this off-road aspect of off-roaders' performance safely and keeping within their limits forms the major part of this book.

In permanent 4x4, take-you-by-surprise grip situations are licked at any time. But a vehicle's design purpose can lean either toward on- or off-road use. See next.

1.2 The compromises

Compromises?

Real life. Get used to the idea that there are potential compromises involved in making an off-roader suitable for both on- and off-road conditions. The requirements are different and the machinery is different. This will not be news to you but whilst the laws of physics cannot be denied, designers get better and better at giving them a good run for their money. Where cost is less of an issue and the engineers are given a free rein, remarkably high standards of on-road and off-road performance can be achieved. Elsewhere, the mix of vehicle characteristics, of course, can be optimised in either direction – towards on-road or towards off-road.

Problems and solutions. An example: 'Ride vs handling' is the age-old problem for saloon car designers wanting to make their product softly sprung and comfortable and at the same time corner flat as if on rails. The two aims are usually conflicting in design and layout requirements but not even competitors would be deny that Jaguar's reputation for combining the qualities in their sports saloons is close to the best.

Off-roaders are a battleground for conflicting design requirements – mostly concerning suspension movement. Off-road you need lots, which can yield on-road roll.

Handling

The off-roader problem. By definition, off-road obstacles tend to be big and uneven so that an off-roader needs ground clearance (big wheels, inevitably) and lots of up-and-down wheel travel – usually axle movement and long-travel road springs. It is not too difficult to arrive at something like this on your drawing board but it gets to be tall since ground clearance *and* lots of wheel travel add up to that. Tall vehicles with plenty of axle movement tend to lean over a lot on corners and handle oddly. Body roll is the term you have heard; linguistically extravagant but it gets the idea across.

Body roll and unsprung weight. Big wheels for best ground clearance together with long wheel travel so the wheels can ride over large bumps amount to a tall vehicle with a high centre of gravity; add softish springing for a decent ride. Turn it sharply and it tends to lean out of the turn. (We'll see about anti-roll bars in a minute or two – they do limit roll but also limit axle movement relative to the body and that's bad off-road.) Large wheels on the end of beam axles give good ground clearance over obstacles but also amount to high 'unsprung weight' – ie the bit of the vehicle on the bottom of the springs.

(*Unsprung weight?* If you think about it,

Narrowing the gap between on- and off-road optimisation. Nissan's Patrol has a disconnectable rear anti-roll bar to unleash formidable wheel movement when off-road. On-road the re-connected anti-roll bar minimises body roll.

The more the luxury, the fewer the workhorse attributes. The better the on-road handling, the less the off-road benefits – usually. No brochure will admit to where its product lies on diagrams like these or admit to any compromises but they do show what the designer is up against and how ingenious some of them are in conquering both ends of the scale at the same time. Complexity is usually the price paid when edging off-road workhorses up and to the left.

The usual trade-offs – handling, drivability

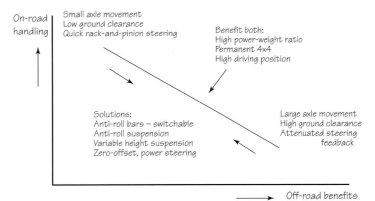

The compromises – function

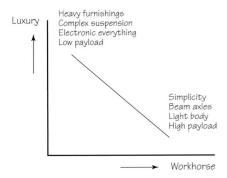

braking and road-holding.

Independent front end. Many off-roaders have independent front suspension with coil springs to reduce unsprung weight but it usually costs them under-axle obstacle clearance off-road.

Make allowances. So a great tough off-roader will not always handle, ride or corner like a top-flight luxury saloon. Handling, ride and cornering are where you must look out for compromises and be prepared to make allowances when you buy an off-roader or SUV.

Performance

Weight, power-weight ratio. The size and toughness of an off-road vehicle means it is usually a lot heavier than an on-road car. This will take its toll in road performance, fuel consumption and, since power-weight ratio is involved, acceleration too. Designers put large engines in off-roaders to raise the power-weight ratio and recover lost road performance but performance at the fuel pumps is the price paid.

Happy medium. Many will find, after trying alternatives, that road-burning performance is something they don't always need and that a mid-range diesel gives them quite enough punch to keep them happy. Probably more important, it is very much more economical than a hefty petrol engine.

there is vehicle attached to the top of the road springs – that's the engine and the bit with the passengers in it – and there is part of the vehicle attached to the bottom of the springs – the wheels and most of the axle too. That bottom bit is the unsprung weight and rides directly on the ground.)

The higher this unsprung weight the more difficult it is to get a smooth ride for the body and passengers. If the springs are multi-leaf leaf-springs (unkindly but appositely referred to as 'cart springs') then they are less responsive than coils to small road irregularities and the ride is even worse.

The best saloon cars have lightweight unsprung components so they can follow the contour of the road with least inertia, staying more constantly in contact with it and thus, as well as giving a smooth ride, also yielding the best grip and therefore

Unsprung weight – beam axles etc – give off-roaders less silky on-road ride but those same axles provide the good ground clearance needed in the rough.

Jeep Grand Cherokee, like many manufacturers' top-of-the-range products, addresses the often conflicting compromises of on- and off-road operation. It also offers (see p 2.8) a range of driveline specifications for different off-road conditions.

PAYLOAD, POWER-WEIGHT RATIO CRITERIA RANDOM SNAPSHOT

Payload kg**	Vehicle	Payload as % of GVW	GVW kg	BHP per tonne of GVW
334	Honda CR-V 2.0L auto	17	1900	66.32
315	Toyota RAV4 3dr	20	1565	80.51
345	Jeep Wrangler TJ 2.5 L	18	1925	60.78
447	Ford Explorer	18	2530	79.23
455	Vitara 2.0D 5dr	23	1945	35.98
486	Freelander petrol	26	1900	62.28
560	Range Rover 4.6 L	20	2780	79.49
565	Toyota Landcruiser VX	19	2960	56.75
589	Nissan Patrol GR 2.8 TDi 5dr	20	2920	43.89
585	Toyota Colorado TD 5dr	22	2680	45.89
590	Jeep Cherokee 2.5TD	26	2230	51.12
598	Frontera Sport 2.5TD	24	2510	45.82
603	Frontera Estate 2.5TD	23	2600	44.23
620	Shogun 3.0V6 5dr	23	2650	65.66
630	Nissan Terrano II 2.7TD 5dr	24	2580	47.77
635	Shogun 2.8TD 5dr	23	2720	45.22
640	Discovery Tdi 5dr	24	2720	40.80
660	Defender 90 HT, 2.5Tdi	28	2400	46.25
665	Range Rover 2.5D	24	2780	48.20
676	Daihatsu Fourtrak TDL 2.7TD	27	2510	40.07
694	Mercedes ML320	25	2727	78.84
700	Shogun 2.5TD 3dr	28	2510	39.04
705	Ford Maverick 2.7D 5dr	22	2655	47.67
715	Toyota Colorado TD 3dr	28	2510	49.00
755	Toyota Hilux DC PU 2.5D	30	2515	31.01
800	Defender 90 HT Tdi HD	31	2550	43.51
834	Ford Expedition (US)	26	3243	70.90
1030	Defender 110 SW Tdi	34	3050	36.39
1139	Defender 110 HiCap PU	37	3050	36.39
1414	Defender 130 DC PU Tdi	40	3500	31.71
1425	Pinzgauer 4x4 (soft top)	37	3850	29.87
1925	Pinzgauer 6x6 (soft top)	40	4850	23.71

Concept – luxury vs workhorse

Overview. Few salesmen are likely to admit, even-handedly, where the product lies in the grand scale of luxury vs workhorse concept – ie where the compromises lie and to what extent. All will portray comfort levels as luxurious, space as huge, off-road capability as Godzilla-like and on-road performance as lithe, smooth, crisp and rapid. Some of these values are a matter of personal priorities but, if you want an off-road workhorse, then additional to the all-important driveline spec, keep an eye on:

- Total payload additional to driver
- Payload as a proportion of gross vehicle weight
- Power-weight ratio – BHP per tonne of gross weight
- Low-ratio transfer gearbox?

These are some of the attributes that tend to suffer as a vehicle is biased toward the luxury end of the scale. Some typical last-decade vehicles are listed in the next column to give you a perspective.

Clever design. Advances have been made in reconciling the on- and off-road design demands but be sure you know:

- There really are difficulties to be overcome – luxury vs workhorse
- What you want of your vehicle
- Where you want it to sit (or where your current vehicle sits), on the either/or see-saw.

If compromises are inevitable, know what you want on the either/or see-saw. Seeking smooth ride (soft springs) luxo-barges often have feeble payload.

Notes:
All the above are 4x4
**'EC kerb weight' = empty vehicle plus driver plus full fuel tank. This has been used and manufacturers' data adjusted where necessary in all the above figures. 'Payload' thus represents what extra the vehicle (with driver) can carry.
DC = double cab on pick-up
PU = pick-up
HT = hard top
TD = turbo diesel
D = diesel
3dr = 3-door, generally shorter wheelbase
HD = heavy-duty springs
SW = station wagon
Tdi = Land Rover 2.5 litre turbo diesel

The perfect 4x4 transmission – principles preview!

As we have a spare right-hand page, let's divulge Leonardo da Vinci's perfect 4x4 system (perhaps it wasn't him but it was someone with similarly bright ideas – possibly Leonardo di Caprio?) The next sections will make more sense if you sneak a look at this in advance ...

Phase 1. The perfect system. All wheels geared (or chained) to each other. If one, two or three wheels go over icy patches there's no problem or wheel spin. The other wheel will continue to give traction – since all the wheels are geared together and go round at the same speed. Even the ones on the ice or mud won't be dead or braked; they'll be turning at the right speed. Eureka – the perfect system!

Solid axles

Phase 2. The compromised perfect system. Someone shot Phase 1's perfect system down in flames. They found it wouldn't go round corners properly – outside wheel travels further than the inside wheel. (They also found on a winding road the front wheels travel further than the back wheels.) Leonardo's friend had already invented differential gears. So borrow three and consider an axle being driven to rotate at 100 rpm. Split the axle, put a diff between the 'half-shafts' and now one wheel can go at 110 rpm whilst the other goes at 90 rpm – or any other split of rpm resulting from the **different loads** at each wheel. Now split the front axle too and fit a diff between the halves. And do it again where the drive splits to go to the front and rear prop shafts. That's three differentials – front and rear axles and one in the middle. Now it can go round corners. Eureka Mk 2!

Split and add a differential here ....

... and here.

... and here ...

... lockable.

Phase 3. The modified, de-compromised, perfect system. They didn't see it coming but you did! The system now permits a natural rpm split between left and right wheels depending on the distance travelled (or load or grip) at each wheel. So differentials permitting these variations can also allow (oops!) one rear wheel (say) on a patch of ice to spin away to its heart's content while the other one stays still. The same thing can happen at the front and centre diffs. So they must be made 'limited slip' or manually lockable. Or some combination of the two such that excess spin will cause the diff to gradually stiffen and eventually lock. That's it; G-Wagen, '99 Grand Cherokee. **Eureka Mk 3!**

Phase 4. Bean-counters' modified, re-compromised, perfect system. It had to happen. Diffs are expensive, especially with locking systems subject to misuse and (horrors!) warranty claims. So a host of cheaper variations appeared, some eliminating front/rear 'hard gearing' altogether, others using 'soft' locks like viscous couplings. We're running out of space so check out the current, post-Leonardo, real-world situation at Sec 2.1 'Types of four-wheel drive'.

1.3 Why four-wheel drive

Halving the load

Terminology. It is worth an initial thought about what four-wheel drive or 4x4 really does do. Incidentally, '4x4' ('four-by-four') means there are four wheels, of which four are driven by the engine. So a normal car, be it front wheel drive or rear wheel drive, is a 4x2 'four-by-two' – four wheels in total, of which the car is driven by two. Some types of truck are referred to as a 6x4 – six (wheels driven) by four.

What it does – and doesn't – do. A 4x4 does not double the power on the road; it takes the power you do have and spreads it between four wheels instead of only two. If a vehicle needs a certain amount of push (tractive effort or traction) to make it go at a given speed or traverse a certain type of terrain, a 4x4, by having twice as many driven wheels as a 4x2, will actually halve the tractive load on a given piece of ground and thus greatly reduce the chance of spinning wheels under power. Four-wheel drive is thus a considerable benefit to effective operation and to safety all the time. (But be sure it *is* 4x4, not 4x2 with 4x4 that engages 'as required' – see 'Pseudo 4x4' at Sec 2.1.)

Off-road ingredients. If 4x4 is now combined with large wheels and large amounts of wheel movement on supple, well-damped springs, the ingredients of an effective off-road vehicle, capable of operating on rough uneven ground, are starting to take shape.

Doubling the effect

Maintaining traction. Thus if conditions are such that an ordinary 4x2 car driving only one pair of wheels could spin those wheels and lose traction, a 4x4 will actually be twice as effective in using the power of the engine to maintain traction.

4x4 doesn't double the power on the road but it does halve the ground stress compared with 4x2 so under power grip is better. But braking, of course, is the same.

Why 4x4? Here's why.

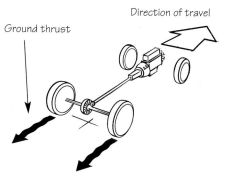

4x2 – all the power on two wheels. High ground stress. Wheels may slip or spin.

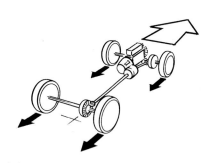

4x4 – same power spread between four wheels. Half the ground stress. Double the traction.

More from four. The diagrams sum this up. All over the world there are bits of ground – oily tarmac, icy roads, glazed snow, wet grassy fields – that will not support the tractive effort needed under certain conditions when power is put through one pair of wheels. Put that power through two axles – four wheels – thus halving the traction required of each wheel, and your 4x4 is likely to get you through, securely and under complete control. This, of course, is irrespective of the size of the vehicle.

Even 4x4s have limits. Of course conditions may be so bad or the traction required so high that even a 4x4 spins its wheels or needs lower gears. These occasions – usually offroad – are addressed later in the book but in general four-wheel drive enhances safety and effectiveness on- and off-road at all times. As we shall see, if you are driving any vehicle with permanent four-wheel drive then you are at a further advantage – always ready for the unexpected rather than having to assess the conditions and then select 4x4 with a separate control lever or wait for some 'automatic' selector to do it for you – *after* sensing incipient wheel-spin.

Vital to remember that whilst 4x4 solves slippery surface traction problems, braking is no different from 4x2 vehicles so have ABS or use cadence braking. (See Sec 3.2)

Traction from all four wheels is the overriding advantage of 4x4 when conditions are demanding. Pioneered by early Range Rovers and now featured on such vehicles as Discovery 3 (left) and Toyota's Amazon (top), both these vehicles have permanent four-wheel drive. Front wheels cover more distance in a turn (above) so as seen in 'Leonardo's' system on the previous spread, a centre differential is needed with this system – see Section 2.1.

1.4 Traction – 4x4 and low range

Typical 4x4 transmission

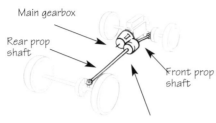

Main gearbox

Rear prop
shaft

Front prop
shaft

Transfer box transfers drive
from main gearbox to front
and rear propeller shafts –
usually with option of high-
and low-range.

Ingredients of traction

Pushing backwards and downwards.
With all this talk about traction, a quick look
at its real meaning – especially in the context
of 4x4 and the 'little gear lever' (or rotary
switch or button ...) for low range. You'll
have scanned the Leonardo system on page
1.7 so will know roughly what's coming.

Traction tends to be thought of as pull –
farm tractors pulling wagons. It's easier to
regard it as push – the bottom of the wheel
pushing against the surface of the ground to
move a vehicle forward. In perfect conditions of low rolling resistance and infinite
grip one-wheel drive would suffice. But
where roads can get wet and slippery and
where no-road conditions are muddy, four-
wheel drive means three wheels can still
push if one gets on a slippery patch.

Push with float – off-road. Away from
the perfect conditions of one-wheel drive,
the real world, off-road especially, is often
soft as well as slippery. Spreading the
weight over a bigger 'footprint' helps prevent sinkage. Big wheels have a bigger
ground footprint than small ones and this
footprint can be enlarged still further in
emergency conditions by letting tyres down

*Traction is
enhanced by
four-wheel drive
on all surfaces,
but other half of
the equation, off-
road, is flotation
– big wheels, big
tyres and, when
needed, low tyre
pressures.*

a little. (There are important speed and safety implications to this – see Section 4.7.) In
addition, big wheels give a smoother ride
over rough ground.

Big wheels? Watch the tyres. A word of
caution. Big diameter 'styled' wheel rims
(18-22 inches) are usually constrained by the
designers to have the same overall diameter
– including tyre – as a 16 inch rim on standard tyres. They are usually therefore fitted
with low profile tyres which are less suitable
for off-road use – see Sec 8.2.

Ground clearance. As we have seen,
large overall wheel diameters also ensure
greater ground clearance over obstacles.
Beam axles keep this ground clearance constant – unlike most independently sprung
front ends – and keep the tyres' tread always
flat on the ground. If your usage is biased to
off-road, beam axles are usually best.

**Grip and gradient – enemies of trac-
tion.** If poor grip can be overcome by driving four wheels instead of one or two and
also benefit from bigger wheels, the other
enemy of traction is gradient – uneven surfaces, steep hills (or heavy loads up not-so-
steep hills). The extra traction you need for
this – 'power', or more accurately, torque –
can come from additional low gears: the
other half of the traction equation – see
below.

The ingredients. So the ingredients of
traction, especially off-road, are:
- Drive to all four wheels
- Big footprint wheels
- Under-axle, under-belly clearance
- 'Power' (torque) – see next.

Extra gears – low range

Lower gearing. Extra-low gears are
available on most – but these days not all –
4x4s. They are not all in the same gearbox.
The transfer box on a 4x4 got its name
because it is what transfers power from the
normal gearbox to the rear axle *and* front
axle thus making it a 4x4. But this extra

Two-speed transfer gearbox – high and low ratio (range)

High range;
1:1 ratio

Low range
gears-down
the drive to
front and
rear prop
shafts

Output gear 'A'
(see differentials dia-
gram page 2.4)

transfer gearbox is what is on the other end of 'the little gear lever' on many 4x4s and is also a *two-speed* affair with a high and a low ratio. The small manual lever is the best way of controlling the transfer gearbox but often, for reasons of cost and easier cab design, manufacturers replace it by a rotating switch and electrical selection.

Doubling the number of gears. Not all 4x4s have a two-speed transfer box but, in those that do, it is a simple solution to providing extra torque through extra gears. It is 'downstream' of the main gearbox and by selecting low ratio it gears-down *all* the gears in the normal gearbox by a ratio of about 1:2 depending on manufacturer. In 'high' range the gears are unaffected. So your 4x4 has a transfer box to effect the four-wheel drive function and additionally to provide what amounts to a

complete set of very low gears so that five-speed box in effect becomes a 10-speed box. Making a single gearbox with ten forward speeds which could be successively selected would result in an expensive, heavy and complicated item.

Low ratio for heavy jobs. The 'low box' is selected for specific heavy duty tasks using as we shall see (Section 2.4).

Low ratio gears available when vehicle has two-speed transfer box – very useful off-road and towing boats out of the water. Not all 4x4s have this – see table at Section 2.1.

Classic application of the low-ratio range of gears afforded by a two-speed transfer box. Using low range drops the gear ratios of all gears in the main gearbox by around 2:1. Trying to move even this lightweight boat on soft ground in a vehicle lacking a low range would result in much clutch slipping, revs and sweaty palms. The low-ratio approach is calm, controlled; see Sec 2.4.

Section 2

Four-wheel drive systems

2.1 Types of four-wheel drive

Selectable, pseudo, permanent 4x4

Don't let them confuse you. This is the most important section of the book. Sweep away the blizzard of trade names – ActiveTrak, Control Trac, Selectrac, Super Select, Torque-on-Demand, All-Mode, 4-matic, xDrive and who knows how many more. There are only three generic types of 4x4 system and the next few pages are going to distil it all, plus all the twiddly bits. Whatever else you don't know about your 4x4 and driving it – you can ditch all the off-road driving stuff in this book if you want – *do* be clear what your 4x4 system is about.

All 4x4s are not the same. Technophobic sales persons, under-briefed brochure writers, too-busy engineers and gloss-over magazine 'experts' often combine to leave you confused about what really is going on. And media persons are all too ready to dismiss explanations as 'too technical' or 'unnecessary'. Wrong on both counts! It's surprisingly simple. (You've already got the gist of it from the diagrams here, haven't you ... ?)

Different approaches. Driving all four wheels all the time but in a way that accommodates the slight differences in distance travelled by left and right wheels, front axle and rear axle (desert picture, p 1.9), is the ideal. We saw this (p 1.7) with Leonardo's 'modified, de-compromised perfect system'! From the design-engineering point of view this is easy to achieve. The 'differentials' (see next spread) that allow the left wheel to go faster or slower than the right wheel have sat in the middle of a normal car's driven back axle for over a hundred years enabling the outside wheel to go further when it turns a corner and can just as easily be installed between the front and rear prop shafts of a four-wheel drive vehicle.

A centre differential adds expense and if you make 4x4 selectable – for use only when needed – then you can, at a push, do away with the centre diff. Some argue, shakily, that 4x4 uses more fuel so the facility *should*

'New developments' – beware the Emperor's New Clothes. There are some smart ideas but the basic categories – this page – remain the same.

4x4 systems – the three generic types

NB. Diagrams do not show low range

Type 1. Selectable 4x4

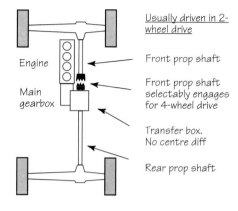

Engine

Main gearbox

Usually driven in 2-wheel drive

Front prop shaft

Front prop shaft selectably engages for 4-wheel drive

Transfer box. No centre diff

Rear prop shaft

Type 2. Pseudo (auto-engaged) 4x4

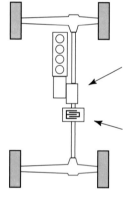

2-wheel drive most of the time

Transfer box. No centre diff. On 'soft roaders' usually no low range either.

Electrically actuated clutch (or other device). If front wheels spin, clutch locks up and brings in rear wheel drive too.

Type 3. Permanent 4x4

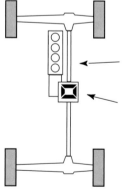

4-wheel drive all the time

Permanently connected prop shaft

Centre diff between front and rear prop shafts. Either:
1. Free and manually lockable, or
2. Controlled by viscous coupling

Typical of their Type. <u>Near right</u>, Type 1, selectable 4x4: Mercedes 461 G-Wagen (manually selected 4x4; also has low range gears and axle diff locks front and rear). <u>Far right</u>, Type 2, auto-engaged 'Pseudo 4x4': Nissan's XTrail, electrically engaged front/rear shafts clutch pack, no low range). <u>Bottom</u>, Type 3, permanent 4x4: VW Touareg (also has auto-locking centre diff, low range, traction control, selectably locking centre/rear diffs, optional front diff lock). Shown with air suspension raised, increasing ground clearance but reducing wheel travel and articulation (See Sec 3.3).

be used only when needed. The result is a bunch of different design philosophies which we'll call, for convenience only (these are not EU- or UN-sanctioned categories!) :

- Type 1. Selectable 4x4
- Type 2. 'Pseudo' (auto-engaged) 4x4
- Type 3. Permanent 4x4

Re-check the basics. Peek back again to page 1.7 which covers the whole 'Leonardo' progression from soap-box to 'bean-counter's modified, re-compromised, perfect 4x4 system'. Keep that in mind (and tongue in cheek) and all this modern stuff clunks into perspective; the trade-name disguises and TLAs (three letter acronyms), like the Emperor's New Clothes, fall away.

Don't forget low range. We're just looking at types of four-wheel drive at the moment so don't forget that all the above types may or may not be combined with a two-speed transfer gearbox. This, as we saw (diagram p 1.11), gears the final drive down by a factor of around two – in effect giving you a 'second set' of extra low gears for heavy duty towing, expeditions or sustained off-pavement operation such as undertaken by many civil engineers.

'Soft roaders'? This is a general usage term but briefly, such vehicles – with their unofficial and purely colloquial category – are designed to give owners the benefits of four-wheel drive traction and safety on snow, ice, wet grass and the like, but without the extra set of low range gears that would be required for really demanding off-road conditions. Most often their 4x4 system

'Soft roaders' – 4x2, with auto-engage 4x4 (no low range) have matured, proliferated and found their niche – ice, snow, wet grass and occasional respectable off-road forays.

'Auto-engaged 4x4' is a fool-proof way of providing 4x4 when required. It disengages at once when traction regained though there may be a manual override..

is Type 2: centre diagram, previous spread – a 'soft', auto-engage connection between front and rear prop shafts such as a viscous coupling or clutches with no centre differential (not a 'shafts and gears' connection). Market demographics being what they are, 'soft-roader' buyers are often not mechanical enthusiasts and manufacturers make the auto-engage systems as simple as possible – as well as (see opposite) taking the opportunity to include some very smart nannying.

The three types of four-wheel drive

Sort it out, once and for all. To make any kind of sensible choice of vehicles for an expedition and operate them properly – even if that 'expedition' is just a twice a week rural shopping run you really do need to know the 4x4 system. Hacking your way through the marketing obfuscation and sales staff gloss-over is the start. Take on board

first that there are really only three generic types of 4x4 system.

Four-wheel drive systems. The basics:

1. Selectable 4x4 . A four-wheel drive vehicle in which the shafting for the front axle drive remains disengaged from the gearbox until 4x4 is selected by the driver, usually by a lever in the cab, is deemed to have selectable 4x4 – see upper diagram overleaf (Type 1). When so selected, the front shaft and rear shaft are locked together and *always* turn at the same speed. There is no centre differential to allow slight differences in rotational speeds. This 'locked together' feature causes some 'fight' between front and rear axles (see also p 2.17) which would normally have small speed differences on corners. If you are off-road or on a loose surface this can be accommodated by small amounts of wheel slippage. On hard, dry surfaces, however, this cannot

---

FAMILIAR WITH DIFFERENTIALS? ... ER, YES, OF COURSE ...

The basic thing. We are so familiar with it that we seldom stop to think exactly what is going on in a diff. Only one pinion is shown here but there are usually two or four. The whole group of bevel gears is attached to the 'carrier' (not shown here) which is almost invariably another wheel which is itself driven to rotate – the gearwheel in the diagram on page

Principle

Gear-wheel 'A' (diagram p 1.11)

This whole group of bevel gears is contained within and revolves with the output gearwheel 'A' in diagram on page 1.11. Principle of 'differential' action: imagine gripping front shaft to slow it down; rear shaft would speed up.

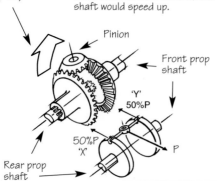

Pinion

Front prop shaft

'Y' 50%P

50%P 'X'

P

Rear prop shaft

1.11 marked 'A'. Think of the pinion as the little swivel bar in the diagram below. The differential takes the rotational 'power' (P) and passes it on to the two output shafts (two times 50%P) – be they front/rear prop shafts or the half-shafts of an axle. If the loads on each shaft are equal ('X' and 'Y' below) they will go at the same speed. When one (say 'X'), due to increased load slows down, the diff action (swivel bar) makes the other one ('Y') speed up. The most usual occurrence of this in transmissions is when one prop shaft (or one half of an axle), due to *reduction* in load or resistance to rotation (slippery mud or ice) spins. Then the other shaft stops: *voila* wheel spin on one wheel and the other one stationary.

Inhibiting wheel spin. What is done to stop or inhibit this wheel spin is to make some other connection between the two shafts which prevents excessive speed difference. (Having got your differential you now have to clip its wings!) This device can be:

1.Solid metal-to-metal diff lock. A sliding dog clutch between the two big bevel gears 'X' and 'Y' in the diagram. This is the principle of a simple manually operated diff lock.

2. Limited slip diff. This is a clutch or viscous coupling (see Glossary) between the gears 'X' and 'Y' that limits slip. A typical modern set-up is that the speed differences between the two shafts is electrically sensed and this actuates a multi-plate friction clutch to bind one shaft to the other and limit excessive slip. This system has the benefit of being highly controllable albeit is dependent on electronics.

3. Traction control. See p 2.7

happen easily and transmission 'wind-up' occurs causing tyre wear, transmission stress and stiff steering. *So with a selectable 4x4 ('Type 1') system you must not use 4x4 on hard grippy surfaces.* When leaving dirt tracks, snow or other potentially slippery surfaces for grippy road you must disengage 4x4 if you have no centre differential.

(NB US use of the term 'part-time 4x4' describes the *usage* not the *system,* meaning you can only use it part of the time, ie not on hard surfaces.)

2. Pseudo (auto-engaged) 4x4. In this type of 4x4 – centre diagram overleaf (Type 2) – the vehicle is in effect a part-time 4x4 (ie a 4x2 most of the time, usually with drive to the front axle) and the 'selection' of 4x4 is done automatically when a lock-up device senses a significant speed difference between front and rear prop shafts.

If the driven axle begins to spin due to lack of grip the other axle is brought into play, usually by a friction clutch pack actuated by electrical speed sensors signalling the different prop shaft speeds. This makes the vehicle a temporary 4x4. Once the speed difference disappears, the vehicle reverts to two-wheel drive. In some vehicles of this kind, such as the Nissan X-Trail and Toyota RAV4, the auto-selection can be overridden and four-wheel drive can be driver-selected by a switch. (It will auto-*dis*-engage above 15-25 mph to preclude a forgotten selection leading to handling problems.)

Note, importantly, that front and rear prop shafts are here connected, not by a differential or any metal-to-metal 'shafts-and-gears' arrangement as in permanent 4x4 but *solely* by the friction clutch. A permitted degree of slip is often designed-in.

The idea is neat in that the entire cycle of sensing spin, needing, engaging and disengaging 4x4 is completely automatic. Moreover there's little shock loading of drive shafts. On the other hand, the device has to experience some wheel-spin before it will engage, albeit reaction times are now very short and Land Rover claim just 15°of wheel spin is enough to summon full torque to the rear wheels on their Freelander 2 (see

HALDEX LIMITED SLIP COUPLING

The Swedish Haldex limited slip coupling is long established for cross-axle or 'Type 2' auto-engage 4x4 applications. If the front and rear prop shafts rotate relative to one another (indicating wheel slip) the wedge-shaped swash plate causes the hydraulic piston pump to generate pressure and engage the clutch, locking the shafts together and thus engaging four-wheel drive – similar to earlier Jeep Gerotor or Honda twin-pump systems. Like RAV4, Haldex, however, has a valve, operated via an electronic control unit (ECU) that can influence the degree of engagement. With the addition of a 'recharge' high pressure pump (Land Rover Freelander 2) it pro-actively engages 4x4 when required – eg from a standstill for max getaway traction. ECU then opens the valve to reselect 4x2.

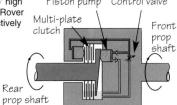

Piston pump   Control valve
Multi-plate clutch
Front prop shaft
Rear prop shaft

Haldex diagram above).

From being treated with some disdain by serious off-roaders and simply not understood by the majority of users, auto-engage 4x4 is entering a new age of sophistication. Far less the cheap option it once was, provided the electronics prove to be durable current systems can elegantly integrate with steering and stability algorithms (RAV4 *et al*) to address a host of dynamic (and static) situations to enhance safety and handling.

By definition, though, auto-engage 4x4 is dependent on clutches of some kind and 'lets go' as soon as the two prop shafts are once more revolving at the same speed –

Full time (permanent) 4x4 spreads drive loads between all four wheels all the time. You are ready for anything – all the time. Functionally the best.

Auto-engaged 4x4 with a difference. Like RAV4, and BMW X5, Freelander 2's 4x4 is pro-actively engaged from standstill to enhance initial takeoff. Reverts to cruising 4x2 but chimes in and out for other dynamic safety and stability requirements. Backs off Haldex clutch at large steering angles. Neat.

'Sending the torque ... ' **etc.** In brochures and magazines there is often indiscriminate mention of 'sending the torque to the wheel that needs it most' as though some nano-committee was making great decisions on your behalf down there in the transmission oil. An over-used, parroted cliché, it is invariably a simple case – easier to grasp – of binding one prop shaft or axle half-shaft to the other to prevent the one on the less grippy surface from spinning.

---

unless there is a manual override. It cannot be recommended (nor is it intended) for arduous off-road work where prolonged difficult conditions may be encountered.

3. Permanent 4x4 . In permanent 4x4 – the system adopted for vehicles such as Terios, Discovery, Range Rover, Land Cruiser, Grand Vitara, – there is positive drive to front and rear axles at all times: 'shafts and gears' – bottom diagram, page 2.2 (Type 3). Such a set-up always has a centre differential between the front and rear prop shafts that accommodates the small differences in axle speeds inevitable on cornering and off-road manoeuvring.

Centre diff locks. However this 'centre diff' is normally 'free' so in extreme conditions there is the possibility that if the front axle had very poor traction (on a patch of ice, for example) and the rear was on dry concrete, then the front axle would spin endlessly while the rear axle stayed station-

Mechanical diff locks are the best solution for worst off-road conditions but have adverse effect on handling. Engage in advance, must disengage when not essential.

SOLUTIONS TO ROLL CONTROL

We started off talking about diff locks ... and here we are talking about body roll. But you can see the inter-relation when trying to optimise on- and off-road performance – see pictures opposite.

Anti-roll bars. This is basically a car-width, U-shaped, bar. The bottom of the U is bolted to the chassis and the ends attached to each end of the axle (front or rear). Roll causes the bar ends to move in different up/down directions, inhibited by the torsional springiness of the bar. Controlling roll, it also, alas, limits axle articulation off-road.

Pioneered by Nissan's Patrol, there are now anti-roll bar configurations (Porsche Cayenne, Jeep Grand Cherokee, Range Rover Sport) that, for off-road conditions and at low speed, can be disconnected. This enhances articulation – the ability of the axles to let the wheels feel for the bottom of the dips.

---

ary – see panel on differentials previous spread, 'The basic thing'.

To preclude this kind of situation, as the Phase 3 Leonardo system (p 1.7) indicates, the centre diff is usually controlled in some way, often lockable – either manually (eg Defender) or automatically (Range Rover or Touareg). In this application the centre diff lock is virtually foolproof if not always quick; automatically engaged and disengaged, albeit in extreme torque conditions (1st gear low range) the lock-up is not, with some automatic systems, 100% positive.

More rapidly responding electronic limited slip differentials are being adopted where prop shaft speed differences are sensed electrically, actuating engagement of an inter-shaft clutch pack to bind the two shafts together. As well as being very quick this can also be made infinitely variable. This relieves the driver of the need to disengage diff lock when it is not needed.

Permanent 4x4 is best. Though getting a run for its money from the latest auto engage systems, permanent 4x4 is the best system of all in that as well as giving best on- and off-road traction with least call upon the track surface for traction, it is ready for anything at any time – the sudden icy patch, the wet leaves on the corner, the sudden soft sandy area in the track. With selectable 4x4 you have to know in advance that you will need it – life is not always like that. With auto-engage 4x4, despite its conceptual elegance, you have to experience slip, however little, before you get full 4x4 – and that can sometimes be too late.

(Once again, as with 'part-time 4x4', US use of the term 'full-time 4x4' describes the *usage* not the *system* – 'full-time' meaning you can use it all of the time, even on hard surfaces and it thus implies the presence of a centre differential.)

4x4 systems – and Names™

Various tunes can be played on the 4x4 systems categorised generically here to accommodate what the market wants. Jeep have been sensible enough to address this – see next spread – with the graded perma-

Controlling single-wheel spin. Mutual aid: 4x4 system meets suspension design. The task is the same – to maintain traction. Early Discovery (above) uses axle articulation (long springs, no anti-roll bars) to keep wheels on the ground. Pinzgauer, with short half-axles (top right), can't do this so opts for 100% locking cross-axle differentials to prevent spin on raised wheels. '05 Grand Cherokee (right) has electronically controlled axle (and centre) diff-locks but adds traction control – individual wheel braking – to quench single-wheel spin. Front diff lock clutch pack backs off during turns; neat.

nent 4x4 options introduced on the '05 model Grand Cherokee, recognising that some customers just want enhanced traction on packed snow and are happy to benefit from the cost and weight saving that accrue from specifying their simpler choice.

Beware of fancy trade names, usually trumpeted as something like SupaTrac™. Jeep seem especially attached to this kind of appellation that befuddles customers as much as it confuses showroom staff. Whatever the marque, get the salesman to say which of the three generic systems on p 2.2 apply and what additional functions it has. Take along the table on p 2.10, look for the big arrow and have the young man tick the squares applying to your proposed buy.

Controlling left-right wheel-spin

Same problem. As with centre diff locks controlling front/rear axle spin, so, on *any* 4x4 system, the problem of controlling sin-

gle-wheel spin across an axle. Summarising the p.2.4 box, two basic systems are used:
- Diff locks (may be limited slip)
- Traction control.

Diff locks. These are precisely the same as centre diff locks:
- Automatic – some kind of limited-slip device often with electronically-sensed gradual engagement, or
- Manually selectable – 100% solid.

Traction control. Here the ABS individual wheel-speed sensors detect when one wheel is spinning and apply braking to that wheel only. This goes some way towards 'locking' one wheel to the other and progress may be resumed; reaction times vary. Traction control is a palliative for occasional use, involving continual brake application, wear and heat. For sustained serious off-road operation a manual 100% diff lock or electronically controlled automatic diff lock is the answer.

Single-wheel spin can be quenched by braked-wheel traction control; or more is elegantly by electronic locking diffs that trigger a cross-axle diff clutch pack.

FINE-TUNED 4X4 DRIVELINE SPECIFICATIONS

Still three generic 4x4 types ... but. We have seen that there are essentially three generic types – the selectable, the auto-engaged (soft-roader type) and the permanent 4x4 as shown in the diagrams on page 2.2. All 4x4 systems, with whatever exotic trade names they are burdened, will slot into one or other of these categories. There are still, however, different means of implementing each system and ways of optimising it for particular applications.

Others will doubtless follow but in early 2005 Jeep were the first manufacturer – who better – to recognise and cater for the different uses to which their products will be put. The Grand Cherokee appeared with a range of driveline

As well as 4x2 (available on X-Trail and RAV4 too), Jeep Grand Cherokee offers permanent 4x4 options spanning a wide spectrum of users. Range Rover Sport offers impressive off-road spec – totally at odds with its sports-car pretensions – but no front diff lock or lesser options.

Grand Cherokee options – note Options 2, 3 and 4 are all variations of Type 3: permanent 4x4

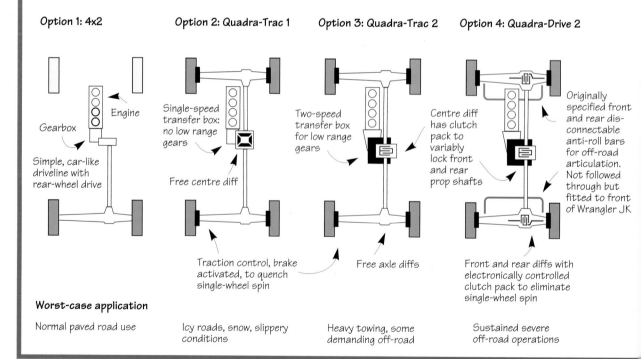

Option 1: 4x2

Engine

Gearbox

Simple, car-like driveline with rear-wheel drive

Option 2: Quadra-Trac 1

Single-speed transfer box: no low range gears

Free centre diff

Traction control, brake activated, to quench single-wheel spin

Option 3: Quadra-Trac 2

Two-speed transfer box for low range gears

Free axle diffs

Centre diff has clutch pack to variably lock front and rear prop shafts

Option 4: Quadra-Drive 2

Originally specified front and rear disconnectable anti-roll bars for off-road articulation. Not followed through but fitted to front of Wrangler JK

Front and rear diffs with electronically controlled clutch pack to eliminate single-wheel spin

Worst-case application

Normal paved road use

Icy roads, snow, slippery conditions

Heavy towing, some demanding off-road

Sustained severe off-road operations

options ranging from a simple 4x2 for people who just wanted a capacious tough vehicle to use on normal paved roads, through two further 4x4 options right up to a maximum off-road performance specification suited for sustained use in severe off-tracks conditions – see bottom caption line in the diagram opposite.

Common-sense wins at last. The three 4x4 drive-lines (Options 2, 3 and 4 opposite) are all variations on the 'Type 3' permanent four-wheel drive theme and the escalating off-road capability at last offers a mature and sensible choice for the customer – a welcome, common-sense, break from the increasingly bizarre parallel upward-spiral of off-road prowess, luxury trim and on-road performance to which some makers seem wedded.

Graded driveline options. As a design concept this top-spec Grand Cherokee (Option 4 specification opposite) seems hard to beat for best possible off-road performance. The Range Rover Sport uses a hi-spec combination of driveline facilities but with normal anti-roll bars, no front diff-lock or graded driveline options. It is further off-road-limited by conflicting high speed on-road requirements that include 20-inch wheels on very low profile road tyres. Unlike the Jeep's iffy ergonomics (p 2.23), however, range-change can be effected on the move – low to high – at up to 30 mph: invaluable in deep sand where a stop to engage high would be unacceptable.

There's a fine-tuned 'Type 2' as well. Jeep's Option 2 here follows a similar philosophy to BMW's X5 design team in offering a 4x4 system bereft of what to some are the confusion of additional levers and controls yet one which will deal effectively with the most common 4x4 application, icy roads and snow. In fact the Jeep layout shown here will to some be superior to the BMW in that there is a centre differential and a positive 'shafts and gears' connection between front and rear prop shafts. BMW's xDrive, now matched by RAV4 and Freelander 2, is smartly programmed and probably as good as you will get while still saving the weight and cost of a centre diff. Where the Jeep options represent fine-tuning of a 'Type 3' permanent 4x4 system, there are also fine tuned and quite clever 'Type 2' soft-roader systems around too.

2.2 Applications

What to do – buying advice

Priorities. Whether or not you use your 4x4 off-road, Section 2.1 is the most important section in the book. The magazines aren't much help; the off-road ones are seldom analytical enough while the others gloss over the 4x4 system – the whole reason for having the vehicle. The brochures aren't much use either, often written by 'creatives' who didn't get the tech brief.

Don't buy a 4x4 ... ! If you just want the ruggedness, space and driving position, some SUVs and pickups are available as straight 4x2 vehicles. Buy one!

Do buy a 4x4 ... ! Hopefully you'll have seen by now there are definite advantages to 4x4 on-road as well as off and, from Section 2.1, that the 4x4 system itself is very important. The more off-road oriented you are the more important are the refinements such as two-speed transfer boxes, diff locks and other means of controlling wheel spin.

Check list. You could do worse than use the diagram opposite as an *aide memoire* – beginning with the bottom line of captions. Then examine – and get the salesman to examine – the headings down the left side of the chart on the next spread. And read Sec 2.3!

Just for you. Between the extremes there are many 4x4s suited to *your* purpose. If you want the 4x4 aspects of a general family holdall just to guard against occasional winter ice plus you have multiple drivers, some of whom haven't the time or inclination to remember about disengaging 4x4 or diff locks on hard surfaces, then go for Type 2 auto-engage 4x4. They have matured well and there are few traction compromises. But if a new route in the Sahara or the Brazilian jungle is on your menu then Type 3 with three locking diffs would be the way to go: you will need all the help you can get!

Read sub-section 2.1 at your leisure. Know the 4x4 systems, grade your choice according to your needs. Check the table on the next spread for 4x4 ingredients.

4x4 SYSTEM FEATURES AND FUNCTION

Fit for purpose? Red boxes.
Red boxes = demanding off-road: Look for checks in row 1, 2 or 3, plus row 6. Row 9, then 7 (with the right tyres and skills!) makes you almost unstoppable in serious off-road conditions.

Fit for purpose? Green boxes.
Green boxes = smug grin over the neighbours' Morris Mino on wet grass or on snow and ice before the gritters got out.

Your vehicle?
If it's not listed here, ask your dealer these questions. Don't accept 'Insta-Tork' or 'Trac-Tronic' – have him read and tick the boxes.

	Daihatsu Terios	Land Rover Freelander 2	Honda CR-V	Nissan X-Trail	Hyundai Tucson	Toyota RAV-4 '06	Lexus RX300	Nissan Pathfinder ('05)	'05 BMW X-5	
1. Four-wheel drive system										
Selectable 4x4 [by lever (L) or button (B)], ie vehicle is usually in 4x2										
Permanent 4x4, with centre differential. Centre diff manually lockable (L)	✓ L						✓			
Permanent 4x4, with centre differential, auto-locked by clutch, VC or other means										
2nd axle driven after front/rear speed difference sensed. Drive is through clutch (electrically operated); reverts to 4x2. Selectable 'Lock' (L)		✓		✓ L	✓	✓		✓ L	✓	✓
As above but clutch is hydraulically operated (H) or 'pre-loaded' viscous coupling (V) connects prop shafts			✓ H							
2. Two-speed transfer box (low range gears)										
Fitted as standard								✓		
On-the-move range change – manufacturer approved (eg. lo>hi at around 20-25 mph)										
Range-change by: lever (L), button/knob (B)								B		
3. Cross-axle wheel spin control										
Axle diff-locks rear (R), front (F), limited slip (LS)				RLS						
Traction control (auto braking of spinning wheel): optional (O), standard (S)		S		O	S	S	S	✓	S	S
4. Automatic transmission, goodies										
Auto box optional (O) or standard (S)	O	O	O	O	O	O	S	O	O	O
Special facilities, eg. Hill descent (H), 'Terrain Response' (T). Disconnectable rear anti-roll-bar (drab). [drfab = rear and front anti-roll bar] to enhance off-road articulation.		H, T					H		H	

(left margin labels for row group 1: 'Hard drive' – shafts and gears; 'Soft drive' – eg. Electrically actuated clutch, viscous coupling. No centre diff. Auto-engaging. Front-rear axle connection)

– EXAMPLES SNAPSHOT

Fit for purpose? Traction control.
Traction control – auto braking of a spinning wheel – is shown with a green box, ie as a soft-roader benefit but, if you don't have a cross-axle diff lock it is beneficial for limited serious off-road operations too

Key – see also first column
S = standard   O = optional.
Feature° = that feature is optional
  eg R° = rear diff lock is optional

Nissan Murano	Toyota Hi-Lux (pickup)	Nissan Navara (pickup)	Jeep Wrangler JK ('06)	Jeep Cherokee	'05 Jeep Grand Cherokee (Q-D2)	Mitsubishi Shogun	Mercedes ML 270	Porsche Cayenne ('05)	Land Rover Defender	Nissan Patrol ('05)	Toyota ('05) Land Cruiser	Toyota Amazon	Land Rover Discovery 3	Range Rover Sport ('05)	Mercedes G-Wagen ('03)
	✓L	✓L	✓L	✓L						✓L					
						✓L	✓	✓	✓L		✓L	✓L			✓L
			✓					✓					✓	✓	
✓L															
	✓	✓	✓	✓	✓	✓	✓	✓	✓	✓	✓	✓	✓	✓	✓
								✓					✓	✓	✓
	L	L	L	L	B	L	B	B	L	L	L	L	B	B	L
	R	RLS	RF	R°	RF			R°		R	R°	R°	R°	R°	R F°
✓					S		S	S	O		O	O	S	S	
S			O	O	S	O	O	O		O	O	O	O	S	S
			dfab					drfab		drab	H°	H°	H T°	H	

2.3 Controls – levers, buttons, ergonomics

(Left) Good old days? Profligate use of cockpit space, pretty disastrous aesthetics but the grandeur of the levers does bear appropriate relation to the functions they control. (Little chance of forgetting the huge, six-inch pull-up difflocks on the 25 year old Type 461 G-Wagen design!) See next spread for real examples of how not to do it! .

(Right) Controls? What controls? BMW's 'soft roader' X5, like Freelander 2, keeps it simple. All 4x4 controls, for better or for worse, are automatic. There are no low-range transfer gears and, like the '05 Grand Cherokee in Options 1 and 2 format (p 2.8) there are no other controls to confuse the driver.

What's to control?

The info. You know about selectable four-wheel drive (Section 2.1), and about two-speed transfer boxes (Section 1.4). You know about the need for centre differentials between front and rear prop shaft when permanent 4x4 is fitted (Leonardo's Phase 2 design, page 1.7, also at page 2.5, left column and the picture at the foot of the facing page here). You noted that lockable diffs (page 2.7) also do a mean traction job with axles when you are badly off-road.

Three basic controls. A sepia-toned look into a WW2 Jeep or a Land Rover of Series 1, 2 or 3 vintage will have you noting three gear levers to control the above, namely:

  1. Selection of main gears
  2. Selection of 4x4
  3. Selection of low-ratio gears.

There's more. These days, though, according to what is fitted to your vehicle, there are controls for the selection of:

  4. Centre diff lock (often automatic)
  5. Axle diff locks (often automatic)
  6. 'Other' – that favourite term for when the list gets too long, here includes traction control (if switchable), ditto ABS, a Land Rover speciality called

Basic transmission controls are main gears, selection of 4x4 and /or low range. But centre and axle diff locks, electronic goodies like stability must be understood.

HDC (hill descent control also available from other manufacturers like Toyota) and, introduced by Land Rover in 2005, 'Terrain Response' – a means of 'tuning' responses of throttle, automatic transmission and diff locks according to the off-road conditions in which you are driving. And, to ward off litigation as much as directional problems, there is often a Stability Control programme of some kind which for off road operation really should be switchable.

The little gear lever – *et al.* The transfer box lever usually looks after items 2, 3 and, if appropriate, 4 – the latter in both high and low range gears. A manual lever is simple and reliable but dash-mounted electrical rotary switches or buttons controlling actuators are a cheaper alternative, do not involve another hole in the cabin insulation and can be electrically inhibited to prevent misuse. So that is what some manufacturers fit.

Foolproof benefits? Such electrical selection, however, *provided it is totally reliable,* can be a boon to occasional users happy to be prevented from getting it wrong by inhibiting features which include ensuring

the main gear selector is in neutral and/or the speed is very low – often 5-8 mph . If these conditions are not met, the selection is electrically blocked until they are. There is much to be said, however, for levers rather than buttons to control a major transmission function. A lever's position indicates what has been selected and it is unlikely to have been selected inadvertently.

Ergonomics. No apology is made for here highlighting and, where appropriate, criticising, poor control ergonomics – how intuitive they are to use, how appropriate to their function, how easy (LEDs or LCDs are)to see in bright sunlight, how proof they are against inadvertent or unsuitable selection, how self-evident in what has been selected. Read and reflect on the box at p 15 on the next spread about control protocols

Totally intuitive. Simple, straightforward examples of their type, Nissan X-Trail (Type 2) soft roader 4x4 manual override, left, and the excellent '04 Jeep Grand Cherokee (Type 3) arrangement, centre, which has a clear neutral on the range change for no-hassle automatic transmission towed recovery. Jeep have retained a neutral transfer gears selection capability even on the button/small lever select system on the '05 model. (See 'Towing your auto', p.2.25). Old-style Daihatsu (Type 1, right) shows exemplary simplicity.

and, when buying, make intuitive simplicity your goal. Taking this message on board will hone your own awareness and selectivity as a vehicle customer, get you a more suitable product – and with any luck the message might one day get through to the designers.

Levers are generally more positive than buttons; more intuitive and have more feel. Buttons can be inhibiting to prevent errors but are reliant on electrics.

Why do you need a centre diff lock? On this early Discovery centre diff has been deliberately (and incorrectly) left unlocked in difficult off-road conditions. Weight transfer to rear on the slope offloads the front wheels allowing them to spin while rear axle is stationary. If you want to smash the transmission engage diff lock now! Needless to say in this situation, foot off the accelerator and dip the clutch, wait a couple of seconds and then engage centre diff lock.

How not to do it. (Left) The upper switch, alongside a PRND caption, looks initially like a mini-auto-box selector. Actually, it's a <u>toggle</u> (!) selector for high and low range gears. Which has been selected? Aha! You won't find out until you take your eyes off the switch and look for it on a captions panel. The switches cry out for a guard. 'Ah', says driver, 'there's Jack!' Stops. 'Pass me the bag, Mary.' Mary passes small heavyish bag, rests it briefly on console, inadvertently pressing toggle switch. (Switch also shields the PRND LEDs in a right hand drive vehicle.) Did the ergonomics chappie have a good lunch?

(Above – others) More how-not-to-do-it ergonomics – a major driveline control, the range change, buried among minor items and again no neutral for the transfer gears. Buttons are a cheap alternative to transfer levers. Levers are more intuitive and logical. 'Let's have the radio on! Ah, looks like a bass boost button there ... ' (Far right) A classic that defies belief! (Yes, a range change!)

When buying do be sure of all control functions and don't assume good ergonomics will prevail. Some current modern designs are astonishingly bad.

The glass soap dish syndrome. Where 'Form follows function' should be the well-worn mantra, too often vehicle designers come up with the automotive equivalent of the oft seen glass soap dish – loose on a chrome fitting, easily dislodged, no drain-hole, a veritable magnet when you have soap in your eyes, and lethal when smashed on the shower floor. Looks cute though.

Controls – what's to get wrong?

Preventing or accommodating? What is there to prevent? Misused controls to select low range can cause severe clonking in the transmission. About the only way of eliminating this reliably and with no possibility

of damage is to do it with the vehicle or shafts (or both) stationary – hence the inhibiting parameters mentioned above ('Foolproof benefits?' p.2.13).

Preventing is cheaper. The majority manufacturer view – cynical or pragmatic – is that since most driving is done on-road and, where selectable, in two-wheel drive, cost can be kept down by providing Type 2 instead of permanent 4x4 or synchro on the transfer box. So preventing drivers from crashing the gears and breaking things – by inhibiting potentially damaging selections electrically – is cheaper than accommodating the need to make selections on the move. A lot of customers, happy to pay less, would support this or just don't think about it.

Levers, not buttons, please. However, many off-road professionals like public utilities, farmers, civil engineers, and armed forces need permanent 4x4, prefer levers to switches *and* the ability to make undamaging selections easily when they want to. And if that means provision of a centre diff and synchro where needed, then so be it.

So that's what's to get wrong. This rather long-winded rationale is important because it points out the sometimes conflicting commercial (price-driven) and user (function-driven) priorities that govern what appears in the market place – or more precisely, in the bowels of your off-roader's transmission system and thus in its transmission controls. Know about it, define your preferences. We got there at last!

CONTROL PROTOCOLS
Time for reflection on the user interface

Position equals selected function. That's what they keep messing with isn't it – the way things are controlled. That's what we have to keep on re-learning. Remember light switches – old-style? A small lever a quarter to half an inch long. When it was up it was off. When it was down it was on. Its position gave you a visual indication of what had been selected. Then came progress. For switches, it was 'toggling': press once for 'On', press again for 'Off'. Momentarily distracted, which have you actually selected? You've come across it at home. Reading light doesn't work. Is it the bulb? Have I switched it on or off? Is it safe to touch that wire? You have to do a continuity check or rummage for your multimeter to be certain.

Toggling ... er ... . After toggling (simple stuff, that) came the time parameter. Press to change mode. Press and hold for two seconds and … . Hold, while pressing the other button … . Hold, press the other button, face north, sing two verses of Rule Britannia and … ! You get the picture. It is all too familiar. You could call it LOTI - loss of the intuitive. No problem if you are using the system every day and have first learned it but the invitation is out for complete confusion and possibly misuse if you are fresh to it.

350 page manual. From the viewpoint of the design engineer, immersed in the system eight hours a day, it is all terrific. Extraordinary control span from just one or two buttons. Far cheaper to produce, let the electronics do the work. For the customer, though, it's er … where's the handbook? (And the handbook is 25 mm thick.) Though such handbooks are often a thinly disguised umbrella against litigation ('We did tell you so you can't sue!'), one 4x4, recently released, has a 350 page English language handbook and five add-on supplements. That's just to drive it. Your friend wants to nip down to the shops: do you throw him the keys and say 'Yeah, take the wagon!'?

Indicator by the switch? There are some mind-boggling examples. Something as funda-

'Hold left and right buttons both at once for three seconds. With the right hand digit flashing, adjust the value and confirm with the left button. The next digit will start to …. ' The number of functions that can be controlled on this bicycle speedometer with just two buttons is amazing. Just don't lose the instruction leaflet!

mental – and hugely important – as whether a 4x4 is in low range or high range. Something that used to be selected by a great big lever, that firstly could never be selected by mistake and secondly gave unambiguous visual cues as to what had been selected. Too embarrassing to mention manufacturers, at least two 'premium 4x4s' have – amazingly – an unguarded toggle action switch to select low and high range. On one, to be sure which one you have selected you have to look, not at the switch, but at a caption on the instrument panel. (Worse, the occupant of the passenger seat might have selected it when you were at the traffic lights and you didn't hear him say, 'Daddy, what's this for?') There isn't even an LED down by the switch. A later model at least has a two-position switch for this, plus an LED, so you can see (in bright sun?) what you have asked the electronics for.

It *can* be done. Nor is this a mere Luddite tirade. ('Modern' is an old-fashioned word – the all-time classic oxymoron indicative of always looking back and long since replaced by 'cool' or 'hip' or 'New!!!' with at least two exclamation marks.) Nevertheless … modern control interfaces *can* be done properly and intuitively. The screens, modes, menus and settings for GPS equipment can pile high but US manufacturer Lowrance, for example, with screen prompts and basic controls have made it all easy and intuitive. Read the book once and throw it away. Likewise DAB radios' 'scroll-and-push-to-select' protocol gives an ergonomics person a nice warm glow and is simple enough for anyone to grasp without a handbook.

Learning for all. Certainly there is a subliminal learning process that we are all, necessarily, going through (or getting confused by). Is the control protocol time-dependent? If it's toggle, is there a remote indicator? Is it hold A and push B? Is it scroll and select? With the same knob or using an 'Enter' button? The folks in the white coats have got to do some learning too. Like it says at the top: time for reflection.

LOTI – loss of the intuitive – is all too common on control functions. Few customers get beyond feeling they are vaguely at fault for not understanding

Tribal wisdom. VW Touareg's
self-explanatory driveline controls combine electro-selection
compactness with intuitive
ergonomics. Pointer indicates
what is selected. Press the button and it pops up so you can
select something else. Centre
diff auto-locks by degrees in
normal high or low range when
sensing front-rear prop shaft
speed difference. Move the
pointer to the 3 o'clock position
to lock centre diff manually.
Note you can only do this when
you are – rightly – in low range.
If optional rear axle locking diff
is fitted, a further pictogram at
the 5 o'clock position is the setting for its manual selection –
again rightly only after low
range and centre diff lock have
been selected. Stability control
'Off' button is usefully alongside. However, like most electrically selected range changes,
there is no neutral. Porsche
Cayenne has similar driveline
but non-intuitive controls.

even axle, differential. In other
words if the front/rear prop
shaft (or axle half-shaft) speeds
differ significantly a clutch or
viscous coupling of some kind
will be brought into play (see
Touareg, left) to do the job. If
there is no auto diff lock you
may have a manual one
(Defender, facing page) or no
diff lock at all, the wheel/axle
spin situation being taken care
of by wheel-braking traction
control – fairly effective but not
the best for prolonged off-road
use. See also box on p 2.4.

Wait for the lights. Where
a diff-lock control is manual,
actual engagement of the diff-
lock may or may not take place
at once. There will usually be a
warning light associated with a
control movement which will
indicate, maybe a moment or
two later, that the selection has
actually taken place. Typically
locking or unlocking a centre
diff will not be immediate on selection as
there are engagement spring inhibitors that
will wait for conditions to be correct.

Transmission controls – conclusions

Choices. As with so many expositions,
when you actually start at the beginning the
conclusions are staring you in the face long
before you actually spell them out. As we've
seen, for their transmission controls, some
vehicles have levers, some have switches.

• Switches can be OK for low-cost, foolproof operation where the ultimate in
off-road performance is not needed.

• Levers are best for total reliability and
ergonomic feedback

• Synchro on the range change is necessary when you need all the off-road performance you can get, day-in, day-out.

All levers are not the same and the facilities they offer can differ widely. Switches
are often burdened with disastrous
ergonomics – shining exceptions X-Trail, top
left p.13, Touareg, above.

Diff-locks. Many vehicles these days
have an automatically locking centre, or

*In-depth pre-
purchase scan is
recommended.
Nail the sales-
man till all is
clear. If you've
already bought,
satisfy yourself
on how your
transmission
controls work.*

Actually using the controls

Transfer lever – etc. As a general rule or
if in any doubt, stop the vehicle, select main
gear neutral and de-clutch (or select N on
the auto box) before selecting range change
or diff locks – levers or buttons. However:

• **4x2 to 4x4.** Nearly all selectable 4x4s
can go from 4x2H to 4x4H 'on-the-fly', ie
at any speed up to about 60 mph. *Always
de-clutch and off-load the throttle before
doing so*, however, to be sure the only
driven axle is not spinning.

• **Engaging low range**, almost without
exception, stop, dip the clutch and
nudge the lever into low. If it doesn't go
in cleanly, you may need to lift the
clutch pedal a little to try again, often
with the vehicle in gear.

Mercedes' G-Wagen has a transfer box on which high or low range can be selected with the vehicle on the move – a life saver when, for instance, you have to start in low range in deep sand and dare not stop in order to engage high range. At last other manufacturers are providing this capability. Defender is one of the few drivelines where – usefully – low range can be used with or without centre diff lock – see also Touareg opposite.

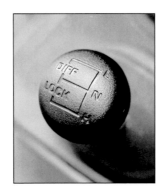

• **Engaging high range** from low range, again, almost without exception use the same procedure as above, moving the lever the other way. But see Sec 6.1 where on-the-move methods (not applicable to button-type selection) are discussed – useful in bad off-road conditions or when starting a heavy trailer.

• **Synchro transfer box?** The Mercedes G-Wagen (and now the Discovery 3, Range Rover and an increasing number of enlightened designs) has a synchro transfer box designed to enable selection of high or low range on the move – low to high at up to 30 mph. (Invaluable when, say, in deep sand, you have to start in low range but would not dare stop to get into high range.)

• **The lights.** As already mentioned, watch for the warning lights to confirm selection has actually taken place.

• **Wind-up; getting out of 4x4.** Vehicles with selectable 4x4 may, even on loose surfaces, suffer from a degree of transmission 'wind-up' due to lack of centre differential; when you try to deselect 4x4 you may find the lever virtually immovable. To relieve the wind-up (stress in the shafts), select reverse and go backwards for 10-20 metres, at the end of which dip the clutch and the lever will usually move freely – or respond to a sharp fist-thump back into 4x2.
This phenomenon is more likely to occur on trucks (with, long, torsionally flexible

propeller shafts) than on domestic SUVs or light 4x4s.

• **Centre diff locks.** Centre diff-locks can usually be engaged while moving, *provided there is no front/rear wheel spin at the time of engagement*; but dip the clutch before doing so to cut off drive to the single driven axle and render any inter-shaft spin impossible.

• **Disengage diff locks** when no longer needed; especially the axle ones – see next spread.

Know what you can do on the move. 4x2 to selectable 4x4 is usually OK; also centre diff lock. Dipping clutch first in both cases precludes shaft speed differences.

*Mitsubishi Shogun transfer gears sequence (right, upper) is logical – 2WD high, 4WD high (free centre diff), 4WD high Lc (locked centre diff), 4WD low Lc (locked diff) – with a neutral in between for on-the-move changes. Jeep Cherokee ('04) is less logical for many with the two 4WD high positions transposed. Jeep's terminology is strange too '4WD part-time' here meaning 'selectable 4x4 with centre diff locked, you can only use this mode *part* of the time', ie not on hard surfaces. Likewise '4WD full-time' means you can use it *full* time – even on hard surfaces – so the centre diff is not locked. Got it? System is OK, nomenclature and ergonomics unusual.*

Freewheeling front hubs

The principles – only. Once again a confetti of tinsel trade names (helped in some cases by badly written manuals) confuses what is going on in the case of freewheeling front hubs. The basic idea is a carry-over from the concept of having selectable 4x4. As well as in most cases saving the cost of a centre differential, proponents of selectable 4x4 – the ability to run a 4x4 vehicle in two-wheel drive (2WD) – cite fuel economy. This is actually a debatable contention.

Carrying on this line of reasoning, however, since in 2WD there is no *drive* to the front wheels, the front prop shaft, diff and drive shafts are all rotating needlessly and thus also absorbing energy. If, whilst in 2WD, you can temporarily disconnect these temporarily redundant shafts from the front wheels then you will save fuel.

First there were 'manual hubs' where turning a key simply withdrew some splines disconnecting the wheel hub from the drive shaft. Then came 'freewheeling' or automatic hubs in which the front wheels could freewheel in 2WD but when the shaft was powered, as when 4x4 was engaged, the shaft would drive the front wheels. The principle was the same as that of a bicycle back wheel.

Freewheeling hubs are sometimes standard on Type 1 4x4s (see p 2.2) or may be fitted as aftermarket accessories.

The hardware. So summing up in a bit more detail, there are:

Freewheeling front hubs allow front prop shaft, drive shafts and diff to be stationary when in 2WD. Auto or lock settings manually selected. Fuel savings debatable.

1. All-manual hubs
2. Automatic hubs
3. Two-position automatic hubs –
all coming under various fancy trade names. So the full picture is:

- **Manual hubs – item 1 above** – which can be set to 'free' (disconnected from the drive shaft) or to 'engaged' (locked to the drive shaft). Simple.
- **Automatic hubs – items 2 and 3 above.** These can be of two kinds:

1. *Auto only.* When the vehicle is in two-wheel drive, the front drive shafts are not driving the front wheels, leaving the shaft stationary (thanks to the freewheel) and thus saving fuel. When 4x4 is selected, drive is applied to the shaft and the shaft tries to overtake the wheel; in this case the hubs are engaged. The pawl mechanism in the diagram shows the principle though it is not as crude as this in practice – because it also works in reverse too. The hubs disengage when the vehicle reverts to 2WD (see below) after you've backed a few yards.

2. *Auto hubs with override locked mode.* These are two-mode hubs. In 'auto' they function roughly as the pawl mechanism in the diagram, ie in reverse the front wheels would not be driven, even in 4x4. When set to 'locked' the wheel is locked to the drive shaft – just what it sounds like, as though there was no magic hub there at all. This is the mode you would use for most deliberate off-roading.

4x4 to 4x2 – hub disengagement. All the above on the 'auto' mode, of course, relates to the case of a vehicle going from 2WD to 4x4, ie a previously dead drive shaft being powered up and transferring drive to the front wheels. Once this has happened and you want to revert back to 2WD, the hubs have to disengage. If it was a noisy, clackety pawl arrangement as in the diagram the front wheels could overtake a once-more stationary shaft without any problem. But because the freewheel mechanism consists of balls going up ramps and the like, you actually have to *reverse* the vehicle a short distance after selecting 2WD in order to dis-

Principle (only!) of freewheel hub

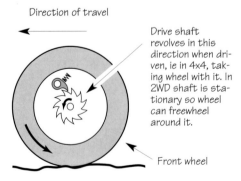

Direction of travel

Drive shaft revolves in this direction when driven, ie in 4x4, taking wheel with it. In 2WD shaft is stationary so wheel can freewheel around it.

Front wheel

engage the drive to the hubs. If you forget to do this then the front prop shaft will, on selection of 2WD, not be driven by the engine but the axle half-shafts and diff gears will still be connected to the wheels.

Handbrakes

Transmission brake. A transmission handbrake is one where a single brake drum grips the propeller shaft just aft of the gearbox. It is extremely powerful. If your vehicle has a transmission handbrake, as many Land Rovers have, *do not use it with the vehicle moving* at all. Regard it as a *parking* brake only. Using such a parking brake with the vehicle in motion puts exceptional stress on the axle half shafts and can lead to their failure – "Snapped off like a carrot ... ", as the well known saying goes!

Electric parkbrakes. The levers vs buttons camps get even more sharply – and justifiably – divided when it comes to the new generation of electrically operated park brakes.

• **First the critique.** Taking the '05 Discovery 3 as an example, looking at the switch, incredibly, there is no visual indication as to whether it is on or off – see pic p 2.22 and 'Control Protocols' page 2.15. Notes, warnings, ifs and buts, red and yellow warning lights and four pages in the owner's handbook cover operation of this item. Emergency use is non-intuitive. (Don't even think about a flat battery or other electrical failure!)

• **Then again ... .** The park brake self-applies when the vehicle is stationary (a two-edged weapon). Some may regard it as merely a helpfully power-assisted function like power steering.

No-rollback parkbrakes. This can be unwelcome in severe off-road conditions where (see Sec 4.4) you may wish to swiftly roll back down a hill after a failed ascent.

Axle diff locks – non-automatic

Engaging. As a general rule, axle diff locks should be engaged with the vehicle stationary; dip the clutch when doing so to

get into the habit and to ensure you are not trying to mate a stationary wheel with a powered spinning wheel at the moment of engagement. Proper diff locks (as opposed to limited-slip differentials) usually consist of a somewhat brutal dog-clutch arrangement so the total synchronising of left and right drive shaft speeds has to be the aim. Some manufacturers permit engagement of rear axle diff locks at speeds up to 7 km/hr (walking speed) and the selection electrics are often inhibited by a speed sensor above this speed.

If your particular instruction book permits engaging at higher speeds on the move this usually implies some kind of hold-off device but, with a manual gearbox, still dip the clutch to make sure a spinning wheel is not suddenly curbed by engagement of the diff lock.

In-use speed limit. It is potentially dangerous to leave an axle diff locked on road or at high speed. Many vehicles have an audio warning buzzer above a set speed, around 20 mph, or the diff lock will throw out (maybe with a bang!) if subjected to high speed and cornering.

Disengaging. Disengage the axle diff lock as soon as it is not needed, especially the front one. an engaged front diff lock makes the steering feel as though it has been welded solid. In really demanding conditions, say a mix of rock and soft mud, you will be engaging and disengaging the front diff lock all the time. First of its kind at the time of writing, the '05 Jeep Grand Cherokee has a front ELSD (electronic limited slip differential) that releases the diff-locking clutch pack during turns – an elegant concept plugging in to the stability control system sensors and precluding the transmission 'fight' (or 'crow-hop' as Jeep call it) that would otherwise occur and tighten up the steering feel.

A final reminder ... .

Grippy surfaces. Remember the golden rule: never engage selectable 4x4 (Type 1) or any differential lock when using the vehicle on firm grippy surfaces.

Unless design permits it, engage axle diff locks only when both halves of axle revolving at same rate. Disengage as soon as it is not essential. Don't use on-road.

2.4 Low range – when and how

First gear low box ideal to control steep descents, occasionally 2nd. Always 1st with automatic transmission – see next spread..If there's no hill descent control or equivalent be prepared to administer cadence braking – see Sec 3.2.

Low range – 'power' and 'control'

Low range for *power.* As we have seen, selecting low range on the transfer box is not just another gear but affects *all* the gears in the main gearbox (including reverse), gearing them down by around 2:1.The obvious uses of the low range are thus occasions when you want a great deal of 'power' or tractive effort – towing a car out of a ditch, ascending a very steep slope, getting out of deep mud or sand or pulling a fallen tree trunk out of the way.

Low-range gears have two distinct applications – power for extra steep inclines and control to restrain a vehicle on a steep descent or crawl over rocks.

Low range for *control.* Less immediately obvious uses for the low ratio include the provision of control rather than high tractive effort. Examples of this might be steadying the vehicle on a very steep descent without use of the brakes or, classically, allowing the vehicle to crawl over rocks slowly, steadily, without jarring – with your foot off the clutch pedal and without use of the brakes. Low box, first gear excels in this kind of exercise and can often be used with minimal throttle opening or even at idling revs. Rock crawling is a particularly appropriate application where there is otherwise the tendency to 'fall down the far side' of boulders and land with a thump.

Low 1st – too low? Low range first, because of its enormous 'power' capability, is often too low for slippery surface conditions and it is easy to spin the wheels inadvertently through the application of more torque than the ground can take. So 1st-low should be used mainly when grip is very good, when momentum is not required and when there is little danger of spinning the wheels – usually when considerable tractive effort is needed. A common application is in affording engine braking down very steep slopes (see Section 4.5, 'Descending steep slopes'); though surprisingly (Section 4.8) some sand demands it.

Top gear in the low box is a good gear for loping along tracks. Often about the same rpm as 3rd high but when difficult patches appear you're already in low range.

Saharan boulders epitomise the 'control' case where low range 1st gear gives steady rock-crawling capability (centre diff unlocked). 1st gear start is sometimes appropriate to heavy towing but higher gears in the low box provide general off-road flexibility (below left). Avoid the temptation to 'use the clutch as another gear', ie don't slip the clutch.

What to start off in

Low 2nd – rule-of-thumb. Second is a good rule-of-thumb starting-off gear for most low range situations – muddy conditions, steep slopes and the like even with a heavy trailer. In snow you may even find using 3rd gear low range is the answer to preclude wheel spin on take-off. Because tractive effort available is then more closely matched to what the ground will take, there is less risk of wheel spin and the lost traction that results. As indicated in Section 2.6, with

Gentle right foot! Moderate momentum and 2-low or 3-low here.

automatic transmission select '3' (to preclude too early a change into higher gears); this can sometimes also be the solution with manual transmission where conditions demand the delicate touch.

Low 3rd, 4th, 5th – versatility. Third, fourth and fifth gears in the low range are good 'getting about' gears with manual transmission ('D' or '4' in auto) for the better parts of derelict mountain or desert tracks, for getting across the field or for forest tracks that are a bit tight for high range. They bring out the vehicle's versatility and the ease with which it traverses cross-country terrain. You can make a respectable speed in low-box 5th or 'D', yet drop all the way down to 2nd without a range change when the going gets more difficult (see Section 4.2, 'Driving on tracks').

Driver still the key. We shall see in the ensuing Sections specific examples of what gears to use. And also that there is more to maintaining traction than just selecting a low gear; driver sensitivity is half the battle – see Section 3.2, 'Gentle right foot'. (Also Section 6.1, 'High/low range overlap'.)

Thus there will also be times in slippery mud when a very gentle start in 3rd low will successfully drip-feed torque to the wheels when 2nd would have them spinning.

Lowest gear isn't always best. First low is often too low, over-torqueing the ground and generating wheel spin. 2nd-low is good rule of thumb start-off gear.

2.21

'Terrain Response™' – etc

Help for the uninitiated? Variously regarded as an innovative off-road aid, a gimmick or the final barrier to learning proper off-road driving sensitivity, Land Rover's 'Terrain Response' (TR) driveline control system aims to tweak the response curves of throttle, automatic transmission change points and electronic diff lock settings according to broad, pre-defined terrain types selected by the driver. Low range or raised suspension driver prompts are given. Thus there are driver-selected settings for:

- Normal driving
- Snow and wet grass
- Mud and ruts
- Sand
- Rock crawling (some models).

Each setting implies discrete response characteristics for the driveline components. Thus 'Snow and wet grass' gives very gentle throttle response and a start in 2nd gear high range or 3rd gear low range to give a

Simplicity and direct communication between driver, vehicle and terrain is usually best for learning the skills. Response modulation may sometimes help novices.

softer torque delivery and lessen the risk of inadvertent wheel-spin. Conversely, when set to 'sand' throttle response is more aggressive and gears are held for longer.

Two-edged weapon? On this point, however, there are a great many types of 'sand', and these settings, as configured in the initial versions of the TR system, are suited only for deep churned soft sand. Unbroken dune sand with a delicate load-bearing top crust (See facing page and Sec 4.8, page 4.29) demands exactly the opposite driving technique. There is thus the well-known 'double-learning curve' familiar to users of camera auto-exposure systems (still got any pictures of grey snow?), where you have to know what the automatics are trying to do and then make allowances for that. The knowledge required to make the automatics work often exceeds the knowledge needed to get along without them.

Similarly rock crawling – one of the few conditions where traction control may be better than a locking diff – often puts less strain on transmission components with the diff

Introduced for 2005 model year, air-sprung Discovery 3 driveline controls feature (clockwise from top centre): electrically operated park-brake (see p 2.18); electric hi/lo range selector (switch position and instrument panel caption confirms selection, invaluable 30 mph on-the-move changes possible); Hill Descent (yellow button); air suspension setting switch; and (rotary knob) Terrain Response mode selector. Note there is, surprisingly, no cursor on this knob; selected mode is ascertained from illuminated pictogram (in bright sunlight too?) and dash information panel (cf Touareg, on p 2.16.) Optional LCD 4x4 info panel (left) gives valuable overview on what is going on – drive modes, HDC, diff-locks, steering angle. The latter is especially useful in muddy ruts to alert driver to 'railway-line effect' (see Sec 4.2).

There are 50 types of 'sand'. And no automatic system will be smart enough to learn them all. Vehicle carefully rolled to rest (left) without brakes on marginal 'pie crust' dune. Note how some foot-prints have broken the delicate crust, others not. Gentlest possible throttle is required, not the brutal programming of 'TR'. In soft de-bogging (right) a cautious 'boot-full' of throttle may be needed at first, followed by 'the midwife's touch' when back on 'firm' ground. Drivers must learn, not just push buttons!

locks free. TR tightens them up.

With the various hill descent systems, (Sec 4.5 and 6.4) it can be argued, as above, that if you are savvy enough to recognise a serious steep descent situation requiring you to select HDC, then you don't need any automatics to look after what to do next. A similar argument can be wheeled out, with slightly less foundation, with TR.

Some novices will find it useful, if only psychologically, and regard it as no more of

'05 Jeep Grand Cherokee chrome T-bar (lower right) is a toggle switch to select (at 3 mph max) low or high range – no indication which until instrument panel caption is consulted. Inadvertent selection would be unlikely. Confusingly, though, button to its left is just a caption while similar 'N' button (right) selects neutral in transfer box – in-button light confirms. Despite such inconsistent ergonomics, availability of a definite neutral is rare and useful, facilitating towed recovery – see p 2.25 'Towing your auto'.

a gimmick than an automatic transmission. Others will argue that it dulls and confuses the sensitive feedback between driver, vehicle and terrain that must prevail in demanding off-road driving – see photos above.

Middle path. Another, simpler, approach in a world where a multi-purpose vehicle's on-road throttle response is given a high priority and sharpened, is merely to change the throttle mapping when in low range, ie a given movement of the throttle pedal elicits less rapid engine response. A slower throttle response in low range is now standard in all 'non-TR' Land Rover products giving a slower accelerator over uneven ground. Jeep (left) has a similar arrangement but Toyota keep it simpler still and – sensibly –leave it to the driver.

'TR' and 'Type 2' 4x4. Interestingly, in 'one-robot-helping-another' mode, TR makes a useful contribution to auto-engage 4x4 in Freelander 2, interacting elegantly with the stability control system. It also loosens off the coupling when large steering angles are sensed.

Luddite reaction or valid criticism? Make your own mind up about the content of this spread as well as the ergonomics of your control system!

2.5 Automatic transmission

Basic knowledge

Standard procedure. The tolerance and smoothness of an automatic transmission, makes it ideally suited to off-roader applications. Almost invariably, but especially in the case of a diesel engine, a suitably integrated automatic transmission will result in smoother progress at lower engine rpm than would be the case with a slightly tense driver operating with a manual gearbox. For those new to automatics, standard operating procedure can be summed up briefly:

1.Most automatic gearboxes are five- or four-speed units with automatic lock-up on at least the top ratio above a certain speed to minimise torque converter slippage.

2.'**D**' *enables* (ie permits the use of) all forward ratios. '**4**' enables the lower four – ie it will use 1st, 2nd and 3rd and 4th but not change above 4th. Similarly of '**3**' and '**2**' which enables 1st and 2nd only. '**1**' enables 1st-only.

3. Select '**N**' on the main gear selector before making a transfer box selection. If it will not immediately engage, apply the brakes, engage '**D**' briefly, go back to '**N**' and try again. See Section 6.2 for low box to high box on the move on some automatics.

4. If you are stationary for any length of time, engine running, select '**P**' or '**N**' rather than let the vehicle idle 'in-gear' which will unnecessarily heat up the transmission fluid.

5. If you are in '**P**' or '**N**' apply the footbrake before selecting a forward or reverse ratio to avoid creep.

6. Remember there is usually no 'gate' between '**D**' (top ratio) and '**3**' in some vehicles so for a sudden acceleration requirement and to force a very rapid change-down all you have to do is 'slap' the selector lever back into the '**3**' position. This will often give you quicker response than a 'kick-down'.

7. In the best systems you don't have to think about kick-down or slapping through

Automatic transmission has definite advantages for off-road work as well as its obvious on-road benefits. Gentle changes preclude damage, enhance traction flow.

to third. Automatic means automatic !

Controlling the automatics

Automatic transmission off-road. Though traditionally most off-road operations are carried out by vehicles with manual transmission, this is no more than a statistical fact rather than validating any preferences. That there is considerable advantage in the use of automatic transmission off-road is attested by the fact that many military users specify it.

Advantages and disadvantages. The most obvious advantage of auto transmission is that of ease of operation for the driver. This is important for the military or public utilities user whose mind will be on other things as well as driving but is immeasurably beneficial for reducing fatigue and maintaining alertness in extended off-road operation such as expeditions, aid work or simple day-to-day use in areas where poor tracks, rocks, pot-holes and the like demand frequent slowing down to negotiate difficult terrain.

There are also significant benefits in terms of vehicle durability and protection from driver misuse and transmission shock loads. Off-road performance is considerably enhanced by an automatic's quick seamless changes of gear in 'lift-off' situations but most of all in sharply deteriorating conditions such as soft sand or deepening mud where, with a well-matched engine/transmission pair, virtually undetectable downshifts keep an unbroken tide of torque flowing to match the vehicle's need while the driver attends to choice of route.

The only disadvantages are higher initial cost and theoretically increased brake wear though, as already indicated, major professional users with cost-effectiveness in mind compare this with the higher maintenance and repair costs of misused manual vehicles and still come down in favour of automatic.

Simple, but knowledge still needed. A 4x4 with auto transmission can be operated on a minimum-knowledge basis by, say, a fleet or pool operator with disparate drivers of differing experience; for these or the inexperienced a basic knowledge will suffice. On the other hand refinement of operating effectiveness and vehicle capability will result if time is taken to learn to get the best from the system – see Sections 6.1, and 6.2.

Auto and low range

Auto – use low range. An auto will struggle manfully in high range off-road but do keep an eye on engine rpm and don't be tempted to remain in high ratio when you should be in low in difficult off-road conditions. This is an easy trap to fall into if you have not much previous off-road experience with a manual gearbox vehicle and cannot relate engine rpm to low-range ground speeds.

Poor engine braking. As indicated above, in comparison to a manual transmission, you will find an auto has surprising gradability in high range but, particularly off-road, engine braking is inherently poor even in low range. Engage '1' low range to obtain best engine braking on a descent but you will usually find cadence braking (see Sec 3.2), ABS or one of the hill descent programmes will be necessary. Engage 1st low range early for if speed is too high this will not engage – see next paragraph.

Steep up and down. A steep climb followed by a steep descent sums this situation up well. Whilst you will probably be able to climb a steepish slope well enough in high range on 'D', you will need low range '1' for the descent. To save doing a range change at the top of the incline the technique should thus be to engage low-range before the obstacle, select '3' (see below why), make the ascent and, at the top, with forward speed at a minimum, pull the main selector back to '1' in order to get maximum retardation for the descent. If you are over the summit and select '1' with the speed too high, it will not engage; you will stay in 2nd or 3rd with little or no engine braking – see Section 6.3 for emergency procedure.

'Lift-off' elimination of wheelspin. The reason for selecting '3' before a slippery

ascent or other potential wheel-spin situation is that as soon as the wheels begin to spin the auto sensors will recognise the reduced torque and change up; this will tend to eliminate wheelspin as soon as it occurs – in just the same way as you would lift off the throttle with a manual transmission to quench wheelspin near the top of a steep loose slope. Selecting '3' rather than 'D' ensures change-up is not too high.

Muddy, 'forest floor' situations. The same applies for 'forest floor' slippery mud situations. Even though the main ratio actually in use may be 1st or 2nd, having the selector in '3' ensures that, as soon as wheelspin (reduced torque) is sensed, the gearbox will change up to 3rd to eliminate spin but not change into an inappropriately high gear.

Towing your auto

Beware! Do know the score. Danger of severe transmission damage lurks for an automatic 4x4 being towed if things are not done properly. Most 4x4s with auto require both the main gear selector and the transfer box selector to be selected to neutral before they can be towed – all wheels on the ground. Not all auto-equipped 4x4s have a neutral position on the transfer box so must be put on a trailer. Some have a limited-speed, limited-distance towing caveat which usually indicates that there is a lack of an available neutral in the transfer box and that the automatic gearbox will have damaging lubrication problems if these limits are exceeded.

Some, like the 'P38' Range Rover have a magic formula ('Put a 5 amp fuse in position 11.') in order for the transfer box to find neutral. Read the manual and remember these things.

Raised front wheels? Eek! Raised front-wheels towing can be harmful unless a prop shaft is removed; know your vehicle. Never mind if the recovery service truck has arrived and wants to get on with things. Just be absolutely sure your vehicle is being towed properly.

An auto needs the help of low transfer gears just like a manual. Staying in high range in demanding off-road conditions will cause transmission oil to overheat.

Section 3

Preliminaries

3.1 Mind-set

Smooth operation, making the vehicle flow over the ground (right) rather than jolt is an indication of the required mechanical sympathy. Work your vehicle well (left) but be kind and take the drama out of the driving.

Mechanical sympathy

Preparing the ground. There are some important preliminaries, some nurturing of attitude, that you will find beneficial – either as a precursor to taking your new and seemingly large off-roader on the road for the first time, or before taking your now comfortably familiar 4x4 off the road for the first time. They may even benefit the experienced as a recap; the things you knew all along but could maybe brush up on. Not that you really need to of course ... !

Aim smooth. All machinery responds well to being treated with mechanical sympathy – even rugged off-roaders. There is more to this than just following maintenance schedules and keeping the oil topped up; that is vital but is not the whole user-interface picture. Smooth driving operation is the aim; no stabbing the brake or throttle, no forcing the gear levers, no thudding into holes or over bumps.

Be kind. Using the full capabilities of your 4x4 need not preclude your being kind to it. It is a very tolerant vehicle but clunks in the transmission, prolonged wheel spinning, misuse of the clutch and harsh treatment of any of the controls, engine or suspension should be avoided. Specifically:

Be smooth and gentle with your vehicle. Using the power is not the same as being brutal. Avoid transmission clonks and let the clutch grip fully when it has to.

1. Transmission controls. (Gear lever and transfer box lever.) Moderate force and moderate speed is the best way to use these levers – firm and gentle. If it is difficult to engage low range, leave the transfer lever where it is, dip the clutch, engage first gear and let the clutch up slightly to reposition the gear wheels. Keep the clutch down and try again. Similarly, difficulty engaging first or reverse (or noise in doing so in some older vehicles) may be eased by dipping the clutch, quickly engaging a higher synchro gear (say, third) and then trying again.

2. Riding the clutch. Don't slip the clutch or 'use it as another gear'. Don't 'ride' the clutch either; by this is meant resting your foot on the pedal with slight pressure so as to be able quickly to disengage it. It is natural enough for a properly cautious or inexperienced driver negotiating a difficult piece of terrain to want to be able to use clutch and brake with the minimum delay but riding the clutch – in effect reducing the pressure of the clutch springs – will encourage clutch slip and cause premature wear. Have the clutch fully engaged and your foot clear of the pedal, even if its only a centimetre, whenever possible.

3. Wheelspin .... As we shall see in more

detail, wheelspin is lost traction and *prolonged* wheelspin will scoop earth from under the wheels, digging a hole and worsening the situation. It is not good for the transmission either. A fast spinning wheel suddenly getting grip can cause shock loading on the transmission and the possibility of transmission damage.

3a .... but.. There *are* circumstances – certain types of mud with the best mud tyres – when controlled, short-period wheelspin will permit the tyre to cut through to drier ground and obtain traction where none existed before – see page 4.27. The same approach in sand would be disastrous. So you must become wheelspin-aware, know how your tyre tread is faring and, as we shall see, make judgements.

Pride – learn when to back off

Minimise the drama. Probably the most golden of the rules governing difficult off-road driving is to admit defeat early and reverse out. Good off-road driving is achieved with the minimum of drama. Huge water splashes, spinning wheels and flying clods of earth are rarely necessary. Even the best drivers perpetrate these fireworks occasionally if they have misjudged the terrain –

and usually feel a little sheepish afterwards.

Back off, try again. Often such drama stems from fear of failure and then trying too hard. You will learn from this book, and with practice, that part of the learning process is acquiring the procedures for initially getting it wrong – typically the failed steep slope scenario (Section 4.4). You will learn that getting it wrong first time usually does not matter; you will learn to relax. When a very steep slippery climb stops your vehicle and the wheels begin to spin, back off at once; try again, possibly with a little more speed and in a higher gear. Holding the vehicle with uncontrolled wheelspin will cause excessive damage to the ground, will usually worsen the vehicle's chances of making it up the slope and, in some cases, will cause a vehicle to slew sideways-on to the slope and possibly roll. See Sec 4.4.

Wheelspin alert! The same goes for stretches of deep mud or sand – though the two are quite different. If you do not make it through the patch first time and there is any *sustained* and ineffective wheelspin, stop before you bog deeper, reverse out and try again using a different route or different tactics. Do not be too proud to admit that you got it wrong.

If it isn't going to go it's no big deal – reverse out while you can and try again. Getting through second time is better than having to be towed out on the first try.

3.2 Gentle right foot

Max-power climbs often need sensitive throttle-foot lift-off near the top to preclude wheelspin.

Wheelspin under power and lock-up when braking: two versions of the same thing – a discontinuity of rolling contact between the wheel and the ground.

Gentle throttle

Reading the ground. You will have seen, or will see, that effective use of the low range and realising the extraordinary potential of your vehicle depends a lot on a driver's appreciation of how much traction the ground itself will take without allowing *inappropriate* wheelspin.

Excessive throttle. As with a car on ice, too much throttle will 'over-torque' the driving wheels and make them spin. You could consider this as over-torqueing the ground, for the ground will only take so much push from the tyres before they slip. With such low gearing in the low range gears, this is especially the case in slippery conditions. Drivers will quickly develop a delicate throttle foot and learn when the conditions

Continuous rolling contact. Conceptually, this is how your wheels and the ground should interact. Too much throttle (wheelspin) or too much brake (wheel slip) will break the relationship. Traction and accurate control will be lost.

are putting the vehicle on the verge of wheelspin.

Spinning wheels dig. Spinning wheels represent loss of traction, often a loss of directional control as well and can also result in ground being scooped by the spinning tyres from under the wheel and the vehicle becoming stuck. In some cases (Section 4.7) this scooping will get through slippery mud onto drier ground – but not always. Alertness is the keyword. So there are many good reasons for acquiring a sensitive throttle foot and not choosing too low a gear. Both will avoid wheelspin and help to maintain traction.

Traction control. As already introduced in Section 2.1, traction control, when fitted, will monitor, and inhibit, inadvertent wheelspin and considerably assist in maintaining traction under limiting conditions.

'Terrain Response'. Both Land Rover and Jeep use a change to a less sensitive throttle response in the low range gears to make torque control easier for the driver. Land Rover take it further on some models with 'Terrain Response', tuning a number of drivetrain parameters according to driver-selected terrain types. Depending on your viewpoint this can be regarded as a driving aid or an obstacle to your progression up the learning curve of developing your own sensitivity to terrain conditions – your own 'gentle right foot'. (More detail at Sec 2, page 2.22.) Toyota don't interfere with the driver/throttle interface on level terrain.

Gentle brake

Excessive brake. Wheelspin represents a throttle-generated discontinuity of rolling contact with the ground – the ground and the periphery of the wheel are not in stationary contact with one another. Exactly the same situation arises in the case of excessive braking on slippery ground. One or more wheels lock up and slide over the ground resulting in a discontinuity of rolling contact – the periphery of the wheel and the ground are not going the same speed. In one case the wheel is slipping past the stationary

All manner of clever automation takes care of situations like this now – Hill Descent Control and half a dozen similar pro-grammes. If you don't have that you'll probably have ABS to stop the wheels locking when you brake. No ABS? Hard manual braking will lock the wheels. The back-stop is cadence braking – the driver's foot on/off the brake as fast as he can. It never fails.

ground; in the other the ground is (relatively) slipping past the stationary wheel.

Cadence braking

Same foot, same cure. The same cures may be used to nail wheelspin and wheel slip. Lifting your right foot off the throttle will stop wheelspin and lifting your right foot off the brake will stop wheel slide or skidding. In the case of braking, though, you applied the brakes because you wanted to stop. So re-apply them more gently.

Cadence braking – sheer magic. Best of all, employ 'cadence braking' technique – repeated jabbing of the brake pedal with your foot, quite gently, as fast as you can so that the wheel never gets a chance to lock. It's a kind of manual ABS. Though it takes will-power to take your foot off the brakes to do this when you are trying to slow down, cadence braking is remarkably effective.

Cadence braking on-road too. Cadence braking, discovered and taught long before ABS was invented, works well on-road too – probably even more spectacularly. Off-road tyres often lack the on-road grip of tyres designed specifically for tarmac (see Section 8.2) and many is the case of a desert-tyred off-roader in rain on tarmac overseas being saved from certain collision by frantic cadence braking; frantic but controlled ... !

ABS – automated finesse. Anti-lock brakes (ABS) – as many will know, employ a very fast form of automated cadence brak-

ing to obtain the maximum retardation on the most difficult surfaces without locking up any of the wheels. You will hear and feel, through pedal feedback, the brake relay working. So in the case of a vehicle fitted with this feature you will get maximum available braking and retain directional control – *for given ground conditions.* Beware, however; ABS will not reverse the laws of physics. If you are on ice, packed snow or slippery mud there is only so much any braking system can do. ABS and cadence braking will give the best possible braking for those conditions but, to repeat, neither can change the laws of physics.

Engine braking

Elegant, gentle. Engine braking, of course, is a very controlled and gentle way to achieve retardation as we shall see in the Sections to follow. But even that should not be regarded as an infallible solution to every problem, especially when it is very slippery; you can still finish up with sliding wheels – see Section 6.4. And, with selectable 4x4 (Type 1, p 2.2), remember that when you are in two-wheel drive your engine braking is only acting on two wheels, not four.

Wheel slide on wet tarmac or slippery mud or ice? Back off the brakes and re-apply with rapidly repeated gentle jabs. That's cadence braking – sort of manual ABS.

3.3 Geometric limitations

Clearance angles

Appreciating clearance. Common to negotiating all types of obstacle off-road is an appreciation of under-body clearance angles, clearance under the chassis and axle differentials and the amount by which the axles can articulate (move up on the near-side and down on the offside – and vice versa – see next spread).

Clearances, under-chassis angles. True off-roaders tend to be high and have lots of ground clearance, which is how they perform so well cross country. A few moments to study the accompanying diagrams, how-

ever, will help to refine your judgement on the kind of thing that can and cannot be done without touching bodywork or chassis on the ground. Under-axle clearance is relevant to the size of a single isolated rock on the track between the wheels that can be driven over without fouling, but under-belly clearance relates to the (bigger) size of ridge undulations that can be crossed.

Ramp angle – belly clearance. The angle measured from the chassis at the centre of the wheelbase down to the periphery of front and rear wheels is the ramp breakover angle, usually called the ramp angle. Its significance is self-evident since it governs whether or not you will 'belly' the vehicle on a hump. Such a hump taken without thought of the ramp angle can result in getting bellied with the wheels grappling for traction and the vehicle's weight taken directly on the chassis on the top of the hump – see photos at Section 5.1.

Underbelly damage. Depending on the design of the vehicle and provision or otherwise of skid plates, bellying can result in damage – usually to the exhaust system. If it bellies on the transfer gearbox the unit, as well as the gearbox mountings (not designed to take the weight of the vehicle or any ploughing operation) can be wrecked.

Variable suspension. Some upmarket 4x4s, in pursuit of improved ride (and to counter the inevitably high unsprung weight of their axle assemblies) are fitted with air suspension. This, for added cost and complexity affords the opportunity to provide variable-height suspension for off-road use. This is now a fairly widespread option. Whilst early versions offered insignificant lift – 25mm or so – modern versions can effect a 50-100mm increase. This is at the cost of articulation – see next spread.

Axle clearance. Under-axle clearance is a more obvious limitation since it is always less than under-belly clearance. Do not be tempted to allow an axle diff casing to plough out its own path. Deep ruts, rocks submerged in soft mud or encountering hard or rocky going will cause the vehicle to

Clearance angles – what they are

Be aware of under-axle clearance and how it differs from belly clearance. Low-set towing hitch can cause tail end to dig in on steep ascents or crossing ditches.

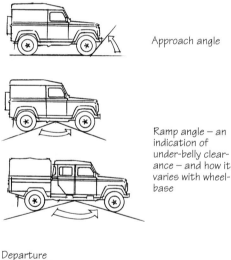

Approach angle

Ramp angle – an indication of under-belly clearance – and how it varies with wheelbase

Departure angle – and how a towing hitch can affect it

Under-axle, under-belly clearances

Double-wishbone, independent suspension. Less ground clearance on bump than beam axle but is close with air suspension extended – sacrificing articulation

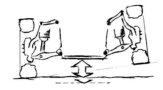

Beam axle. Constant ground clearance

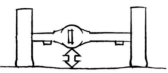

Underbelly clearance is almost invariably greater than under-axle clearance

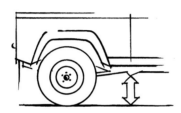

Know where parts of the vehicle may touch the ground. Tow hitch (top), commonly forgotten and here leaves a rear wheel hanging. If a G-Wagen bellies, it will be on massive girder chassis, not on vulnerable exhaust or gearbox.

come to a sudden damaging stop when the axle differential housing hits the obstacle. If in doubt, get out – see Section 3.4 on marshalling.

Approach and departure angles. Approach angles (diagram, left) are large on most 4x4s but remember that tail overhang and departure angle is the one that will catch you out most often going up a very steep slope (see below). Regarding the common problem of 'hitting the tail', the departure angle is further reduced when a low-set towing hitch is fitted and it is not uncommon for an inattentive driver to dig the tow

hitch into the ground while going forward up a very steep incline and then find that he cannot reverse back because the tow hitch prevents him doing so.

Big wheels, short wheelbase. The biggest wheels and the shortest wheelbase will give best under-chassis clearance angles – a Defender 90 or Wrangler on big tyres will do better than a pickup; their short rear overhangs also yield the best departure angles.

Long wheelbase and tail overhang call for more caution on rough ground – especially with aft-mounted fuel tanks.

Clearance angles – what they mean

The significance of – left to right – approach angle, departure angle and ramp angle.

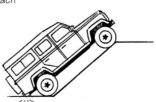

Axle articulation

Maintaining traction. As the picture at the foot of p 2.7 shows, there are two ways for a 4x4 to maintain traction on wavy ground: allow the axles so much rocking freedom that the wheels always stay in contact with the ground, or accept that this cannot be achieved and when one wheel leaves the ground nail the resulting wheelspin with traction control or locking diffs (see p 2.6).

Axle movement. Articulation is the rocking movement of the axles relative to each other – the amount by which one axle can move, left wheel up, right wheel down or vice versa, in relation to the chassis and its fellow axle. So it represents the degree to which your vehicle can keep its wheels on the ground on undulating 'twisty' terrain and thus retain traction under difficult conditions. Articulation is thus a geometric limitation, albeit one of the less obvious ones. As we saw on p 1.4 and the pictures and panel on pp 2.6 and 2.7, lots of articulation is at odds with good on-road handling, normally constrained by anti-roll bars, and some designers have targeted a best-of-both-worlds solution by providing automatic or selectable roll control – Nissan Patrol, and the 2006 Jeep Wrangler JK, for instance, have disconnectable anti-roll bars.

Longitudinal articulation angle. This term is a way of encapsulating wheel movement vs wheelbase as a single parameter. For a given wheel movement, a longer wheelbase will have a smaller longitudinal articulation angle – see below.

Axle articulation keeps wheels in contact with the ground and producing traction. A short wheelbase vehicle will be more agile than one with a long wheelbase.

Navara achieves exceptional articulation – the more notable for being leaf sprung at the back. Offside tyre is frighteningly close to wheel arch roof – but, thanks to well-designed bump stop, not touching!

Air suspension. 4x4s with air suspension instead of steel springs often have the capability to extend the suspension units to afford more under-belly clearance off-road – VW Touareg, Discovery 3, Range Rover, Cayenne. This establishes a new 'static' suspension datum but wheel movement either side of this for bumps or dips after raising the suspension is more limited. So the real articulation with suspension raised is less than with it in the normal position.

Turning, leaning, wading

Manoeuvrability, lateral lean. As with under-belly clearance, in terms of manoeuvrability, inevitably the shorter the wheelbase the tighter the turning circle. Whether Darwinian evolution saw off-roaders coming is not clear but we all seem to be equipped with a well-developed and self-preservational fear of lateral lean in vehicles. The angle to which an off-roader can lean laterally without tipping is surprisingly high; comfortably, we all chicken out before we reach it. Keep it that way! As covered in Section 4.6, 'Traversing slopes', the limit is in any case a static figure and should not be relied on when driving. Local bumpiness and the effect of even minor steering corrections make a considerable difference

Longitudinal articulation angle

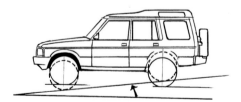

NB For a given wheel movement, a longer wheelbase will have less effective articulation on uneven ground.

Turning circle is an important geometric limitation and related to wheelbase. Despite a commendable max steering angle, Mercedes GL's 3075mm wheelbase gives it a 560mm larger turning circle than Discovery 3.

and a limit of half the figures given is recommended.

Wading depth. Maximum wading depth for most off-roaders is around 0.5 metre – the limiting factors being water spray on the ignition harness of a petrol engined vehicle and height of the air intake. *Under no circumstances whatever, should water be allowed into the engine air intake.* As shown at Section 4.10, there are preparations and precautions to be taken before wading to this depth.

Inspection first. When close to any of the above geometric limitations a preliminary survey on foot is what is required,

preferably with someone to marshal you through or round the obstacle when you resume the driving seat. It is pointless to risk damage or getting stuck for the want of properly surveying the obstacle first. This is fully dealt with in the next spread.

If you are near to the limits, get out and take a closer look – see next spread. Traversing lateral slopes be sure small dips don't increase tip angle beyond prudent limits.

Side slopes always feel worse than they are – but don't press your luck! Independently sprung Discovery 3 demonstrates prodigious articulation on test track, using traction control to steady the airborne wheel. (Below) Know your vehicle's wading limits before committing to deep water. How much deeper does this get? Was there a pathfinder? See next spread.

3.4 Look before you leap

Always worth it. An on-foot survey will delay you and is usually mucky or wet. It is, however, far preferable to damaging the vehicle or finding you have a major recovery problem on your hands.

On-foot survey

Inspect before you drive. It is invariably beneficial to do an on-foot survey of difficult obstacles before committing the vehicle. The aim of the survey is to pick the best route and ensure there are no previously unnoticed hazards such as rocks to foul the axles, deep ruts hidden in undergrowth or the lie of an obstacle under snow. A reconnaissance also gives you the chance to test the firmness of visible ground – soft mud or the strength of the sand crust on a dune.

Even if it's the 50th time that day, always make an on-foot inspection of difficult/unknown obstacles. Omitting it will risk getting your vehicle stuck or damaged.

Prod before you drive. An on-foot recce is especially important when fording streams and rivers where there is no established safe path. Nor will it be easy since you will have to establish not only the firmness of the river bed but also its evenness. Dropping into an underwater rock hole or suddenly descending to a depth that will drown the engine will require fundamental and major recovery procedures. Water deeper than about 35 cm demands that wading plugs be fitted to the clutch housing and cam-belt drive housing in some Land Rover vehicles. (See 'Wading', Section 4.10.)

Marshalling

External guidance – marshalling. If you are not alone, an invaluable adjunct to negotiating difficult ground with small clearances is to have your passenger marshal you through from outside the vehicle. Only someone outside the vehicle can properly see all four wheels and where they are going – and see the exact clearances under the axle casings (see photos Section 4.9).

Wading recce

On-foot inspection especially important in rivers where hazards are hidden.

On-foot pre-inspection establishes feasibility – the aquatic imperatives and method shown far left and left below. On the steep hill – and gully right – the driver can see far too little to be safe. Just the on-foot recce may be enough but, if in any doubt, a marshaller can see all four wheels and gives precision guidance. On rocky ground this can also avoid tyre sidewall damage on rocks.

Overall view, take it steady. A marshaller should stand 5 to 15 metres ahead of the vehicle – facing it – where all the wheels can easily be seen. Guidance by the marshaller should be given unambiguously and entirely by hand and arm signals rather than by voice. At the risk of stating the obvious, be sure there is just one marshaller who is in total charge and make a conscious effort to take things one step at a time. Situations in which marshalling is required frequently spawn two or three people all shouting half-heard directions at one time; the general tension often generates a feeling that something decisive and effective must be done, immediately...! The calm and measured approach is to be preferred!

Marshaller in control. Obey the marshaller completely. Try not to take your eyes off him or her to make your own judgements on a situation you cannot assess as comprehensively as someone outside the vehicle. Stop if you are not happy but once moving, the marshaller is in control.

One marshaller only in control. Directions by signs, not voice. Stop if you're not happy; otherwise always obey the marshaller. He's the one who can see all four wheels.

Marshalling signals

Advance   Go back   Stop   Steer in this direction

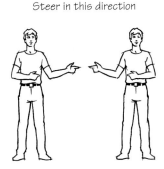

Hand signals for marshalling are simple and unambiguous, given close-to or at a distance.

Section 4

Operating techniques

4.1 Towing – on-road

Preliminaries – the theory

Theory matters? There will be many who, faced with pulling *that* trailer (no choice) with *this* vehicle (no choice) are of a mind to doubt the value of theory and just get on with it. An understandable view from a busy operator but airline pilots, similarly limited in choice of type or design of the aircraft they fly, do benefit a great deal – and safety is immeasurably enhanced – by knowing what is going on aerodynamically. There is much folklore and many rules of thumb associated with towing and it is helpful and refreshing to know that what goes on really is quantifiable now and every parameter may be taken into account – from the spring rates of the towing vehicle (tug) to the types of bushes fitted to the suspension.

Famine and feast. A capable design analysis computer could produce enough information and study of variables to fill a book on this subject alone. The object of this section, in just eight pages, is to steer a middle course between the information famine of preceding years and the feast of data now available. The good news, for readers braced for another 'breakthrough' and overturning of received wisdom, is that virtually all the rules of thumb are valid. Knowing why, though – and their limitations – is absorbing and there are enough surprises to make it worthwhile reading further.

Trailer dynamics

Stability. Overriding priority will be given by all operators examining this subject to the question of stability and safety and brief treatment will be given therefore to:
- Straight line stability.
- Oscillation or weave.
- Steady turn stability.

Straight line stability. Consider a towing vehicle (tug) of infinite mass – the implication being that the towing pin moves in an undeviating straight line, uninfluenced by the trailer. The trailer behind it will tow straight for the same reason a dart or aircraft flies straight; as soon as the trailer deviates due to a gust or random side-load, the tyres will then be at an angle to the direction of motion and as a result a side-force will be generated by the tyres to push the trailer back in line behind the tug.

When trailer weight exceeds around 75% of tug weight, the laws of physics dictate you are entering a critical zone for stability. Be aware of the theory of trailer dynamics and know what is going on.

However hard-nosed and down to earth the job, knowing the theory will make operations safer.

With imaginary non-deviating tug, trailer displacement gives rise to tyre slip angle which in turn generates restoring side-force to put trailer back on course in single or decaying series of swings. If trailer can influence tug (diagram opposite, far right) complex swings can be self-sustaining.

Yaw angle and tyre slip angle

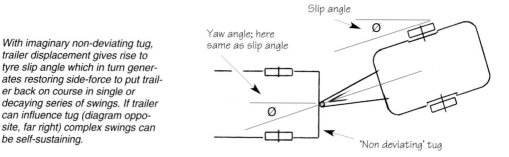

Slip angle

Yaw angle; here same as slip angle

Ø

Ø

'Non deviating' tug

As the trailer approaches zero slip angle the side-force also reduces until, when it is in line again, the side-force has disappeared. Fairly obvious stuff but it is important to consider this – the concept of slip angle and tyre side-force – before going on.

Right – an illustration not designed to scare but inserted (from a complete computer sequence) only to indicate that the result of a given combination of parameters and driving techniques can be predicted as a matter of routine. (50 mph, 2000 kg trailer, CG aft of axle, severe avoidance manoeuvre, .22 g braking.) How to avoid it in absence of precise data is less easily predicted; knowledge of general theory, care and caution are best ingredients. Diagrams below – dynamics of tug/trailer interface with decaying or increasing oscillation can be analogous to swinging a school ruler on a pencil. See text.

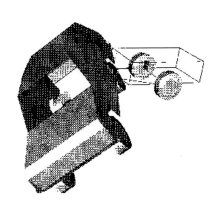

Oscillation, weave

Concept of decaying or increasing oscillation.

Few who have seen TV pictures of caravans 'mysteriously' turning over on motorways will need a definition of weave, yaw or snaking. However, do distinguish between decaying (convergent) and increasing (divergent) oscillation; the difference between what is mildly alarming and peters out and the ever-increasing swing that can result in an accident. Take an ordinary school ruler (the type with a hole in one end) and let it swing on a pencil held in your hand – diagrams below.

The middle diagram (the hand remains perfectly still) corresponds exactly to the tug of infinite mass mentioned opposite where the tug continues undisturbed on a perfectly straight course. The swing of the ruler gradually decays to nothing. The third diagram corresponds to a tug that can move. As you

know, moving your hand in a particular way can make the ruler swing with increasing amplitude. In moving your hand (holding the pencil pivot) to make the ruler swing you are instinctively introducing an appropriate frequency and phasing of your movement to make the ruler swing as wide as possible. Try analysing *exactly* what you are doing and you will see how difficult it is to pinpoint the phase lead and frequency you are introducing. This is mentioned because although the computer, when given the tug/trailer dynamics to sort out, can apply the equations of motion and all the myriad modifying influences with tireless brilliance and accuracy, it reflects the number of variables and how critical they are when the overall stability result is considered.

Exact prediction of dynamics is possible. But the myriad criteria and their varying influence make it impractical to attempt in every case.

Decaying and increasing oscillations

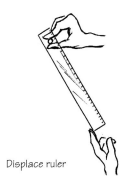

Displace ruler

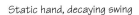

Static hand, decaying swing

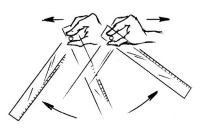

Moving hand, increasing swing

Whiplash effect. Let us therefore resort once more to an analogy, again using the school ruler. This time hold it in a horizontal plane, with your thumb and forefinger over the hole. Flick your wrist left and right and you will see as you do so that the ruler trails, moves and then overshoots the action of your wrist – what may be termed a whiplash effect. Get the combination of thumb-grip (damping) and wrist-speed wrong and nothing much happens; get it 'right' and a perfect 'whiplash' takes place; again you will note there is a particular combination of parameters that 'excite' the system and these are related to the weight of ruler, speed of motion, damping, etc.

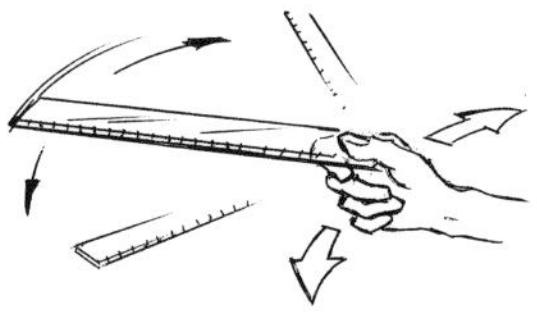

The parallels between these three 'ruler cases' and a tug and trailer –

• The decaying oscillation

• The increasing oscillation due to hand movement and

• The 'whiplash' effect – closely related to the above.

– will be seen at once. With the ruler / pendulum the restoring 'side-force' is provided by gravity and inertia where in the case of the trailer the side-force is provided by the tyres.

Forward trailer CG benefits stability in weaves but too far forward will exacerbate problems in sharp turn manoeuvres. Aim for trailer CG 10-20 cm ahead of axle.

Applying the analogy. It is clear so far that lateral motion of the *tug*, at given phase differences and amplitudes, is a fundamental influencing factor in the generation, sustaining and 'amplification' of lateral oscillation. Because it will affect what we can do about it, it is worth now probing just a little deeper into the actual situation with a tug and trailer.

We have considered the ruler (trailer) swinging about the pivot point (tow hitch) for convenience because that is what actually happens. But we must now grasp the fact that a trailer (or any other 'body'), given a turning motion, will *naturally* want to rotate about its own centre of gravity (CG). Spin a Coke bottle on a table and it will spin about its CG. If you constrain one end while it is revolving (trailer nose hitched to a tow-

hook) it will turn about *that* point but is still trying to rotate about is own CG so will exert a reactive lateral force on the hitch.

CG position. Remember the start point here is a conceptually displaced trailer to the right of the vehicle and the tyre side-force at the trailer then influencing its behaviour. Look at where, in a typical tug / trailer combination, the tug and trailer CGs are located and how this affects the influence of trailer on tug – diagrams opposite (upper)

In a swing, a forward trailer CG (ie tyre side-force acting *aft* of the CG) tends to reduce yaw angle Ø; in effect reducing the angle between the tug and trailer (the pale grey lines). So this permits the oscillation to decay giving a result like the middle diagram on the last page (no hand movement). The *aft* CG, on the other hand tends to increase Ø because tyre side-force is acting ahead of the CG. This encourages an increasing swing. Most readers will already know that a forward CG is best for trailers. When we look to the next sub-section and diagram, however, we will find that the CG should not be *too* far forward.

Steady-state cornering

Extreme forward trailer CG. You might perhaps have felt that the further forward the trailer CG the better would be its stability, but at extreme forward CGs in fast bends there is a *destabilising* effect of the trailer on the tug that actually increases with forward movement of trailer CG. The computer confirms that moving the CG even 30 cm ahead of the axle in an accelerating steady turn can, in certain circumstances, cause breakaway of the tug towards the centre of the circle ('tuck-in') and subsequent rollover. The lower diagram opposite makes clear what is happening. Although it is tyre side-force acting about the trailer CG, you may find it easier to think of it as 'centrifugal force' on the mass represented by the CG; either way, the trailer CG, being far forward, tends strongly to push the nose of the trailer (and the tail of the tug) towards the outside of the circle. There comes a time when the rear tyres of the tug can no longer hold on

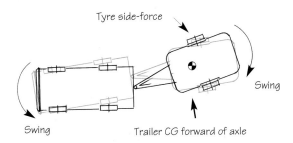

Tyre side-force

Swing

Swing

Trailer CG forward of axle

Assume trailer displaced to right, so tyre side-force is from right. Tyre side-force tends to turn trailer about its own CG, imparting motion to tail of tug that is stabilising (forward CG – left) or destabilising (aft CG – below)

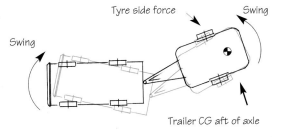

Tyre side force

Swing

Swing

Trailer CG aft of axle

and the tail of the tug breaks away to the outside of the turn and the trailer, in hot pursuit, can provoke a rollover. The practical application of this information? Take corners slowly.

The compromise

Moderation in all things. In concept, therefore, we have a conflict. The weave damping case demands a forward CG and the steady-state turn is sensitive to a too-far forward CG. Whilst *all stability problems are more critical with a high trailer weight*, your particular combination of variables and cornering methods will dictate your choice of CG position. *On most of the initial computer runs a CG about 10-20 cm ahead of the axle gave the best margin for stability.* There are also, as we shall see, other practical factors that favour limiting the forward CG position such as keeping a moderate trailer nose load on the tug's towing hitch.

Evening–up the (side) loads. Clearly to minimise the effect of the trailer on the tug (where a trailer of comparative weight to the tug is used), we must aim to spread the cornering forces evenly between all the wheels involved. In an *ideal* world: same load, same tyres, same tyre pressures on all axles. The world is not ideal so we must instead be sure of the following:
- Do not overload the rear axle of the tug.
- Tyre pressures appropriate to axle load; if in doubt err high.
- Trailer CG forward but not too far.

High trailer weight makes things worse – everything! Drive with extra care; you are fighting the laws of physics!

Fast or tightening steady turn with far-forward CG on heavy trailer can eventually cause the tug rear tyres to lose grip, permitting tail end to slide to outside of turn due to excess 'centrifugal force'. Long tug rear overhang makes things worse as trailer has more leverage.

Extreme forward trailer CG

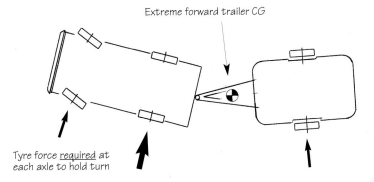

Tyre force <u>required</u> at each axle to hold turn

Practicalities

Safety first. No apology is made for the over-used cliché nor for the accent so far in this section on stability and safe operation. Provided the dozens of relevant parameters are known, the behavioural characteristics of any tug/trailer combination can be predicted on computer models but in the real world they are not known and awareness of the principles of what is going on is doubly important. In many parts of the world, and here the UK is included, legislation for trailer operational safety is skeletal and flimsy. Though complex, it extends to little more than construction and basic use and no regulations cover regular testing or functional checks to what are, in many cases, infrequently-used vehicles. Apart from catch-all 'roadworthy condition' regulations, no periodic tests (brake function etc) are laid down.

Surprisingly, trailer operation is under-legislated with no periodic or age-related tests. Under-used trailers are prone to rusting-up or jamming of brakes.

Your responsibility. It thus behoves the user more than ever to ensure that trailers are in first-rate condition. Readers of this book will in some cases be those using heavy trailers up to and exceeding the weight of the towing vehicle. Be aware that, even using a large off-roader tug, *once you are past a trailer weight of around 75% of the weight of the towing vehicle the simple laws of physics dictate you are entering a critical zone in regard to stability, steering and braking; unrelenting care in operation is your responsibility.*

General towing considerations. The diagram opposite encapsulates all the crite-

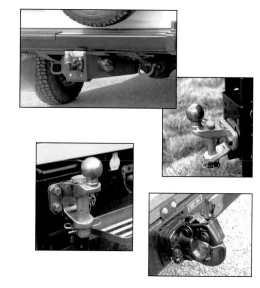

From top: 3500 kg limit ball – also with twin rear tow-rope shackles. Combination 3500 kg tow ball/jaw with variable height hitch – essential for twin-axle trailers (see Item 6, opposite). Four-bolt-fixing hitch cleared for 3500 kg on ball, 5000 kg on pin. High-rated 'NATO' pintle for use with towing eye.

ria relevant to optimum load and stability in a trailer and should be studied carefully in relation to the trailer/tug combination you have. Nose load is critically important to towing stability when setting up a given trailer.

Some typical approved off-roader maximum gross trailer weights						
Trailer/braking	On/off road	Defender with 2.5D kg	Defender, any other engine kg	Discovery kg	Range Rover kg	New Range Rover kg
1. Unbraked trailer	On road Off road	750 500	750 500*	750 500†	750 750	750 500
2. Trailer with overrun brakes	On road Off road	3500 1000	3500 1000	3500** 1000†	3500 1000	3500 1000
3. 4-wheel trailer with coupled brakes (see above).	On road Off road	3500 1000	4000 1000	4000† 1000†	4000 1000	3500 1000
*750 kg for 110 with self-levelled suspension. **Discovery Mpi 2750 kg †Not Discovery Mpi*						

Towing variables – seeking the optimum

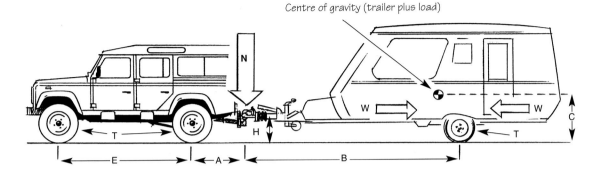

Centre of gravity (trailer plus load)

Go slowly through the variables:
1. A:E – minimise the ratio (small A, big E) when considering a towing vehicle.
2. A:B – minimise the ratio (small A, big B) when considering a trailer.
3. C:B – C not to exceed 40% of B, so keep CG low.
   C not to exceed 95% of trailer track (small C, wide track).
4. E:B – Small E, big B makes for easier reversing.
5. T – Tyre pressures – hard: use GVW settings (Sec 8.2) unless off road (Sec 6.4).
6. H – Same for trailer and towing vehicle. *Specially important with twin-axle trailer.*
7. **N** – Trailer nose weight. More nose weight equals more anti-weave stability but less cornering stability (lower diagram, previous spread and Note in Trouble Shooting table next spread) – 7% of trailer gross weight is a guide, BUT:
   1. Do not exceed limits of ball hitch or coupling head – usually 100–150 kg.
   2. Remove twice this amount from towing vehicle payload – ie if N = 75 kg, take 150 kg off listed max payload of vehicle when working out how much else you can carry in towing vehicle.
8. W – For a given nose weight, concentrate load close to trailer axle to reduce moment of inertia.

Note. CG position. To calculate CG position you need to know trailer gross weight (weighbridge), axle-to-hitch distance (drawbar length) and nose weight (bathroom scales or weighbridge). Then:
CG position (in cm, ahead of trailer axle) = Nose load in kg times drawbar length in cm divided by the trailer gross weight in kg.

Braking and weight. Braking method and capacity are especially important. Design and regulatory limitations applicable to some sample Land Rover products are shown opposite and give an indication of what to look for; note the large difference between on- and off-road cleared towing maxima. See also Section 6.4 Towing off-road. Above 3500 kg trailer gross weight coupled brakes are mandatory but will be beneficial below this for their sensitivity. Single or twin line air or vacuum brakes with various reservoirs may be fitted. Fitment of such systems requires specialist knowledge and workmanship and should only be carried out by specialists.
Tow hitch, coupling head strength.

Remember that the widely used 50 mm ball hitch is limited to a 3500 kg trailer gross weight. Above this use one of the hitches shown opposite. Nose load must normally not exceed 150 kg.
Rear axle load. The effect of trailer download on the rear axle of the tug has already been shown to be very relevant to stability – some, but not too much, is required. The download on the towing hitch is also like having additional payload far aft of the centre of the vehicle load bed – check the diagram at Sec 8.1 (3rd spread) and you will see that 250 kg carried on the tailgate actually increases the rear axle load by 341 kg. The same applies to trailer nose load; see Note 2 under 'N' (Item 7) in diagram above.

Nose load is critical to stability. Remember too strength limits of the tow hitch. Nose-load is tug payload. Take double the nose-load off your residual tug payload.

A substantial tow car with four-wheel drive raises the important tug/trailer weight ratio as well as enhancing traction on wet sites. Kia Sorrento, voted towcar of the year, beneficially also has short rear overhang. Front-mounted hitch useful for precise manoeuvring.

Driving with a trailer

Always check brakes. Although light, unbraked trailers will seem not to affect the vehicle very much it is wise to check overall braking action as soon as possible after starting off. Trailers with overrun brakes – especially if they have not been used for some time – can suffer from grabby, non-progressive brakes due to rusty brake drums and a test on a clear piece of road is essential before setting off with a newly loaded trailer. Whilst coupled brakes should be more progressive, a test is still wise since the trailer may not be proportionally braked and still exert some residual push on the towing vehicle during braking.

Braking, general. Whatever the regulations permitting use of some trailers without brakes, braked trailers are more stable than unbraked. That said, *any* braking situation will exacerbate a marginal stability or safety problem. Keep this always in your mind together with the need to avoid braking

As soon as you are moving, check braking response. Always keep maximum space between yourself and vehicle ahead. Keep tug and trailer in line for braking.

except when the trailer and tug are in line. These considerations should lead to a conscious and consistent effort to drive with as much space between you the vehicle ahead as possible so that you are never called upon to brake suddenly or fiercely. Often your cargo (horses, say) will dictate this anyway.

Reversing. Reversing with a trailer is a well-known difficulty for drivers not used to it. In general, trailers which are long relative to the wheelbase of the towing vehicle (such as articulated trucks) are easier to reverse than those that are short. Those that are shorter than the wheelbase of the tug are all but impossible to reverse any distance. As with all aspects of operating your off-roader, do not be afraid to admit you have got it wrong. If a trailer is that short, it will also be light and uncoupling to manoeuvre it by hand will save the difficulty of reversing it.

Auto-reverse brakes. Overrun trailer brakes work on the principle that a braking tug will cause the trailer to push against the

Gross trailer weights above 3500 kg demand a ring-hitch and coupled brakes – a special vehicle modification. Top and centre (left) show electrically driven compressor unit and associated couplings for air brakes (as opposed to vacuum brakes). Lower shot shows heavyweight turn-table trailer which is stable but brings its own reversing problems.

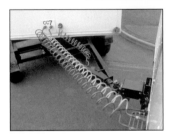

an inhibiting catch before and after doing so. Currently, all new trailers with overrun brakes have an auto-reverse fitment that senses the difference between overrun and reversing and no driver action is required. Be sure you are aware of which brake type you have.

Excessive braking. Harsh braking when towing causes the trailer to increase download on the towing vehicle hitch (hence need for centre of gravity constraints, diagram previous spread). This produces a rotating moment about the rear axle and a resulting offloading of the vehicle front wheels which can, in slippery conditions, produce front wheel lock-up. This will not happen with ABS brakes and the risk can be reduced by use of cadence braking (Sec 3.2).

Electrics. Lights, brake lights and direction indicators should be checked with the trailer and electrics connected.

Towing off-road – see Section 6.4.

Does your trailer have auto-reverse brakes? Or must you operate a catch before and after reversing?

hitch and in doing so apply its own brakes. Reversing such a trailer would ordinarily therefore cause the trailer brakes to come on and you must get out of the vehicle to apply

Towing – trouble-shooting summary	
Symptom	*Things to do*
1. Weaving	Move trailer CG forward, reduce trailer weight, reduce moment of inertia (concentrate weight closer to the trailer axle), increase trailer and tug tyre pressures, fit a hitch yaw damper, increase trailer drawbar length, reduce speed.
2. 'Oversteer' cornering (tendency to 'tuck-in' when cornering)	Move trailer CG further *aft* (but not less than 10-20 cm ahead of trailer axle), *reduce cornering speed*, increase tug rear tyre pressures. small reduction in tug front tyre pressures, reduce trailer weight, increase trailer drawbar length.

Note. You will see that, from the point of view of trailer CG position, the two conditions above are (literally) 'swings and roundabouts': improve the weave (swing) stability by moving the trailer CG forward and you could be in danger of encountering divergent oversteer on sharp/fast bends (such as roundabouts). Tendency to weave will in some cases be due to an inherent conditions (in relation to your load) you can do nothing about – such as tug rear overhang, for instance. You may be compelled here to move trailer CG further forward than you would wish in order to quench tendency to weave. In these circumstances it may be the right decision so long as you ensure your cornering speeds are reduced.

4.2 Driving on tracks

Typical unsurfaced tracks have moderately fast sections for which 5th low range may be ideal, enabling you to change down to a cautious 2nd for the really rough bits without a range-change.

Sympathetic flow

Driving – smooth, calm. On tracks, even rough ones, your driving technique should aim to have the vehicle flow smoothly over it rather than jolt and jar. This will usually mean adjusting your speed downwards and varying it according to the unevenness immediately in front of the vehicle – typically slowing at the apex of a rise or the bottom of a dip, however small they may be, You will probably find a general speed that will cope with it all and yield a smooth ride. If your vehicle has coil springs front and rear you will find it easier to achieve a jolt-free ride, albeit there are clever things that can be done with multi-leaf springs to give a pliant, stiction-free ride. The application of the mechanical sympathy mentioned in Section 3.1 will do much to foster an appropriately smooth driving technique for these conditions. Taking a calm and unhurried approach will also help; correction – it is fundamental.

Aim to flow smoothly over rough terrain – don't let the vehicle jolt and jar. High gears in the low box very useful for rough tracks.

Which gears? High range 2WD in maybe 3rd gear is often quite adequate for driving on unsurfaced tracks, depending on the smoothness and frequency of rough patches but, as mentioned before (Sec 2.5, 'Low range – when and how'), the high gears in the low range can be very useful on rough tracks. Such tracks usually have short, difficult sections for which the steady control of the low range will be required without constant use of brake and clutch .

High gears, low range. Thus taking a track in, say, top gear low range will allow the driver to make a good pace without excessive revs yet change right down to 2nd or even 1st when the ultimate low speed control and torque is required; this without the need to change transfer gear range. There is, of course, quite an overlap between speeds in the high and low range gears – for example 4th or 5th low box being equivalent to 2nd or 3rd in high. To get a clear picture of the overlap between high and low range gears, see Sec 6.1, 'High/low range overlap'.

Automatics. As in many aspects of off-road driving, a well-matched auto gearbox is the ultimate aid to smooth driving – stress free for driver and vehicle.

Railway line effect

Slippery ruts. Driving along a deeply rutted track where the ruts are cut into slippery ground can be like driving along rail-

Deep ruts with slippery sides (right) can mask normal steering feedback. You can be unaware your wheels are not pointing straight ahead. When grip is available, vehicle suddenly veers. Discovery 3's '4x4 info' display (above) is a valuable aid in this respect – also allowing you to keep head and arms inboard, safe from hostile vegetation.

way lines. Turning the steering wheel left or right does not have any effect since the tyres will not grip on the steep slippery sides of the ruts. The danger of this situation is that you can be driving along with some steering lock applied (which the vehicle is not responding to) and not know it. When the vehicle reaches level ground or a patch where traction permits it to respond to the steering lock applied, the vehicle will suddenly veer off the track with possibly dangerous consequences.

Wheels straight ahead? Since this condition is not met every day it is doubly important to have the possibility in the back of your mind that the conditions may be of this type when you are in ruts. The way to preclude the occurrence is to monitor the self-centring of the steering. Periodically and very briefly reduce your grip on the steering wheel by keeping just a light frictional touch with the palms of your hands, letting it regain, through castor action (see

Glossary, Section 9.1), the straight ahead position. Also a visual check from the driver's window will establish which way the wheels are pointing. When using the window in this way beware of branches of shrubs or trees flicking in your face.

Traction

Existing wheel tracks. If there are already wheel tracks along the unsurfaced road you are travelling, this can affect the traction of your vehicle – for better or for worse. On wet or muddy tracks or in snow it is best to follow in the tracks of a previous vehicle since, in general terms, that vehicle will probably have cut through to the drier ground beneath and this will offer your vehicle more traction. See also Section 4.4, 'Climbing steep slopes', and Section 4.7, 'Weak ground' .

Desert and bush. On sandy tracks in desert or bush or on routes over desert plains avoid the tracks of previous vehicles – often you will have to divert from the track in order to do this – since they will have broken the thin crust that normally forms on windblown sand. Beneath this crust is soft sand offering less flotation; this is likely to be badly churned which will make flotation and traction even worse. See 'Sand', Section 4.8.

Beware driving with non-gripping steering lock on. Let self-centring castor-action periodically align your wheels in deep ruts.

Fast relatively smooth tracks are one of the delights of 'off-road' driving but you should always be on your guard against sudden deterioration – typically a transverse gully or runnel – and the reduced braking the loose surface causes. Muddy tracks call for a delicate right foot.

Deep ruts, gullies

Under-axle clearance. Rough tracks will sometimes deteriorate into deep V-shaped gullies due to water erosion or extra deep ruts caused by the passage of trucks with larger wheels than yours. Keeping in such ruts will lead to grounding the chassis or axle case of your vehicle and anticipation is needed to take appropriate advance action. As the diagram shows, you should aim to get out of the ruts early so as to straddle the gully. (In extreme cases you can use a hi-lift jack for this – see Section 5.1.) Care will be necessary to avoid steering up one or other of the gully walls which could lead to the vehicle being trapped with its side against the gully.

Be on the lookout for ruts that have become gullies. They will run you out of under-axle clearance.

Steering feel. As indicated in the previous spread, because of the depth or slipperiness of the rut or gully, you may well lose the natural feel of the steering and find it hard to know exactly which way your wheels are pointing. Worse, the combination of the wheels' natural castor angle and the terrain under it can cause the wheel to want to turn towards a steep upslope – ie the side of the rut or gully. For this reason keep a firm grip on the steering wheel and check the wheels are pointing where they should be. To ensure front and back wheels are surveyed all the time when driving over gullies, use a marshaller ahead of the vehicle giving you precise directions. If you do not have a marshaller then lower the driver's window and observe the front wheel yourself – being careful, as ever, not to let your concentration blind you to the hazard of tree branches passing close to the vehicle.

Steering offset

Design nicety. As explained in the Glossary, steering offset is the distance between the centre point of tyre contact on the ground and the point where the extension of the wheel steering pivot (the notional

Rain or flood erosion can cause deep ruts to become gullies and there is the danger of the vehicle slipping down one side. Careful guidance by a marshaller who can see all the wheels is the only way to negotiate this kind of obstacle. New Range Rover has small steering offset making steering feedback more reliable here.

'king-pin') also touches the ground. The smaller this distance the more reliable will be the feel of the steering on off-road obstacles where left and right wheels may be subject to differing forces. Design-wise, it is not easy to achieve with 4x4s and has only in recent years been acknowledged as desirable but it will lessen the feedback of one-wheel obstacles. Interestingly, the designers

of Jeep's 2007 iteration of their hallowed icon (see p 7.26) took the opportunity to reduce the steering offset of the Wrangler JK from 50mm down to 14mm to reduce this one-wheel-in-cold-treacle effect when tackling variably rough ground off-road. Lest these gentlemen should crick their backs taking bows, early Suzuki Vitaras had a steering offset of only 8mm!

You will lose – or get false – steering feel driving gully sides. Get guidance and/or look out of the window.

Ruts that become deep gullies

1.

2.

Do not stay in badly eroded deteriorating ruts (1). Get out of ruts and (2) straddle the gully. Vehicle must be carefully guided in gully to sit evenly across it. If necessary, cut steps with a shovel to give tyres a positive footing with sliding down the gully side – and use a marshaller.

4.3 Ridges and ditches

The ridge/ditch problem – wheelspin

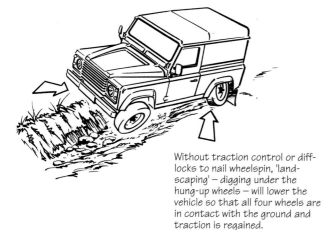

Without traction control or diff-locks to nail wheelspin, 'landscaping' – digging under the hung-up wheels – will lower the vehicle so that all four wheels are in contact with the ground and traction is regained.

Diagonal suspension

Ridge – a mirror-image ditch. Ridges and ditches have particular significance in the context of suspension travel and wheelspin as shown on page 2.7 and the box on page 2.6. They can be encountered both on tracks and across open country. Though one is a mirror image of the other, ridges and ditches can introduce the same problems for the vehicle – grounding the chassis or hanging diagonally-opposite wheels in the air and losing traction by reaching the limits of articulation (see page 3.8). The method of crossing these obstacles will require judgement according to their size since the recommended method of crossing a small ridge –

Diagonal approach usually best but wheelspin is the main hazard. Know vehicle's articulation limits. Methods of crossing vary according to size of the obstacle.

diagonally – will lead to trouble if it is applied to a big (or abrupt) one.

Articulation – again. Much has been written already about articulation in other parts of the book but it is a fundamental factor in the performance of a 4x4 off-road and a basic cause of probably 90% of all failed traction situations – the ability to put four wheels on the ground and get each wheel to contribute to forward motion of the vehicle. Long ignored, manufacturers , happily, are waking up to this and now offering diff locks, and, second best, traction control.

Size determines technique

Potential hazards. The diagram shows the potential hazards – one wheel on each axle on the bump stops and the other hanging in mid air. The best *general* advice is to take ridges and ditches diagonally with as much momentum as you judge to be prudent. If that seems like the ultimate escape clause, remember that some obstacles are better taken at right angles (if you can) to avoid risk of diagonal hang-up; others are best taken diagonally (if you can) to avoid jarring or hitting the tail as you exit – check the table below. Consider these obstacles in three sizes:

1. Small ridges and ditches. These may be taken at right angles within the limits dictated by vehicle under-belly clearance and rear overhang (departure angle). However this does mean that the respective front and rear axles will hit the obstacle square-on and probably impart a severe jolt. By taking the obstacles diagonally the vehicle will hit the bump or dip one wheel at a time and flow over the obstacle with a rolling motion but without any shock loading. Indeed if, when

Ridges and ditches: diagonal approach vs right angles		
Approach	*Advantage*	*Disadvantage*
Right angles	Precludes diagonal hang-up	May jolt, belly vehicle or hit tail
Diagonal	Avoids jarring	May cause diagonal hang-up

Two approaches. Diagonal suspension encapsulates the ridges and ditches problem. Defender's simple approach – lots of articulation – keeps wheels on the ground. ML Mercedes' arthritic suspension movement enhances on-road handling but, shy of diff-locks for this market, needs traction control to curb wheelspin– see pp 2.6-7.

driving quickly over a plain, you encounter a shallow ditch which you had not seen earlier, alter direction immediately to take it diagonally. Don't hit it square-on.

2. Medium-sized ridges and ditches. These may be classified as those that will give problems of under-belly or departure angle clearance and therefore cannot be taken at right angles. With these ones you thus have no option but to take them diagonally. The technique outlined above should be used.

3. Tall ridges and deep ditches. On-foot inspection and the assistance of a marshaller will almost certainly be necessary. These are obstacles that definitely cannot be taken at right angles and also, if taken slowly diagonally, may result in diagonally-opposite wheels lifting to allow (if you don't have axle diff locks) wheelspin and loss of traction. In these cases you have two options:

a. *Provided the going is smooth enough,* take the obstacle diagonally but fast enough for momentum to carry the vehicle past the momentary lifting of corner wheels.

b. *Provided it is permitted,* 'landscape' the

ground with a shovel to remove the top of the ridge or edge of the ditch that will cause grounding of the chassis or tail end or suspension of the wheels and then proceed as at 1 above.

Learning gently. As with so many skills it takes longer to write and read this advice than to apply it. You will quickly learn to judge which situation you are in and how it relates to your vehicle's articulation and the presence or otherwise of diff locks. As ever, so long as you do not jolt the vehicle badly or ground the chassis it does not matter if you do not get this right first time – at least on small and medium obstacles. Do not be afraid to take it gently at first or admit you got it wrong; back off and try again – no damage has been done. (See also 'Self recovery', Section 5.1.)

Judgement required: speed and diagonal approach can help. Digging under hung-up wheels may be needed.

4.4 Climbing steep slopes

Taking the slope at right angles

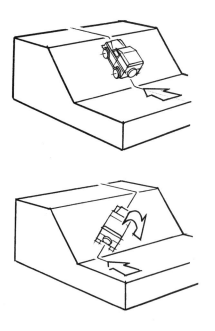

Going up a slope at right angles to the lip of the ridge is safe; a diagonal approach can provoke a rollover down the slope. The risk is made worse by any wheelspin.

Grip, gradient, momentum

Grip is invariably the limiting factor on steep slopes. The right gear (usually 2nd or 3rd low) and a sensitive throttle foot is the answer. Keep at right angles to the slope.

Grip and gradient. The twin problems with steep slopes – gradient and grip – usually reduce themselves to one in cases where a 4x4 has a two-speed transfer box with a set of low range gears (see page 1.10 and diagrams page 1.11). Such a vehicle will have the power and appropriate gearing to climb a continuous slope of not far short of 1-in-1 or 45° if the grip is there.

That gentle right foot. Grip is far more likely to be the limiting factor and we have seen in Section 3.2, 'Gentle right foot', how use of the right gear (not necessarily the

lowest one) allied to a sensitive right foot can eliminate the wheelspin that can result from insufficient grip. Climbing steep slopes is the classic application of sensing grip and being gentle with the throttle – and, see next spread, admitting defeat early in cases of wheelspin. Don't floor the throttle when you get wheelspin in the vain hope of getting up the slope; the vehicle could slide sideways off course and may tip – see diagram, right.

Go straight at the slope. Whilst a walker would take diagonal tacks up a steep hill to reduce the gradient, you should take the fall line direct in a vehicle, ie take the slope at right angles, head-on. The diagonal approach is for ridges and ditches, not for steep slopes. This is to ensure the vehicle is laterally level – your walker can stand up straight when traversing a steep hill; a vehicle leans over (see 'Traversing slopes', Section 4.6) and is in danger of tipping down the slope in extreme cases.

Momentum, traction, throttle control. Common sense steep slopes need no more than common sense tactics: if it is reasonably smooth and not excessively steep take a bit of a run at it in the right gear and do not over-torque the wheels to provoke wheelspin. Select the right gear before the slope and stay in it; only an automatic will do a smooth enough and quick enough change if one is needed. But on really difficult slopes, as ever, an   will be needed. Such slopes are unlikely to be smooth and tramping out the chosen route to locate any local bumps, tree stumps or rabbit holes that might cause a wheel to lift and spin will be useful.

Extra grip – from the steering wheel. If the track is rutted – and this can apply on level ground too, including churned sand – limiting grip can be enhanced by moving the steering wheel from side to side (11 o'clock to 1 o'clock) and cause the tyre sidewalls to contribute grip.

Don't over-torque the ground

Higher gear ... . Unless you are tackling an unusual and exceptional climb such as 40° on rough dry concrete, 1st gear low box

Classic example (below) of a 2nd gear low range slope needing a bit of momentum at the bottom and a readiness to lift off the throttle towards the top. One of the rare 1st gear low range slopes (right) where grip permits full use of vehicle's ultimate climbing ability.

will be too low and will provoke wheelspin. Most 'normal severe' climbs will be best tackled in 2nd gear low box, or, if there is any amount of run-up available, 3rd. Use the most run-up momentum you can, having established the ground is smooth enough to permit it, since the more you can utilise this, the less will be the demand for grip from the ground actually on the slope.

... with throttle lift-off. As you near the top of the slope your momentum may be running out and the vehicle will become more reliant on grip and traction. This is the point, quite near to the top, where the wheels are most likely to start slipping or spinning – usually (unless diff-locked) one

of the front wheels due to weight transfer to the back of the vehicle. So it is thus, paradoxically, the point where you may find that *lifting off the throttle helps* keep that 'continuous rolling contact' (diagram page 3.4) without spinning the wheels.

Automatic applications. The equivalent of lift-off to de-stress the ground where traction is marginal will occur on an auto transmission vehicle if 3rd is selected before a steep climb. The gearbox will change to 3rd as the throttle is lifted and reduce the risk of wheelspin. Selecting 3rd (ie ensuring no up-change beyond 3rd) will make sure the transmission does ,not change up too far when you lift off the throttle.

Take a run at it – as far as the terrain will allow – and be prepared to lift off the throttle near the top to preclude wheelspin.

Failed climb, recovery

First-time scare. If you are losing grip on a steep climb don't boot the throttle and accentuate the wheelspin; de-clutch and apply the footbrake. Your first failure on a very steep climb – nose of the vehicle pointing at the sky, brake leg trembling, maybe a dead engine and a plan view of the world in your rear view mirror – can be mildly scaring; it can sometimes also be mechanically traumatic for the vehicle if a driver tries to bluff it out or attempt impossibly quick sequences of control selections during the 'recovery' descent. Remember 'Mind-set' on page 3.3; admit defeat early. Pause awhile, (there's plenty of time), back off and try again.

Slowing the adrenaline. Observing – and practising – the following procedures makes a fail-and-try-again climb so matter-of-fact that both driver and vehicle have a far easier time. Knowing this means you do not cane the vehicle unnecessarily hard in a white-knuckle attempt to get up first time. Climbs can fail with or without a dead engine:

1. Forward motion ceases, engine running, wheels spinning – grip problem.
2. Forward motion ceases, engine stalled – gradient problem.

After failing, come down at right angles to the gradient. Going backwards, steering castor action is also reversed. Grip the wheel firmly to prevent 'runaway'.

Practise it – yes you can. Using the following procedures you will come back down the hill with both hands on the steering wheel (important, that), feet off the pedals – ie not on clutch, or footbrake but covering the throttle. Engine braking controls your speed of descent and no frantic use of gear lever or handbrake is needed. It looks complex first time you read it but, you can practise it, book in hand, if need be. There is no rush. (Procedure for manual transmission shown; Auto procedure is shown in brackets.)

Case 1: Failed climb, engine running. If you have failed the climb through wheelspin and loss of grip:

1. Clutch pedal down, hold the vehicle firmly on the footbrake, engine idling. (**Auto:** allow engine revs to die, brake, engage **'R'** low box, gently release brake, jump to step 4.)
2. Engage reverse gear low range.
3. With *both hands* on the steering wheel and leading with the clutch, release the clutch and footbrake. The vehicle (engine still idling) will start back down the slope fully controlled by engine braking. At this stage your feet can be off all three pedals – ie you are in reverse, clutch fully engaged and engine idling. Remember that *in reverse, steering castor action is also reversed and there is a tendency for the steering wheel to 'run away' to full lock if you do not hold it firmly.*
4. Keeping both hands on the steering wheel, go straight back down, at right angles to the slope, to less steep ground.
5. Note. The admit-defeat-early credo is very important in a traction failure on a hill – ie with wheels starting to spin. If you do not quit the moment it is clear you are not going to make it, it is very

likely the vehicle, wheels spinning on a slippery surface, will slew sideways-on to the slope and there is a risk of it capsizing down the hill – diagram previous page. Even if it does not do this, the spinning wheels – usually one front wheel with its diagonally opposite back wheel – will scoop depressions in the ground to make your next attempt more difficult.

Case 2: Failed climb, stalled engine. If you have failed the climb and stalled the engine in the process (see also diagram sequence right):

1. Engine is dead. Hold the vehicle on the footbrake, clutch position immaterial. (**Auto**: go to step 5.)

2. Engage reverse gear low range and remove left foot from clutch.

3. With both hands on the steering wheel, slowly lessen the pressure on the footbrake until your foot is off it. The vehicle is now held by the engine.

4. The vehicle may begin to move backwards on its own and in so doing 'bump'-start the engine. In which case let it continue back down the slope, under full control of engine braking, keeping both hands firmly on the steering wheel.

5. If the engine has not started under gravity, take one hand off the wheel to operate the starter motor briefly – with the vehicle still in reverse gear and clutch fully engaged (photo above right). This will invariably kick the engine into life and you are, as in 4 above, slowly descending back down the slope in full control, in gear, clutch fully engaged, left foot on the floor, both hands on steering wheel to resist any steering 'runaway', right foot hovering over throttle. (**Auto**: foot still on brake, select **'N'** or **'P'**, start engine, engage **'R'**, both hands on wheel, slowly release footbrake.)

6. Just as you would climb the slope at right angles to the gradient, make sure you go straight back down the slope – still at right angles to the gradient. When you reach less steep ground, use the controls in the normal way.

Dead-engine failed-climb – so straightforward and calm it is worth shutting off the engine to use this procedure even if it has not stalled. Stalling engine puts very high stresses on it. Try to de-clutch before it actually stalls. Feet off all the pedals (but throttle-ready), touch starter.

Recovery sequence, stalled engine

1, 2

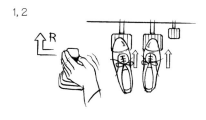

These procedures take far longer to read about than to do. They are really very simple. Practise on gentle slopes, then steeper ones.

3, 4

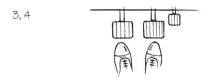

5

See list, adjacent column. 1, 2. Clutch, footbrake, into reverse. 3, 4. Feet off all pedals – but throttle foot ready. 5. Touch the starter briefly; both hands on steering wheel. 6. Reverse back on mirrors.

4.5 Descending steep slopes

The view over the nose comes only when you are committed to the slope; so recce on foot first. At the point of commitment you can often only see sky or the far side of the dip.

Gear to use

Remove the drama. The extraordinary agility of a 4x4 may make your first really steep descent an intimidating experience. A 45° downslope itself is unusual enough but to this angle you add the fact that you are looking even further downward over the bonnet; the result can seem vertical, especially when you are hanging forward in your seat harness. But this is an experience that you get used to remarkably quickly – usually after just one steep descent. As with climbs, the aim is to take the drama out of the situation and utilise the vehicle's facility for keeping you in control.

Get out and look. A 45° slope is extreme but there are many lesser slopes that can still seem very steep and, as with the climb, an on-foot inspection is advisable to ensure that your planned route is safe. This is doubly important since when you come to the edge of a steep descent you can sometimes see nothing over the nose of the vehicle except the other side of the dip; only when you are actually pointing down the slope can you see the ground immediately in front of you – too late, if you didn't recce and got it wrong!

For this reason, among others, stop the vehicle for the on-foot inspection at least two metres before the edge of the slope – engine off, in gear, handbrake on. This will give you time, when you do start the descent, to get the vehicle fully in gear and with your foot off the clutch for the descent.

Rule of thumb, 1st gear low range. Using 1st gear low range will in nearly every case result in a perfectly controlled, feet-off-all-pedals descent. Actual retardation will depend on whether you have a diesel or petrol engine, whether or not it has a manual transmission and the condition of the slope but the rule is a good one and a safe one. It is important to remember that due to its higher gearing and the way it

Stop two metres from the edge (engine off, 1st gear, handbrake) and inspect on foot. Plan to use engine braking in low range.

functions, *automatic transmission offers poorer engine braking* down steep slopes

The rationale. Your aim is to obtain maximum retardation without resorting to the brakes which can result in wheel locking and sliding. As always your aim is to preclude any possibility of discontinuity of rolling contact (see Section 3.2, 'Gentle right foot') – ie no wheelspinning or, in this case, sliding.

Does sliding matter? Surely, say some, a locked wheel gives more retardation than a merely braked one but the *raison d'etre* for ABS brakes applies on nearly all off-road surfaces and certainly on mud, ie, as you will dimly remember from school, the coefficient of sliding friction is less than the coefficient of static friction.

Ready for throttle. If the ground is too slippery even to provide the grip for the retardation of the throttle-off engine and you begin to slide, be ready to use the accelerator to help the wheels 'catch up' with the vehicle and eliminate any wheel slide.

The ideal descent is with both feet on the floor and the engine doing the braking. Be ready to use throttle if the retardation is too strong and the wheels begin to slide.

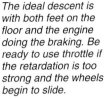

Ready for exceptions. There may be occasions – long descents of loose ground or extremely slippery clay – where low range 2nd gear will be better in order to preclude an initial sliding-wheel glissade. One or two exceptions are covered at Section 6.4. Some descents – see photo page 6.9 – will actually demand 3rd low range and considerable throttle to prevent nosing-in on a soft surface. As before, it is best to select the gear for the whole descent and stay in it.

Brakes

Brakes? Never... An easy generalisation – and for good reasons – is to counsel against ever using brakes on a steep slippery descent. Braking on wet, muddy or loose-surface slopes – even with the excellent sensitivity of some 4x4's discs – can easily cause one or more wheels to lock and the loss of directional control in the resulting slide could be dangerous. The use of engine braking down steep slopes makes, in general, for a very safe, controlled way of keeping the vehicle from gaining speed and there is no danger of overheating the brakes. Often you are able to take both feet off the pedals

and rest them flat on the floor while the vehicle trundles gently down the slope with the engine idling.

But... There are times when engine braking is not the infallible solution (see Section 6.4, Advanced driving, Downslopes) and the sensitive use of brakes or, preferably, cadence braking (Section 3.2) can help. If your vehicle is fitted with ABS brakes – and they are one of the systems that can cope on- and off-road – then brakes may be used on a slippery downslope. There is a very good case, however, for getting into the habit of using engine braking first.

Hill Descent Control. The proliferation of variously branded iterations of Land Rover's initial Hill Descent Control system (HDC – see also pp 2.10, 6.8) enables a driver to leave an automated mix of ABS and engine braking to the black boxes on many vehicles facing a steep descent. Do learn the basic common-sense procedures above, however. Don't let the automatics destroy your learning curve. It has also been said, with some validity, that if you can recognise situations requiring HDC then you probably don't need it.

Rule of thumb – 1st low and do not use the brakes. But... see Section 3.2 for cadence braking and ABS is magic in reserve. Accelerate if necessary.

4.6 Traversing slopes

Assessing the ground

Side slopes are different. From the last two sections – 'Climbing steep slopes' and 'Descending steep slopes' – the doctrine of always taking such obstacles at right angles to the slopes implies that traversing a slope is dangerous. And so it can be when the angle of gradient is severe. There will be times, however, when, on less severe slopes, you do need to traverse a slope laterally. Like your first steep climb and descent, your first traverse will be unnerving. Unlike climbs and descents, however, you will not quickly get used to it. And that is a good thing since the consequences of getting it wrong on a traverse are a great deal more serious than getting it wrong on a climb or descent.

Trust your instincts. There appears to be a built-in safety feature of human perception that makes a traverse feel a lot more dangerous than it is in relation to a vehicle's absolute tipping limits. Your vehicle will actually tilt to quite high angles on perfectly smooth ground without rolling over but to the driver, a traverse along a slope even one third of the maximum permissible can feel alarming. Follow your instinct and do not traverse slopes that feel dangerous. As ever, carry out an on-foot reconnaissance first and be on the alert for:

1. Slippery surface. Assess the surface to be sure it is not so slippery that the vehicle will slide sideways down the slope.
2. Bumps and dips. Look out for dips that the down-hill wheels may encounter and bumps that the up-hill wheels may roll over – rabbit holes and sawn-off tree stumps in particular. If you are not aware of them both will suddenly and

Side slopes don't feel right. Trust your unease and treat them with great caution. Inspect on foot looking for bumps or hollows that can affect vehicle's lateral stance.

Side-slope and escape manoeuvre

A static rig-test tip angle is often around 40° but the dynamics of real driving make this dangerous to approach. Escape manoeuvre applies if you feel you are getting close to tipping.

alarmingly increase the tilt of the vehicle and further the risk of it tipping over.
3. Secure load. Any load in the back of your vehicle should be secure and as low as possible. Be particularly wary of roof-rack loads. Passengers should sit on the up-hill side – or dismount.
4. Marshalling. If there are any doubts about the effect of the terrain or if there are obstacles to avoid, then use a marshaller (see Section 3.4) to see you forward and make sure he or she keeps an eye on all four wheels.

The on-foot inspection is especially important. Look for bumps or dips that affect lateral lean. Every inch of ground irregularity makes approximately 1° difference to lateral lean – a 4" bump equals 4°. Digging away the hillside ahead of the up-slope wheels can lower the actual tilt angle. Lateral slopes that are also slippery – and that can include grass when wet – demand special caution.

Escape manoeuvre, restraint

Be ready. The recognised escape manoeuvre is to steer down the hill if the vehicle slips or seems too close to the maximum tip angle. Think about this in your on-foot recce. Is it actually feasible to steer down the slope, what are the consequences? Is there a gully at the bottom?

As with normal steep descents, the nearer you can get the vehicle pointing directly down the slope the less the danger of lateral tipping. If you feel the machine getting laterally unstable turn down the hill quickly and give a little burst of throttle. The centrifugal force of the quick turn, further enhanced by the blip of throttle, will help keep the vehicle upright.

Restraint. Some means of restraining the vehicle may be practical such as passengers hanging on to the up-slope side – about the only time add-on running boards and steps really come into their own in off-road conditions! Or a rope can be used, attached to a roof rack. It goes without saying that using people pushing on the vehicle flanks from the down-hill side is not an acceptable risk!

'Escape' by steering down the hill, with a touch of throttle.. But plan the contingency in advance.

4.7 Weak ground

Ground stress – horizontal, vertical

Reading the ground. Soft ground is weak ground – vertically and laterally as well. The vertical context is well known – the tendency for a vehicle to sink in it – and the lateral connotations mean it will not take much thrust or braking from wheels without degenerating into slippery wheelspin or slide; the gentle right foot on brakes and throttle (Section 3.2) comes into its own in such conditions. Read the surface and adjust your throttle foot accordingly: getting the traction where you can, backing off where you can afford to do so in order not to lose the traction you do have – and occasionally (on the right tyres) applying a carefully judged burst of wheelspin to get through slime onto drier grippy ground (see photo upper right, next spread). Read the ground.

Soft ground is weak laterally and vertically – so it's gentle right foot again. Lock the centre diff, read the ground, judge what it will take without spinning the wheels.

'Fifth-wheel' traction. On the limits in rutted ground, turning the steering wheel from side to side, 11 o'clock to 1 o'clock, is effective in getting that little extra traction from the tyre sidewalls – especially with bold-tread mud tyres. It works in sand as well, as we shall see, where it has been churned by previous vehicles.

'Green lanes' are classic examples of low vertical and low horizontal ground strength – a mixture of the soft and the slippery.

Ground stress components

A 4x4 under power. Decreasing weight or tyre pressure (weight per unit area) and exercising care with throttle and brakes reduces both components of ground stress.

Horizontal stress: throttle, brakes

Vertical stress: weight per unit area

Resultant:

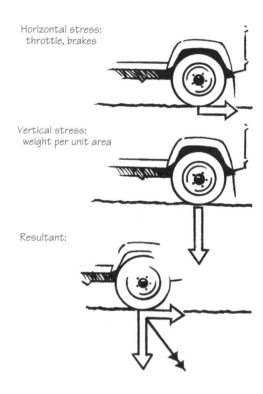

Horizontal load – throttle, brakes. The most immediate control you have when encountering weak ground is from within the vehicle – the horizontal stress on the ground created by the vehicle's linear motion – forward, back or braking. You should be in four-wheel drive if it is selectable – and the centre differential on a permanent 4x4 should be locked so as to preclude the possibility of one axle spinning any faster than the other. No hard and fast rule can be laid down as to the 'best' action then to take. Some situations will demand

Examples of ground that is vertically weak (soft, left), horizontally weak (slippery, below left) and close to the limit on both (right).

you accelerate on the good going to take you through the soft and slippery patch using momentum, others will demand you slow down to take it gently because it is uneven or of extended length. The only invariable rule is to gain momentum where you can without hazarding the vehicle by crashing over bumps or potholes and to also heighten your awareness of the risk of wheelspin. To minimise this, choose the highest gear you judge will get you through without over-stressing the engine – this will often be 2nd or 3rd low range. As for brakes, remember they stress the ground in the same way as driving torque at the wheels and insensitivity will result in sliding and less of that all-important rolling contact shown in the diagram on page 3.4.

Low range 2nd or 3rd will usually be the best gears for soft ground.

Tyres and tyre pressures

Tyres. Section 8.2 deals with tyres in more detail but the subject is inseparable from weak ground operation so some coverage is given here. Differentiating between vertical and horizontal stress in weak ground is important. As already mentioned, some weak ground needs cutting into to get to the firmer ground beneath: an aggressive, probably quite narrow, very open tyre tread for mud. Mud is slippery and thus horizontally weak but in some cases (not all!) can be relatively shallow so is less weak vertically.

Soft-shoe approach. Other types of weak ground need the 'soft-shoe' approach – more tyre width to give flotation on bog or peat or moorland where the surface is fragile and damage has to be minimised; this ground is notable for being vertically weak – to the extent, sometimes, of being virtually bottomless. Salt marsh, or sebkha, as it is called in desert regions, is a classic and dangerous example (see next spread).

Sand is a special case (next Section) but is also classifiable as vertically weak and thus needing maximum flotation; for special reasons it also requires a very mild and particular tread pattern. As Section 8.2 makes clear, tyres can only be 'best' in one set of conditions and 'compromise' or all-purpose tyres are exactly that – a compromise. As you see above – a fairly thin layer of slippery mud on a reasonably firm base ground – the fattest tyres are not always the best.

Tyres can effect a 'cutting' or 'floating' role. Reduced tyre pressures increase flotation and ride comfort but MUST be accompanied by reduced speed.

Vertical load – per square inch. Once you have your chosen tyres and are on your chosen terrain, vertical load per unit area – the tyre pressures, rather than total vertical load – is the factor of which you will have easiest control. You may not think tyre pressures would make much difference since the total weight of the vehicle will usually remain the same, sitting on the same four tyres. But bear in mind that 'emergency flotation' pressures (Section 8.2) can be two thirds of road pressures or less. This means the tyre footprint size increases (see diagrams Section 8.2) and the weight of the vehicle is spread over a correspondingly larger area so that – as in recognising the benefits of 4x4 which spreads the thrust over four instead of two wheels – you are asking less of the ground that is already having difficulty in supporting the vehicle's weight.

Weak-ground tyres for 'cutting' and 'floating'. Michelin XCL (right), excellent in mud/clay – open, bold, self-cleaning tread but noisy, L-rated (75 mph max, see Section 8.2) and not very grippy on wet roads. High flotation version (265/75 x 16) of Goodrich All Terrain (left) is S-rated, quieter and grippier on-road but tread pattern is not as ultimately effective as XCL or BFG Mud Terrain on mud/clay. No one tyre can be good at everything but the BFG All Terrain is exceptionally versatile – and notably effective in deserts.

Horizontally weak (slippery – left) and vertically weak (soft – below) ground need appropriate tyres and techniques. Note (left) how narrow a good mud tyre really is – here being used with controlled wheelspin to cut through to better traction. Flotation (below) is absolutely on the limits; left tyre has broken the crust, right tyre just holding on. See next Section and photo on page 4.30.

Reduced tyre pressures – when and how much. Reduce pressures only when needed – then re-inflate (see Section 4.9, 'Rock, stones, corrugations'). The golden rule is: *do not run with low tyre pressures without reducing your speed*. With inappropriately low tyre pressures the steering and handling of the vehicle will be adversely affected. Much more importantly, however, if you don't slow down serious overheating of the tyre will occur which could lead to tyre damage or blow-out. Tyre pressures for particular conditions will vary according to:
- the vehicle,
- the axle load and
- construction of the tyres.

Typical axle loads and off-road tyre pressures for Land Rover vehicles are given in Section 8.2, 'Tyres'. Rule-of-thumb guidance figures are shown below:

1. Tracks and poor roads – 80% of road pressures, maximum speed 65 kph (40 mph).

2. Emergency flotation pressures – about 60% of road pressures, maximum speed 20 kph (12 mph).

Vertical load – reducing the total. It is common sense that reducing the overall load will give the vehicle a better chance on weak ground also enabling a greater reduction in tyre pressures to be used. In practical terms few users will be able to dispose of payload to suit the going but the principle is worth remembering for the case of recovering a bogged vehicle - see Section 5.1, 'Self-recovery'.

Previous wheel tracks

Where others have been. As already mentioned (Section 4.2, 'Driving on tracks'), if the weak ground is wet or muddy, it will usually pay to follow the wheel tracks of a previous vehicle since that vehicle will have cut through to firmer ground and you may be able to take advantage of that. If the weak ground is sandy see next section.

Tyres MUST be re-inflated before exceeding the low pressure speed limits. Choice of tyres is important for frequent soft-ground operation – see Section 8.2.

4.8 Sand

Initial rules

Different types. It is said that Eskimos have 50 different words for snow. There are probably at least as many different types – and conditions – of sand. Let's be clear what 'condition' means: churned, virgin, untrodden, crusted, wind blown, coarse, aggregate, fine rounded, superfine ... and more.

Wet sand, damp sand and a dozen types and conditions of dry sand each lead to different expectations of vertical and horizontal strength (flotation and surface shear strength) as well as behaving differently as far as compaction strength is concerned. Each thus demands, first, recognition and then different driving techniques.

You will cover many miles on sand without difficulty but, when the bearing strength starts to get marginal, being instantly ready with throttle (and the right gear) to get you through a short soft patch is critical. And, in conditions of deteriorating flotation, avoiding wheelspin, is nowhere more important – since soft sand can be very deep. Stop before serious wheelspin develops and reverse out while you can.

There will be times when the terrain will demand on-foot inspection of tricky sections and 'stamping out' to ascertain firmness – approaching dune edges is a classic example (provided you have been able to stop on a firm enough patch to do a recce!). Again, in limiting conditions or following a bogging, the vehicle will have a far better chance if tyre pressures are reduced – see diagrams and tyre pressure/speed tables at Section 8.2, 'Tyres'.

Initial rule-of-thumb. Initial guide rules are therefore in order if you are to get through the sand rather than trying to learn all the different varieties of problem at once.

1. Dry sand. If you are running out of traction or flotation, keep off previously churned or broken sand. Make your own new tracks.

2. Damp sand. Follow previous tracks which will have compacted the sand and

There are many types of sand – all with characteristic bearing strengths. If the going has been churned up, break out onto unbroken sand. It will be stronger.

Innocuous-looking sebkha (salt marsh) can be extremely treacherous. Here one vehicle has strayed less than a metre off the track and sunk into the salty mush. Going right off the track can lead to a major recovery problem – if you are lucky, See next spread.

made it firmer.

3. Wet sand. Keep off altogether. It can contain areas of 'floating' sand, or quicksand – bottomless with virtually no vertical strength.

4. Sebkha (salt flat). Very dangerous – unpredictably soft and bottomless. If a well-used track goes over a sebkha it will have compacted the surface (seemingly from beneath) into a smooth, relatively strong route. Do not stray off the hardened track by even a tyre's width.

Sand types - the detail

Dry sand. Being an aggregate of small grains and large grains, nature's windblown sand, helped by night dews and diurnal heating and contracting, forms a surface crust which has more strength than the sand beneath; it is stronger in the cool of the morning than in the heat of the day. Use these characteristics to your advantage and be very careful not to break through into the soft sand beneath by excessive use of the brakes; think of the analogy of driving on a pie crust.

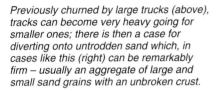

Previously churned by large trucks (above), tracks can become very heavy going for smaller ones; there is then a case for diverting onto untrodden sand which, in cases like this (right) can be remarkably firm – usually an aggregate of large and small sand grains with an unbroken crust.

1. Sandy tracks. Sandy tracks, by reason of the previous passage of vehicles, have no pie crust. Difficulty is likely where there has been a lot of previous truck traffic, even on sand sheet in open desert. Three things will happen here – the ruts will get deeper, the depth of churned sand will increase and the width between the ruts will increase. This is simply a function of the size of the previous vehicles, their wheel diameter and the width of their axles. As ever, be ready to admit defeat early before getting into real trouble, and steer out of the track onto virgin ground if you can. The higher gears – 3rd, 4th and 5th – in the low range (centre and rear diff locked where applicable) will probably be best for tracks of this kind. The advantage of being in low range is that it will enable you to accelerate through suddenly worsening conditions without the risk of being unable to restart, having stopped to change from high to low box. For this reason do not stop except on firm going – or if you do have to stop be

gentle with the brakes. As the going gets heavier, more churned and more demanding you will find you have to be firm with the throttle and use a lot of the torque at your disposal; this is different from the technique used on virgin sand.

2. Virgin sand. Some previously untrodden desert sand is remarkably firm and strong. But if you are close to the limits of flotation when on virgin, unbroken sand in the open desert (or once out of the ruts on the track) you have to be more delicate with the throttle in order not to break the crust of clean sand supporting you. The same goes for the brakes and steering. On some dune surfaces there is a good case for letting the vehicle come to a rolling stop without brakes at all. Similarly, when stopping your vehicle on sand remember that restarting when facing up a slope is almost impossible and you should therefore stop on level ground, or, if possible swoop round the dune surface so that you *always stop with the vehicle facing downhill.*

Previously unbroken sand, particularly, has a 'pie crust' that can be surprisingly strong. But be careful with throttle and brakes or you'll break through to the soft stuff.

3. Sand dunes. Keep away from small, closely packed dunes (photo opposite). Lines of dunes larger than 4–5 metres are usually sufficiently spaced-out to permit driving between them and taking a run if you have to cross a saddle. Expect the firm bits to be the valley floor or half way up the dunes remote from the last sand-fall. Cross dunes at the low saddles if you can (photo previous page). No vehicle will ever get up one but if your dune crossing must involve a sand-fall descent, recce to ensure you'll not go over the edge into a wind-formed and inescapable bowl. Gain all the momentum you can in the valley floor and the firm part of the ascent, slowing as you hit the softer bit near the crest and come to a stop/pause at, and at right angles to, the crest. At this point you can still go back. If OK, 2nd low over the edge (sinkage will be huge – photo below) and power your way down, holding the steering wheel tightly to keep wheels pointing down the slope. (See Sec 9.1, 'Glossary', Steering feel.)

Dune formations will have firm areas dependent on position relative to crest, valley and wind direction. Salt flat is inherently dangerous. Keep off, except on tracks.

Two lessons in one. Reversing out before you get too badly stuck is nowhere more important than in sand. Here sand tracks have been used too. See photo page 4.27, earlier in this sequence checking out bearing strength near dune edges. That photo shows one wheel OK, other one just breaking through.

If you have to stop to await another vehicle only do so on firm sand – preferably pointing downhill: as mentioned above, drive on, swoop round the dune till you get a firm, down-pointing place to stop. If needed, walk back from there to help with the digging and pushing.

4. Fesh-fesh. Fesh-fesh is a thin crust of fine gravel or sand over flour-like dust with very little surface strength. Maximum flotation and instant application of power will be required to avoid getting stuck.

Damp sand. Sand that is damp – such as it might be after a rain shower or even morning dew – just makes driving easier. The water binds it together, strengthens it, gives more flotation and on tracks actually makes it compact to yield considerably more strength than the dry, churned-up sand had before the rain.

Wet sand. It becomes a matter of judgement and definition to say when damp sand gets to be wet sand. Beach sand will frequently behave as dry, cut-up, churned sand where it is dry and become considerably firmer where it is washed by the tide –

The picture says it all. Sand-fall shows how soft sand can be when not crusted. Sand-fall descents will be blind until you reach the crest. Always recce. Always take them at right angles, hold the wheels firmly dead ahead as steering feel is lost.

Small, closely packed dunes are a pig – not enough room to take a run, not enough space between – and usually made of very fine sand too (right). Despite permanent 4x4 and rear diff lock, the locals seem to know what to expect. Fesh-fesh (above) – a sudden sinking feeling and clouds of powder-fine white dust in the mirror; evil stuff.

though this is not an invariable rule. The warning sounded earlier refers to really wet sand of the kind encountered where a river or stream meets the sea or sometimes in a wadi with recent rain a few days previously. Here a kind of 'floating' sand is encountered. This is akin to a quicksand where motion by the person or vehicle on it just causes further sinkage.

Sebkha (chott or salt flat). Sometimes also marked on maps as 'chott', a sebkha forms where lakes used to be and consists of a crust of dried salt-mud usually covering soft, bottomless moist salt-mud underneath. The crust is of variable and unpredictable strength but appears to have the curious characteristic of consolidating from underneath when progressively heavier vehicles run over it under certain critical conditions. Thus a track over a sebkha usually consists of wheel marks indented probably no more than a few centimetres into the surface – implying that the surrounding ground is firm. Yet, as mentioned, this is not the case and straying off the track even a tyre width or a metre can sometimes result in disastrous sinkage – see photo, previous spread. A vehicle stuck in sebkha will quickly sink to the chassis and sometimes go on sinking.

It is usually impossible to effect self-recovery and even assisting vehicles should have very long tow ropes or winches in order that they themselves stay out of the soft spot.

Sand tyres

Sand vs 'desert'. In a perfect world each kind of terrain demands its own specialist tyre. And ideally that applies to the many types of sand structure and conditions that we may encounter. To that though, you must – practically – add the term 'desert' since such regions comprise a mixture of sand, small stones and rock. For many years Michelin's XS (with the ability to accept pressures as low as 0.6 bar) was the best desert tyre for its unsurpassed prowess on all types of sand – especially the delicate unbroken crusted type found on the up-wind side of dunes where you are fighting for every gramme of weight bearing strength. But the XS, though coping well with desert, had slightly vulnerable sidewalls and was frightening on wet tarmac.

The crown must now have passed to BFGoodrich's All Terrain. Possibly one or two percent down on the XS on crusted dune sand but exceptional for it's ability to deal with all-round desert conditions – at reduced pressure (1 bar) on soft sand, at medium pressures (1.8) on sand/track/rock mix and, fully inflated, grippy on wet tarmac. See Sec 8.2 for pressures, loads.

Desert tyres are particularly important in achieving optimum performance in sand. All sand has increased bearing strength if cold, dewy or rained-on.

4.9 Rocks, stones, corrugations

This kind of rocky going is perfectly feasible if you have a low-range transfer box – a 1st gear crawl, with no diff-locks engaged. Tyre sidewalls – see next spread.

cle. Making the same mistake over rocks will likely bring the vehicle to a very abrupt halt and be likely to damage components as well. A separate-chassis 4x4's robustness and resistance to 'battle damage' should be regarded as accident insurance, not part of deliberate everyday driving; monocoque 4x4s are even more vulnerable. Take every precaution to ensure you do not run the vehicle into contact with heavy stones or rocks. Underbody 'skid plates' should be regarded as emergency protection only, not as something to facilitate a kind of snowboard progression over boulders.

Tyres. Tyres too are potentially very vulnerable to damage on rocky ground – especially the sidewalls of radial-ply tyres – but this and overall operating costs can be reduced by attention to:

1. Inflation. Be sure the tyres are fully inflated to road pressures before traversing rocky going – even if this means re-inflation after deflating for previous soft ground. Life is like that off road; you must get used to changing inflation pressures regularly.

2. Sidewall awareness. The most vulnerable parts of a tyre on rocks are the sidewalls. The best on/off-road tyres are radials but these, with their thinner, more flexible sidewalls, are particularly prone to 'bacon-slicer' damage, so-called because the action of the tyre sidewall against an intrusive sharp rock. Develop 'sidewall awareness' when driving over

Risks – chassis, tyres

Rocks – 25 cm high. The sections dealing with use of the low transfer box and the methods of driving on rough tracks (Sections 2.4 and 4.2) will prepare you for the techniques best suited for driving over rocks and stone. The rough definition applicable here to 'rocks and stone' is that stones are taken to be anything from gravel up to fist-sized stones and rocks are taken to be over fist sized and up to about 20–325 cm high – the maximum permitted by the underbody and under-axle dimensions of most 4x4s on 16 inch wheels.

Clearances. What you have read about clearance angles and under-axle clearances at Section 3.3, 'Geometric limitations', is doubly important in the context of driving over rocks and stones. Getting it slightly wrong on clearances when traversing mud will probably scrape earth from the obstacle and take paint off the underside of the vehi-

Take every precaution against grounding the vehicle on rock. Use a marshaller when clearances are tight. Rocks 20-25 cm are about the maximum size to drive over.

When forced onto limiting rocks use a marshaller and great care. Grounding hard ironwork on rock is absolutely not an option.

rocks and use a marshaller in bad conditions.

3. Cross-ply tyres. Where operations are almost exclusively off-road on rock or stone – such as fleet operations in quarries – the more damage-resistant qualities (at full inflation pressures) of cross-ply tyres could help keep operating costs down. It is essential, however, to accommodate the following criteria:

a. Virtually all 7.50 x 16 cross-plies are 'L' speed rated (see table Section 8.2), ie limited to 125 kph (75 mph), so should not be fitted to high powered vehicles operating on-road.

b. Cross-ply tyres have higher rolling resistance so will reduce fuel economy.

c. Cross-ply tyres have marginally less grip than radials so handling on-road would be affected.

Stony tracks and plains. Not all your rock/stone traverses will be over on-the-limits boulders. Stony tracks or vast stony plains in the desert will be very much less hazardous. Well inflated tyres and an alertness for potential further hazards, however, will be important. As with corrugations (next spread) braking will be much less efficient on loose stones.

On-foot survey, marshalling. All the points mentioned so far point to the need for looking at a difficult rocky stretch or obstacle on foot and then being marshalled across by a helper. The marshaller can see all eight sidewalls, the underside of the vehicle and axles – and this will ensure that no damage is done.

Low-range control. The relevance of low range and its ability to control the vehicle's forward motion steadily (rather than just making considerable power available) is nowhere more applicable than in traversing large rocks. First gear, low range (centre and axle diff not locked) clutch fully-in, low engine speed, will enable the vehicle to crawl steadily – without heaving, jerking or lurching – over the very worst rocky terrain.

On-the-limit rocky going demands 1st low range for control. Cross-ply tyres can lower costs in continuous rock/stone operations BUT note speed limitations.

Corrugations

'Harmonic' speed. A special manifestation of something between stony going and rough or unsurfaced tracks is the phenomenon of transverse corrugations across graded earth, sand or gravel tracks – regular, wave-form undulations that can stretch for tens of kilometres in front of you on remote area routes. The corrugations, also called 'washboard' in America, have a peak-to-peak distance of 0.5 to 1 metre and can be as much as 20 cm deep. They are formed by the action (and harmonics) of the suspension and tyres of the track's major-user vehicles on the soil. This latter is an important point since the technique to adopt when driving over them involves using the natural harmonics of your own vehicle's suspension to minimise the apparent roughness of the ride. There will be a speed of driving – usually between about 40 and 65 kph (25–40 mph) in medium weight 4x4s like Land Rovers and Toyotas – where the effect of the corrugations *on the vehicle body* will be minimised. The italics are used as a

Transverse corrugations on track demand a 'harmonic' speed to reduce the vibration on the vehicle. Body shake is reduced but unsprung components go through hell.

reminder that the suspension and unsprung parts such as the axles are undergoing a rare form of torture over such ground, even though the body and passengers may be (relatively) more comfortable.

Reduced brake effectiveness. An indication of the ordeal of the unsprung components will be clear when enduring the acceleration to these speeds and when decelerating from them. (If you still have any doubts about what the suspension is going through, look out of the driver's window at the front axle.) It is vital to remember also that, since the wheels are virtually jumping from the crest of one corrugation to the next, they are in touch with the ground for a fraction of the time they would normally be. *Steering and particularly braking effectiveness will be dramatically reduced* when going rapidly on corrugated tracks.

*(Left) Rivers usually produce rounded rocks
(previous spread) but sharp-edged rocks
can do terminal damage to tyre sidewalls.
Only a marshaller can see all eight.*

*'Harmonic' speed on moderate corruga-
tions reduces jarring on body though suspension still suffers. Coil springs are better
than leaf here. Remember dramatically
reduced steering and brake effectiveness.
Travel on such tracks is invariably accompanied by thick dust clouds (below left).*

Incompatible corrugations

Big wheels and little wheels. Most
light/medium 4x4s and pickups run on 16
inch wheel rims with very roughly similar
suspensions – it is this combination that
forms corrugations on most tracks in the
first place. However, driving such a vehicle
on a track where the corrugations were
formed by, say, a four-ton truck will be
especially unpleasant since the suspension
harmonics of the truck will not match those
of your smaller 4x4 and there will be no
'harmonic speed' where the ride appears to
smooth out.

*Dramatic reduc-
tions in braking
and steering
effectiveness take
place when dri-
ving on corru-
gated tracks.*

4.10 Wading

Streams like this are photogenic but generate swirl holes. Recce on foot first.

Preparations

Think ahead. Think of wading as a wet, blind and usually cold manifestation of every other type of obstacle and hazard you may come across. This is not meant as an unduly gloomy warning so much as a reminder that the same kind of potential problems can lurk beneath the water as you may see on dry land and that advance knowledge of them is no less important.

The same obstacles can lurk – unseen – under the water as on dry land. Plan, and recce, ahead. Be sure that breathers on gearboxes, axles etc can't ingest water.

Breathers, intakes. All internally lubricated components that can get hot will have an air vent. The reason is simple: as it heats up, the air pressure inside rises and would tend to blow lubricant past the oil seals. Then comes the really bad bit;, as it contracts later, it would tend to suck water or dirt back in by the same route. Engines have sump breathers of this kind but, with current emissions regulations the venting usually is back into the air intake.

However, gearboxes, transfer boxes and axles will each have a breather to allow heated expanding air out. If these vents get to be underwater during wading – as they can in older vehicles – the unit cools, contracting the internal air and ingesting water. Most manufacturers now fit long nylon tubes onto these vents with the upper end of the tube safely high in the engine compartment.

Know your vehicle. Know the situation in your vehicle. Very early Land Rovers, for instance, had small bell-shaped breathers on the top of each axle which could not only ingest water but the oily vapour round them caused dust and sand to stick and in time block them up. It is not a quick job but if you are not equipped with long breather tubes and will be involved in lots of wading, then take the trouble to get them fitted.

Wading plugs. Many older Land Rover products are provided with drain holes in the clutch housing between the engine and gearbox and also (where such a belt is fitted) at the bottom of the camshaft belt drive housing at the front of the engine beneath the fan. They are a safety feature to ensure that, in the event of an oil leak in these regions, the oil can drain away and not get onto the clutch or cam drive belt. In case of deep wading, however, these holes must first be blocked off by the insertion of the screw-in wading plugs provided. It is con-

Always walk the stream before commit-ting the vehicle – above, and Section 3.4, page 3.10. Static water like this can be prone to silt bowls; splashes in rocky streams are more predictable (opposite, below). Some, older Land Rovers need wading plugs fitted in clutch housing and, if applicable, in the bottom of the cam drive-belt housing .

venient to keep these plugs (available from Land Rover dealers) and the appropriate 13 mm (or 1/2" AF) spanner handy within the vehicle. It is important that the plugs be removed after wading – not necessarily at once but within a few days. If a vehicle is used for regular wading the plugs should be removed, checked for oil leakage and replaced every week or two.

Engine air intake. Far more obvious than gearbox and axle breathers is the engine's main air intake which must be kept well clear of any possibility of water inges-tion. *Water is incompressible and will destroy an engine if it goes down the air intake.* In most vehicles the intake is high in the engine compartment but (see diagram overleaf) be sure you know the cleared wading depth for your machine and, if in any doubt when on-the-limit wading is envisaged, fit a 'snorkel' or raised intake tube. This is beneficial too in keeping dust out of the air filter.

The on-foot recce

Walking the course. Water obstacles, large or small, should always (as mentioned at Section 3.4, 'Look before you leap', dia-gram page 3.10) be examined first as the

photo above shows. Rubber boots and a long stick are the extras required for an on-foot survey before committing a vehicle. Far better to go in over your boot and get your-self wet than have your vehicle roll into an underwater pit or hollow.

Generally, stagnant water is more likely to be a hazard than a river or a stream as flowing water tends to prevent a build-up of silt. The silt in a stagnant pool or mud hol-low can be several feet deep and very soft. Ensuring that the bottom of the pool or stream is firm enough along all of your pro-posed traverse is essential and it will inevitably take some time to do thoroughly. Markers may be necessary (such as sticks) to be sure the vehicle follows the route you have proved on foot.

Always walk through first with a stick. Better to get wet legs than have your vehicle stuck in an underwater hol-low.

What to do

Wading limitations, how to proceed.
The maximum advisable wading depth for most 4x4s on 16 inch wheels is about 0.5 metre – about 5-6 cm (a thumb length) below the top of the wheel rim or, perhaps more memorably, 5-6 cm higher than the top of the average calf-length rubber boot. Note the implications of this – your brakes will be completely immersed in water but the radiator cooling fan will be clear and so, probably, will the exhaust pipe exit. For wading at depths up to the particular vehicle's cleared normal wading depth the following precautions are advisable:

1. Gear and speed. Despite the huge splashes the magazines show, low speed is the requirement for wading. Low range with a gear appropriate to the amount of power and control over rocks required – and enough power on tap to avoid succumbing to unforeseen sinkage. Keep enough rpm to preclude water entering the exhaust pipe if it is submerged. Speed should be low but fast enough to keep a small bow-wave ahead of the bumper, reducing the height of the water behind the bumper, to keep water away from the fan. In practice, low range 2nd gear is usually about right.
2. Keeping the ignition dry. If you are using a petrol engine-equipped vehicle it is important to keep the ignition dry. The right bow-wave will help. A sheet of plastic lowered in front of the radiator will stop water cascading straight through and onto the fan, reducing the chance of spray over the electrics; it will also prevent liquid mud from blocking the radiator matrix. Additionally an old blanket, sack or other heavy fabric can be draped over the engine behind the fan to keep the harness dry; remember, however, this can be a fire hazard so keep it well clear of the exhaust manifold. *Do not remove the fan belt* as this will stop the water pump and damage the engine.

Normal wading depth limit 0.5 m – just below the top of the wheel rim. It is VITAL not to let water near the engine air intake – through splash or any other cause.

3. The electronics. Wet ignition leads may stop the engine , then dry out and allow you to go on. Wet electronic control units (ECUs) are less tolerant and quit terminally. Know where they are in your vehicle (amazingly in some vehicles they are on the floor under the seats) and be sure they never get wet.
4. Essential – keep engine air intake clear of water. As already mentioned, major damage to engines can result if even small amounts of water get past the air filter and into the cylinders. Never risk this happening. Choose another route where the water depth is less.
5. Don't stop the engine. Do not stop the engine whilst wading if the exhaust pipe is below water level. If you do, water will enter the exhaust system – including the catalytic converter. In rare cases water can siphon back to the engine causing catastrophic damage.
Ignore pictures you may have seen of Camel Trophy vehicles almost submerged in water; these vehicles will have been specially modified with raised air intakes for the engine; or you may be looking at a picture of a vehicle with a destroyed engine.

Wading depth

A typical wading depth limit of around 0.5 m puts the water at about bumper height or just below the top of the wheel rim on a 16 inch wheel.

At max normal wading depth a bow-wave (above) produces a dip aft of bumper that keeps water away from fan. Yee-hah spray splash-up in shallower water (top left) is fun but be sure of your ground – literally. Raised air intake permits deeper wading for diesels. Pre-attached tow rope useful precaution.

Afterwards

After wading. It is essential to dry your brakes after wading, especially if your vehicle has drum brakes. Whilst still in low range, drive a short distance applying the brakes lightly; this will squeegee the discs or linings dry. Remove any plastic sheeting or other engine protection used for the operation. The wading plugs need not be removed immediately if further wading is envisaged but see previous spread about regular use. Remember the handbrake too will be wet.

Getting stuck, recovery and precautions. Covered fully under Section 5, recovery principles remain the same but are complicated by the lower part of the vehicle being under water. Anticipation is the key – such as pre-attachment of a tow rope (or pre-extension of the winch line) so that you do not have to grope with the problem under water.

Drive fast enough for a small bow-wave about 20 cm high. No huge splashes. Squeegee the brakes dry after wading – low-range, against light brake.

4.39

4.11 Ice and snow

More traction, same brakes

4x4, 4x2 differences. Most readers of this book will have experience of driving on snow and ice in ordinary cars. Indeed many will have bought a four-wheel drive vehicle partly because it will give them more reliable transport in wintry conditions. Though traction in snow is best in temperatures below -20°C and less good between zero and -20°C, the basic principles of being very gentle with both the throttle and the brakes will apply in just the same way on a 4x4 as it does on a 4x2. But it is well to establish first just what the differences are between the two types of vehicle:

1. Double the traction ... As we have seen, the 4x4 has double the traction of a 4x2. In snow and ice conditions this should be regarded not as a means of putting twice as much power on the road but as a means of putting the same

4x4s are better than 4x2s on snow and ice for traction – but remember your braking is very similar. ABS is good – but cannot change packed snow into dry tarmac.

power on the road spread between twice as many wheels. This asks less of the surface in terms of grip and so you are thus less likely to get spinning wheels.

2. ... but the same braking. What is often forgotten in the feeling of confidence that a 4x4's tractive performance in snow generates is that the method of stopping is the same as that of any normal car – four wheels on the ground, each one's rotation retarded by brakes. Indeed, 4x4s are generally a lot heavier than normal cars and have a correspondingly increased amount of kinetic energy to arrest. Beware, therefore, of letting your feeling of invincibility extend to the braking department when you are on snow or ice. A 4x4 will brake no better, and possibly less well, than a 4x2.

3. ABS – very good, but not magic. ABS anti-lock braking will give you *the best braking possible under the circumstances* but will not reverse the laws of physics. It will eliminate the human error of locking the wheels; it will yield the maximum retardation possible from given surface conditions – as well as enormously improving directional control – but it will not turn ice into dry tarmac. The surface conditions are still the limiting factor.

Gentle right foot – again

Driving technique. The driving techniques employed for snow and ice are generally similar to those used for slippery mud or wet grass.

1. High gear. Select the highest gear that is feasible for the conditions. ('D' with automatic transmission; some autos even have a winter setting for the gentlest step-off.)

2. Diff lock – centre. Engage the centre differential lock (if manually selected) – and *disengage it as soon as non-icy ground is reached.*

3. Diff lock – rear. Don't engage this unless you are obviously stuck, ie stationary with one rear wheel spinning. In those circumstances, de-clutch, select

Packed snow at very low temperatures is more predictable than re-frozen melt at higher temperatures but there is no simple solution to snow and ice driving. A very delicate feel at the steering wheel, winter tyres, studs, chains and, of course permanent (or selected) 4x4 do the trick. Lock the centre diff but not rear diff unless specifically needed.

neutral (in auto too) to make sure the spinning wheel is now stationary, and then engage rear diff lock. *Disengage it as soon as non-icy ground is reached*; this is most important since an inappropriately locked rear diff will encourage slip in cornering or manoeuvring conditions.

4. Throttle, brake, steering. Use minimum throttle opening when driving away and accelerating, even if electronic traction control is fitted. Avoid violent movements of the steering wheel. Drive slowly and brake with great caution to avoid locking the wheels. Cadence braking will help (see Sections 3.2 and Glossary at Section 9.1).

On-road – what lies beneath. As with sand, there are, of course, a dozen combinations of criteria affecting snow and ice – mainly concerned with what lies beneath the present surface of the snow. These will extend or reduce the limits of traction of your vehicle; they cannot be quantified in any book but acquire new relevance in the light of a large-wheeled 4x4:

    1. First on the road? If, as if often the case, you and your 4x4 are first on the road after the first snow on untreated roads, this is the best traction you will get in snow. Bold and/or sharp treaded M+S tyres will cut through the soft snow either to the ground beneath or will make the first compressed snow 'rails' for you to travel on. These are as grippy as they will ever be. Conditions get worse from now on.

    2. Second or later? When others have

When you have to get through a good 4x4 is only half the battle; the other half is a sensitive driver – knowing when to feather-foot the throttle, when a burst is needed, when to back out.

been on the roads first, their compressed tracks will make slippery going and, as you will have noticed many times, driving out of the previous tracks will get fractionally more traction. As before,

The same principles apply as for slippery slopes – highest gear possible, gentle and sensitive use of brakes, throttle and steering.

Light snow on a country lane gives an idea of what a tyre gets up to. This is the Michelin XZL mud tyre. A winter tyre (next spread) has a finer deep tread. sipes, and is more effective . Winter tyres' tread compound is softer and optimised for grip in snow, ice, wet and low temperatures. Being first out, or on packed snow makes a difference. See overleaf.

Square peg, square hole. Classic application for the easy-to-use, 'soft roader', auto-engage 4x4 'Type 2' driveline (see p 2.2). Kia Sportage, here, joins favourites like Freelander, RAV 4, X-Trail. Honda CR-V. As X-Trail and latest RAV4, Sportage also has useful override manual 4x4 selection.

What lies under the snow? If you are the first out, it will just be road. Snowfall on top of packed snow will be very slippery. A classic case for diff lock in high box.

four-wheel drive will give more traction but no improvement, *per se*, in braking. On long descents or hairpin bends stay in a low gear.

3. Subsequent snowfalls. Snowfall on top of previous compressed tracks which may in places have slicked-over into streaks of pure ice is the real trap but another well enough known phenomenon in which a large-wheeled and heavy 4x4, delicately driven, will prove its worth in obtaining traction. Braking will be fractionally better than a car by reason of the tyre treads but only as long as it is done gently and on untrodden snow. Again, if you have no ABS, cadence braking (see page 3.5 and Glossary) will pay dividends and the big wheels' ability to steer through and towards snow having no underlying ice will prove an advantage.

Auto transmission, traction control. Vehicles fitted with automatic transmission, traction control and ABS will be at an advantage in wintry conditions but these aids to gentler traction enhance the effectiveness of the 'gentle right foot' driving philosophy; they don't replace it.

Winter tyres

What's the difference? Apart from the studded Scandinavian winter-wear beneficial where there is permanent compacted snow on the roads, many may be tempted to dismiss winter tyres because they look quite similar to normal tyres. They really are different, however: tread depth, void size (the gap between tread blocks), sipe design (the 'knife cuts') and above all the softer tread compound which is optimised (high silica) for wet conditions and low temperatures.

The benefits. Michelin say they start to pay off below around 7°C while it's still wet. As if to address the doubters, they quote 18% reduction in braking distance on snow/ice, 7% reduction on cold/wet and a 6% improvement in aquaplaning threshold for the '4x4 Alpin' compared to their own '4x4 XPC. The Bridgestone Blizzak (US) is another well-reported and competition-winning winter tyre with similar benefits – noticeably improved snow/ice grip, softer ride.

Horses for courses. As ever with tyres, despite huge improvements and convergence in multi-role applications (eg. the excellent BFGoodrich All Terrain – see Sec 8.2) , winter tyres wear quicker in high-tem-

Off-road, prod before you plod
Off-road be absolutely certain of what is
beneath the snow. There is rarely enough
grip to get you back out of a mistake.

Off-road snow demands careful sounding – on foot with a stick (below left). On-road, with the right tyres, hub–high snow will present little difficulty but be circumspect about what you try to barge through after that. Getting bellied on packed snow means a lot of very awkward digging – under the vehicle just for a start.

perature conditions. European users usually have two sets of wheels and the winter set is stored by their local garage during the summer months.

Making it all work

Snowdrifts. Big wheels, a locked centre diff and appropriate tyres driven on all four wheels are ingredients for charging snowdrifts and getting through. Or they can be ingredients for getting it wrong and finishing up sitting on top of a vehicle's length of compressed snow and having to dig the snow out from under the vehicle. Do not be too ambitious with what you attempt to barge through. Anything above hub depth is starting to get marginal for sustained travel; individual small drifts deeper than this can often be successfully tackled. As ever, the low box, probably in 2nd or 3rd (with diff lock), will be the appropriate weapon.

Helping yourself and others. Other traffic and those inappropriately equipped having got into trouble will all too frequently be the cause, in winter conditions, of your not getting through to your destination despite your having, without them, the capability to do so. To free them and yourself from delays, carrying a long tow rope, shovels, gumboots, gloves and some kind of under-wheel traction aid (Section 5.1, 'Self-recovery') will help reduce everyone's problems.

Pulling a car from a ditch with this equipment and careful use of the low range and throttle takes only minutes – see Section 5.2, 'Recovery – towing out'.

Snow chains. If you do not have a full set of four snow chains fit the first pair to the front wheels since this will give you grip as well as steering in slippery conditions. To some extent it will also prepare a path for the back wheels. Since a 4x4 has four driven wheels a second set of chains will be beneficial. If using front snow chains off-road there is a danger, with certain types of chain, that full axle articulation and full steering lock at the same time could enable the chains to damage the front brake pipes. Check with your dealer. See also Section 5.1, 'Self-recovery'.

Snow off-road. As there is not a smooth potentially slippery surface beneath it, snow off-road is easier to cope with than snow on tarmac carriageways. A moment's thought, however, highlights the dangers of minor drifting of the snow covering potentially destructive obstacles such as small rock outcrops or gullies on hillsides. The situation is similar to fording streams in that the dangers are hidden; the solution is the same – an on-foot recce and prodding with a stick in doubtful areas.

Tyres with bold sharp tread patterns are best. Fit only snow chains approved for your vehicle. Off-road snow is generally easier - but probe for hidden rocks or ditches.

Section 5

Recovery

5.1 Self-recovery

Traction aids

The calm approach. Having got 'stuck', self-recovery is the art of remedying the situation without the need to call upon outside assistance. The brutal truth is that in most cases getting stuck is a function of driver error – misreading the ground or the obstacle, or not accurately knowing the limitations of the vehicle. Whilst we all try our best with these things and all gradually get better, equally certain is the fact that we all occasionally make mistakes – often for the best of reasons, like not wanting to overstress the vehicle. Admitting this is at least half the battle for it enables you to go about the remedial action in the right spirit – philosophically cheerful acceptance rather than agitation, embarrassment, bluster or the suspicion that life has just dealt you the ultimate humiliation!

Everyone gets bogged occasionally. If you've missed the chance to reverse out, smile and go on to the next stage – digging and something to go under the wheels.

Knowing the problems. It helps to know what problems may be ahead. The categories in which you may find yourself stuck are shown below. Knowing this helps you see the problems coming and avoid them.

Wheels spinning – two causes. A given amount of power plus a combination of:
- not enough grip and
- not enough weight on a wheel

can cause the wheel to spin without providing any motion to the vehicle. In these circumstances traction control, if fitted, will brake the spinning wheel automatically or, again if you have one, an axle diff lock can be engaged – see pages 2.19 and 2.6. In the case of not enough weight on the wheel (the axle may be at an angle to the chassis and the lower wheel is spinning) see Articulation on the next spread. If grip is the problem in a static restart case:
- try a higher gear and a gentle throttle
- try 'weaving' the steering wheel – from the straight ahead position move it to 11 o'clock, then 1 o'clock so the tyre sidewalls contribute to grip; it helps sometimes in mud and sand.

Adding grip and flotation. If these measures fail, inserting some gripping medium between the wheel and the ground is the next step – stones, brushwood, mats, baulks of timber or items designed especially for the purpose – load spreaders, in effect:
- sand ladders
- metal planking and
- recovery channels.

If you've not come across them before, these all amount to the same thing – a 'plank' of some kind to put under the wheels to stop them sinking and/or also to afford them grip. Beware (see sub para 2 below) of anything that can flick up beneath the vehicle and cause damage.

1. Sand ladders can of course be used in any medium – sand, mud, snow. They are specially made aluminium ladders about 1.5 metres long, 35 cm wide and with rungs only about 15 cm apart (gripping edges outermost). They are thrust under the front – or rear – of the wheels (see diagram) and the vehicle will find grip and flotation on the ladders and haul itself out. If necessary, the ladders are moved round to the front (or rear, if you are going out in reverse) of the vehicle a second, third or fourth time to provide further traction in the direction of travel. Sand ladders of the right type – side members 6-7 cm deep – can be used for minor bridging of ditches.

2. Steel planking (PSP – the perforated lengths of interlocking steel planking originally made for WW2 bush airfields) is used in the same way as sand ladders. PSP is heavier and more difficult to use than aluminium sand ladders; it is too flexible to be used for bridging (and can bend upward to snag the underside of the vehicle) but is excellent for laying over logs or branches to provide a vehicle trackway. Despite the contradiction in terms, PSP is sometimes available in aluminium – see photo and Section 7.4.

3. Recovery channels cover a multitude of variants of the above, often combining the best aspects of sand ladders with less bulk. An articulated version is shown

The same principles apply to use of traction aids in mud or dry sand. Use them before the situation gets too bad and dig sufficient space for them to work first time. Though these shots show forward extraction, going out backwards will often apply.

above (centre picture) and in the photo on p 7.13. The articulation afforded by the rope links makes them easier to push in front of the wheels without – as is the case with ladders or PSP – the danger of the remainder of the unit fouling the vehicle chassis. When you have finished with them, the three sections can be folded up, bagged and stowed within the vehicle.

Flotation – sinking in soft ground.
Although technically there is a difference between a lack of traction and a lack of flotation, in practice the two usually strike together and a joint solution – use of reduced tyre pressures (see Section 8.2, 'Tyres') and/or load spreaders such as sand ladders etc mentioned above – will be the answer. If no load spreaders are carried, branches or brushwood should be used. If sinkage is considerable so that the vehicle is hung up (see next page) digging to remove the obstacle or jacking to permit the channels to be put under the wheels will be necessary.

Use shovels early to save a wheelspinning bogging getting worse. Invest an extra few minutes' digging and get out first time.

Use of sand ladders

Always dig away in front of a wheel before inserting the sand tracks. This helps ensure first-time grip.

Use a marshaller to prevent this. Chassis hang-up is one of the most awkward situations from which to recover. Having to dig the ground from under a vehicle provides good motivation for not letting it ever happen again.

Digging, recovery tools

Under-vehicle obstacles – hung-up on ridges or rocks. Least forgivable of driver-inflicted situations, especially if you have a passenger with you who could have got out and marshalled you over the obstacle, is getting the chassis hung up on ridges or rocks. It is also potentially the most damaging. The price will be paid, however, since the only way out of this predicament unless you have a high-lift bumper jack (see diagram / photo opposite), is actually to dig the obstacle away from under the vehicle with a shovel. It will be difficult using the shovel at full arm's length under the vehicle and in addition the vehicle will be tending initially to collapse down onto the shovel as it is used. Knowing what is involved and having the patience to do it slowly but surely will unfailingly get you out of this situation but you will vow not to let it happen again. If it is immovable rock that you are hung up on the situation is more serious but jacking front or rear to put packing under the wheels will achieve a recovery just as reliably.

Diagonal suspension – wheels in the air. As we have seen (Section 4.3, 'Ridges and ditches') it is possible to get a vehicle immobilised by misjudging the amount of axle articulation involved in crossing a ridge or ditch diagonally. (An axle is on full articulation when one wheel is pushed up into the wheel arch as far as it will go and the other wheel is hanging down as far as it will

Under-belly hang-up on ridges can be damaging and recovery awkward. Exceeding articulation limits is a common way of becoming stuck. Diagram page 4.14.

go.) A very common manifestation is 'the diagonal tightrope' in which, say, the rear offside wheel and front nearside wheel are both on full bump and the complementary wheels are hanging down – with the axle differentials permitting the hanging-down wheels to spin when you apply power (see photos page 4.15). If you have no locking differentials or traction control this situation will stop you but has a very straightforward solution – either pack up beneath the spinning wheels or dig away beneath the full bump wheels as shown on the diagram, page 4.14. It is difficult to get earth packed in tightly enough under the hanging wheels (though inserting a sand ladder, levering up and packing with rocks can work) so almost invariably digging under the hung-up wheels is the solution. As with the case above, the vehicle is trying to collapse on your shovel as you dig but, again, patience will invariably win the day.

Recovery tools. If you are planning a journey in which off-roading and the risk of getting stuck exists (see also Section 7.4), the following equipment is worth taking:
- Rubber boots, gloves, overalls.
- Electric tyre pump for re-inflation of tyres; accurate pressure gauge.
- Two shovels (pointed blades, not square ends like spades).
- Two tow ropes (totalling 25 metres) and shackles (photo next spread) for towing and/or joining the tow ropes
- Articulated sand channels or sand ladders – see previous page.
- Hi-lift jack – if appropriate to the vehicle (see opposite).
- Wood block about 30 x 20 x 5 cm to prevent jack sinkage.

Hi-lift jack – *et al.* The hi-lift jack is a mechanical bumper jack capable of a lift of a metre or more. A vehicle that has been run into deep ruts and is unable to get out could have the front end physically lifted out of the ruts and, by then pushing the jack over sideways, could be 'pole-vaulted' onto more suitable ground. Equally, the front end could also be lifted to insert ladders or branches under the wheels. Hi-lift jacks are

Hi-lift jack can be used to raise a vehicle out of deep ruts and 'lateral pole-vault' it onto easier ground. A valuable recovery tool but must be used with strict adherence to safety instructions – including use of chocks to prevent roll-back.

Easilift airbag (right), inflated by exhaust is also useful lifter but be sure under-belly area or item it is jacking on can take the pressure and not puncture the bag.

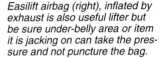

Bottle-jack with custom wheel claw adaptor (above and left), can raise wheel for insertion of sand ladders obviating need for under-axle jacking. Jack direct on rims if necessary using pad.

very effective but are very heavy and awkward to carry; also, as bumper jacks they require the square section of the Defender bumper or special bumper modifications. If you have an operating spectrum in which a hi-lift jack would be a useful recovery tool, it would be worth making modifications to enable it to be carried in a rack and used on appropriate sockets on the vehicle.

Hi-lift jack – safety. Pay special attention to safety when using a hi-lift jack. As a 'mono-pod' it is inherently unstable – see above. *Do not leave the jack unless the operating handle is in the vertical position.*

Wheel jack. The normal wheel jack with a specially made adapter can lift the axle for insertion of sand mats (above, left) and is far

easier than digging to jack under the axle casing.

Winch. Unless required for operating in particular conditions, a winch is expensive and heavy to have as a 'just-in-case' recovery aid. When trying to co-ordinate it with power from driven wheels it is slow in operation, but provided there is something to winch onto it can work wonders in certain self-recovery situations. A capstan winch is best for continuous use; see Section 5.4.

For planned off-roading, carry a full self-recovery kit. Hi-lift jack is versatile, effective for serious off-roading, but is heavy, awkward to stow and needs special care in use .

5.2 Towing out

Use of towing bridle

Ropes and attachments

Second-vehicle safety; long ropes.
Where conditions are likely to be close to the limits of your 4x4's capabilities, you are strongly advised not to go off-roading without a second vehicle. As this and the next spread will show, the potential for recovery where one vehicle is able to help another is a considerable improvement on the situation of a solo vehicle trying self-recovery. Firstly, always use a long towing rope – better still a combination of two. A short rope is easy to stow without tangling but, shackled to another one, will make a long rope to ensure the towing vehicle is not in the same bog or soft sand that has stopped the first one.

Tow rope attachment – vehicle. Tow rope attachment to the towing vehicle should naturally be at the towing hitch if one is fitted. This uses the longitudinal chassis members and the rear cross member to provide a load-spreading attachment point. At the front and rear of most vehicles, beneath the chassis, lashing points are fitted (two front and two rear), principally for securing vehicles on trailers. If a tow hitch is not fitted these can be used (as pairs, not singly) for towing. Better still, and designed to cope with far higher loads, extra-strong lashing/towing rings can be fitted in lieu of the normal lashing rings at the same chassis points on some vehicles (top photo p 4.6). On Defenders, ask for military 'JATE' rings.

Take a second vehicle for safety and to assist recovery if you are going off-roading. Use – and prepare – a long tow rope. NEVER loop tow rope round the axles.

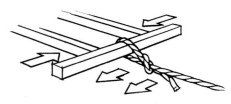

Attached at mid point, tow rope will bend a weak bumper, drawing chassis members together. Move rope close to bumper attachment points.

Too short a towing bridle will have same effect – also putting extreme strain on bridle rope.

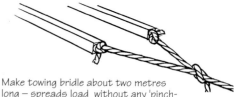

Make towing bridle about two metres long – spreads load without any 'pinching' component.

Standard ball hitch (centre of vehicle) is cleared for 3500 kg pull. If not fitted use a long bridle on the tie-down lashing rings under the chassis. Here these have been replaced by military-spec JATE-rings (photo also on p 4.6)

Bridle and two attachment points. The standard vehicle tie-down lashing points are designed for loads less than maximum towing loads but can be used for normal recovery towing (not snatch towing – see next section) if *both* eyes are used with a long bridle. A bridle is a rope attached to both lashing eyes and joined to the main tow rope two or three metres away of the vehicle. (Do not make this bridle less than two metres in length and do make it of a rope to each lashing ring rather than a single loop through both rings. This way you will minimise rope tension and also eliminate any tendency to draw the chassis members together – see diagram.) Never put a tow rope round a bumper since this will lead to the rope being cut by the bumper's sharp edge. Nor should a rope be put round an axle since this involves the strong likelihood of damaging brake pipes.

Tow rope ends. Ensuring that your tow ropes have properly prepared ends is a very worthwhile precaution. Few things can add so effectively to the problems of having to extract a bogged vehicle than finding that tow ropes have to be knotted round tow points and then need a marlin spike in order to undo the knot afterwards. Spliced-in metal eyes and the use of U-bolts and shack-

U-bolt shackle with a screw-in pin is a reliable and repeatable way of attaching or joining rope without the hassle of trying to undo immovable knots in inaccessible places under bumpers.

le pins (photo above) on properly prepared ropes makes the exercise extremely simple and quick. If you do not have a tow hitch at both ends of the vehicle, prepare a suitable length of rope with U-bolts at each end to pick up on the chassis lashing eyes and act as a two-metre bridle onto which the main tow rope can be attached. The main tow rope should be similarly prepared for your particular vehicle.

Towing autos. If recovering automatics and then towing them home some distance, remember, if there is no neutral on the transfer gears, there is often a tow limit of 30 miles and 30 mph due to lubrication requirements in the auto gearbox (see p 2.25). Over that, the propeller shafts have to be removed or a trailered recovery done.

Ideally don't use bumpers for towing; most bumpers cut tow ropes. In emergency pad with sacking, move rope close to the bumper attachment bolts.

A separate marshaller is invaluable to take up slack, signal the clutches of both vehicles to be engaged at the same time and give the 'Stop' sign – but see p 5.10 if solo. If the stuck vehicle is being towed out backwards its driver is looking the wrong way so a relay man is needed – see photo overleaf.

Co-ordinate power output from the tug and the stuck vehicle. Where the latter is being towed out backwards, its driver cannot see the marshaller so a 'relay' marshaller is needed – distant to left of vehicle here.

Co-ordinated recovery

Use a long tow rope and a marshaller to control the operation. Take your time. Marshaller should use only visual signals, not voice, to co-ordinate both vehicles' power

Meaning, procedure. A co-ordinated recovery is one in which the power and traction of both vehicles – even though one of them, being stuck, has a limited capability – are used together at the moment when the tow is undertaken. This is a common sense point but all too often, in the stress of a vehicle becoming bogged, the point is forgotten and spinning wheels and slack, then jerking tow ropes become the ingredients of minor confusion. A helpful sequence aide-memoir for a normal assisted recovery would be as follows:

1. Marshaller, co-ordinator. Ingredients of a co-ordinated recovery: one stuck vehicle, one recovery (towing) vehicle, appropriate (long) tow ropes, two drivers, a third person visible to both drivers to act as marshaller/co-ordinator.

2. Take your time. If the stuck vehicle is hung up on an obstacle invest ten minutes spade work to ensure the first extraction attempt is the one that works. Even if there is no digging, still take your time.

3. Backwards best? Towing out backwards is sometimes a more reliable option. At least the stuck vehicle has

wheel tracks leading to its present position. In this case, with the vehicles back-to-back during recovery, a second marshaller standing in 'front' of the stuck vehicle is useful to keep that driver in the picture by relaying the hand signals of the principal marshaller ahead of the tug – see photograph. As with reversing back down a hill (Section 4.4), the driver of the stuck vehicle should keep both hands on the steering wheel to preclude steering 'runaway' in reverse.

4. Towing vehicle well clear. Position the towing vehicle so that it is well clear of the conditions that bogged the first vehicle. A long rope is almost invariably more use than a short one for this reason. Attach the rope to both vehicles, position the third person so that both drivers can easily see him and have him marshal the tug forward until any slack is taken up and the rope is tight.

5. Visual signals, simultaneous clutches. Decide on the gear to be used – not necessarily 1st low range; 2nd could well be better. Have both vehicles start engines, engage gear and wait for the signal from the marshaller for both drivers to engage the clutch. As with all marshalling (Section 3.4 'Marshalling'),

Tandem tow

If stuck vehicle is heavy or badly mired a tandem tow, carefully co-ordinated, will usually achieve first-time results.

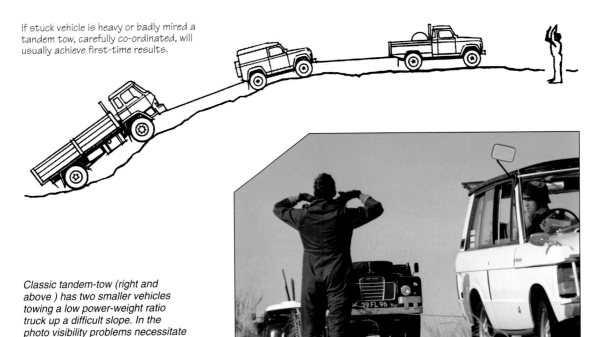

Classic tandem-tow (right and above) has two smaller vehicles towing a low power-weight ratio truck up a difficult slope. In the photo visibility problems necessitate the marshaller standing beside rather than in front of the lead vehicle for all drivers to see him.

this should be a visual not a spoken signal:
- A raised arm to instruct both drivers to be ready and in gear,
- Raised arm describing small circles to instruct them to rev the engines,
- Then drop the raised arm to instruct them to engage the clutches.

6. Marshaller in control. The marshaller should move backwards as the vehicles move towards him, still controlling the operation and being ready to give an immediate STOP signal if he sees any problems. He is the only one who can properly judge how the recovery is going. He too can judge when it is done; he can signal the lead vehicle to stop and the now mobile towed one to come forward slightly to slacken off the rope before disconnecting.

Safety – the danger of breaking ropes

Keep clear. A tow rope breaking whilst under strain can be lethal or inflict serious injury to bystanders in a multi-person co-ordinated recovery. No bystanders or crew should be allowed near a tow rope during the actual tow. Four to five metres is usually a safe distance but the danger area varies with the length of rope and the techniques used – see overleaf, 'Snatch towing'. A breaking rope recoils with whiplash violence. Adequately strong tow ropes are essential as well as rigidly enforced safety procedures in their use.

Pull required. As a guide, the pull required to move a vehicle (as a proportion of its total weight – ie including payload) assuming level ground, is given below:
- Hard metalled road – about 5% of total vehicle weight.

Use a tow rope with a breaking strain about equal to the weight of the vehicle. WARNING. When tow starts, NO-ONE should be anywhere near the tow rope.

White knight! No, not a tow for the 42-tonne artic which was destined to have time to enjoy the scenery, but the procedure in the diagram was used to recover a number of the 4-7 tonners also in the queue behind at this flood washout.

And if it's just you?

Solo rescue. If you are alone and coming to the rescue of someone needing help you can still effect a safe co-ordinated tow-out without a marshaller if you are methodical and brief the other driver. (Diagram, below)

• Lay out the tow rope with a kink in it that you can see with your door mirror.

• Edge forward till the kink moves in behind you and out of your view (see diagram, item 1).

• Continue to edge forward very slowly to take up the final slack, then stop.

• Having earlier briefed the other driver, put your hand out of the window and describe small circles to indicate "In gear, rev up, prepare to engage clutch".

• Drop hand to indicate "Engage clutch" on both vehicles.

Solo tow recovery

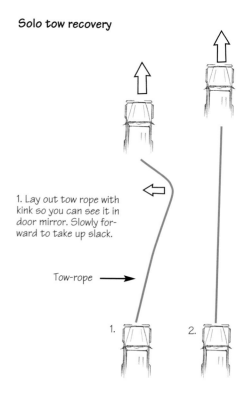

1. Lay out tow rope with kink so you can see it in door mirror. Slowly forward to take up slack.

Tow-rope ➝

2. Very slow when kink out of vision. Then give signs to co-ordinate take-off

If it's just you rescuing a fellow traveller, the recovery can still be coordinated and controlled. The briefing can even be done in sign language!

• Grass – about 15%.

• Hard wet sand, gravel, soft wet sand – about 15-20%.

• Sand – soft, dry, loose – about 25-30%.

• Shallow mud – about 33%.

• Bog, marsh, clinging clay – about 50%.

Rule-of-thumb. It makes sense that the rope to keep in the back of your off-roader is the worst-case rope – the one for marsh/bog/clay. Allowing a safety margin to account for unseen damage to the rope and other exigencies, it should have a quoted breaking strain about equal to the laden weight of your vehicle. For example, when new and undamaged, a 14 mm 3-strand polypropylene rope has a breaking strain of 2.79 tonnes (quoted breaking strains are governed by British Standards in the UK) which would be an appropriate minimum for most medium off-roaders except perhaps a laden dual-cab pickup.

5.3 Snatch towing

Snatch towing is only safe when carried out within very closely defined limits in terms of materials, vehicle integrity, speeds, length of rope, stretch maxima and procedures – in effect R&D conditions. This picture shows what can happen when it goes wrong. The tow vehicle had a chassis that was rusty on the inside. The tow hook was attached to the rusty chassis. When the 'snatch' took place, the complete tow hook and pintle was torn from the tug's rear cross member and, using the energy in the stretched rope, recoiled through front <u>and</u> rear windscreens of this Range Rover. Miraculously no-one was killed.

What is snatch towing?

The rough concept.
First of all, using:
* a very specific type of rope (long) and
* suitably strong tow attachments

the rope is attached to the stuck vehicle and then to the tug. The tug moves forward to take out all the slack. It then reverses towards the stuck vehicle (the 'step-back') for a short distance (about a metre and a half), putting a predetermined slack in the rope and giving a predetermined accelera-tion distance before it again goes taut. With the stuck vehicle in gear and using power, the tug then accelerates in a low gear – 2nd gear, low range. Rope breakage can be almost as dan-gerous as a tow-ing fixture com-ing loose.

What is snatch towing? Too dangerous.
The last edition of this book featured – with appropriate warnings – a carefully quanti-fied example of snatch towing for one spe-cific set of circumstances. and data was obtained under research conditions. These were so specific, so sensitive to variation and so utterly unlikely to be replicated in normal operations that, on reflection, it was felt the procedure could not be recommend-ed. Further, it was felt the only appropriate recommendation should be that snatch tow-ing should not be carried out at all.

Snatch towing is too sensitive to set-up criteria to be safe. Don't do it.

5.4 Winching

Concepts, winch types

Weighty decision; safety vital. The subject of winching requires a book on its own so cannot be covered fully in this Section. But a broad overview can be provided which will enable you to make your choice and get a feel for some of the principles of operation. Give careful thought to the implications of a winch before buying – it is more than an add-on accessory. In general, winches are expensive and heavy, sometimes requiring heavy duty front springs for the vehicle and special chassis reinforcement.

Electrical and mechanical add-ons. Depending on the type of winch, mechanical and electrical additions will have to be made to the vehicle – power-take-off shaft drives, hydraulic pumps or fitment of an uprated alternator or second battery where an electric winch is involved – further increasing weight. Winches require special care in operation since enormous mechanical forces are involved; children, animals, under-informed adults – and that includes spectators – should be kept well away from the vicinity of cables under tension.

Slow operation – can be good. Winches are slow but immensely powerful and usually amenable to precise control. This will be what you want a winch for in most cases. There are many applications for this low speed alone – the slow controlled pull of a boat from the water or of heavy tree trunks. If your business includes recovering defunct passenger cars from ditches or the like, the slow speed and precise controllability of a winch will be exactly what you need.

Slow operation – can be bad. Where a towed extraction is difficult due to poor grip for the tug on slippery ground, extreme boggings can be handled well by a winch – provided the tug can be anchored properly. Such anchors can be ground anchors (see page 5.18) or a strop from the back of the tug to a tree or further vehicle. But for recovering other (still functioning) vehicles

Do you really need a winch? Electric drum winches not best for continuous use. Opt for mechanical drum or capstan winches for continuous heavy duty work.

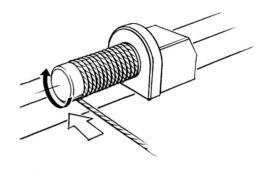

Drum winch (above). Electrical (or mechanical/hydraulic). Geared, heavy duty electric motor, uses around 350 amps. 8–9.5 mm wire rope, probably 30 metres.
Capstan winch (below). Mechanical drive direct from crankshaft or power take-off shaft. Low geared, operates from idling engine. 20 mm Terylene or polyester rope of limitless length.

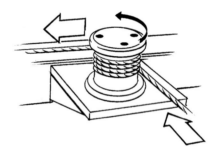

off-road you will find many occasions are better catered for by a vehicle tow with a long rope (see Sec 5.2) and power employed by both the tug and the stuck vehicle. Using a winch to recover a stuck vehicle makes it hard to coordinate the slow speed of the winch with power from the stuck vehicle's own engine and this is where the winch's slowness is a major disadvantage. When you do use this 'drive and winch' technique, care should be taken not to overrun the cable when the towed vehicle begins to grip.

Approved winches. Fitting a winch and ensuring that the stresses involved in winch-

ing are properly channelled into the structure is a specialised skill. Not all 4x4s make
satisfactory bases for winches. You are most
strongly advised to consult your vehicle
supplier when buying a winch and to buy
only winches that have been approved for
your machine. The fitting kit will have been
specifically engineered for it with safety in
mind and so as not to overload the structure. Winches may be ordered factory-fitted
by some manufacturers with some models –
the Land Rover Defender being a classic
example. Additionally there will be a small
Handbook of Winching Techniques issued
with the winch which will summarise how
to prepare and operate the unit. The following few pages cannot deal with the subject
comprehensively.

Winch types. There are two generic classifications of winch:

1. *Drum winches* comprise a drum rotating about a horizontal axis parallel to the
bumper and use 8–9.5 mm wire rope
stored on, and spooled onto, the drum.
They can be driven electrically (occasional short-term use) or there can be
mechanical or hydraulic drive for continuous heavy duty operation.

2. *Capstan winches* consist of a bollard –
like a giant cotton reel – rotating about a
vertical axis. Such winches do not store
any rope; they function by moving
appropriate ropes – usually 20 mm
Terylene/polyester or polypropylene –
which have been wound two or three
times round the bollard and tensioned
on the out-feed side. Capstan winches
are mechanically or hydraulically driven
and are ideal for continuous heavy duty
work with the vehicle engine at idle or
fast idle..

Pros and cons. Relative advantages and
disadvantages of generic and particular
types are dealt with in the table on the next
spread.

*Know your pro-
posed needs for a
winch. Of prime
concern is
whether your
work is intermit-
tent – 'casual' –
or continuous
heavy duty
winching. See
next spread.*

*Capstan winch (above)
powers rope – of any
length – looped round
capstan. 10000 lb
Superwinch E10 (above
right) is among most
powerful electrically
powered winches and
designed for intermittent
heavy duty use; stores
cable on drum.
Mechanical H14(right) is
designed for continuous
heavy duty work.*

Match the winch to the job

Casual or heavy duty. Winching can be
'casual' – towing a boat out of the water or
the occasional use for self-recovery – or
'heavy duty' which implies regular *continuous* use, usually for professional purposes
such as logging or cable laying. Electric
winches are not normally suitable for continuous heavy duty use. Very high amperages are involved, considerable heat is generated and a very high charge rate from the
alternator is required.

A mechanically driven capstan or drum
winch is an altogether more relaxed concept
which operates directly from the engine at
tick-over or very low rpm. It can thus be

*Be aware of the
different generic
types of winch
and the very
broad spectrum
of applications.
A winch ideal
for one kind of
usage can be
quite unsuitable
for another.*

used all day without mechanical stress.

Assess your requirement. Assess your
needs very carefully and accept the fact that
installation of a heavy duty winch will be
necessary where use is continuous and that
such an installation will be heavy and relatively expensive since either mechanical
shafting from a power take-off (PTO) or
installation of a PTO-mounted hydraulic
pump will be required.

Airbag-equipped vehicles. Modern
vehicles with airbags will have triggering
devices for the airbag Secondary Restraint
System (SRS) that are sensitive to specific
crush rates encountered in front-end collisions. These crush-rates could be affected by

Table 1. Winch types and general characteristics

Type	Applications	For	Against
Electric drum winch	Intermittent light, medium or heavy duty use according to specification.	Low cost, simple installation, relatively low weight 54-87 kg. Wide range from light to medium/heavy duty. Easy to use. Minimal maintenance. Wire stored on drum.	Electric motor will overheat if used for long periods. Very high amperage draw from battery necessitates high engine rpm and alternator output to recharge. Installation may need second battery.
Hydraulic drum winch	Continuous heavy duty industrial use.	Can operate for long continuous periods of industrial use with engine at low output or tick-over. Automatic rpm control. Vehicle has capability for other hydraulic tools/applications.	High initial cost for winch and PTO hydraulic pump installation. Needs specialised maintenance for precision components. Engine must be running. Heavy – up to around 115 kg.
Mechanical drum winch	Continuous heavy duty industrial use.	Can operate for long continuous periods of industrial use with engine at low output or tick-over.	High initial cost for PTO gear and drive shafts to winch position. Two-man operation – one controls engine, one controls winch. Engine must be running. Heavy – up to around 112 kg.
Mechanical or hydraulic capstan winch	Continuous heavy duty industrial use.	Can operate for long continuous periods of industrial use with engine at low output or tick-over. Constant pulling power due to rope being constant distance from drum axis all the time. Easy to operate. No limit to length of rope used. Around 63 kg.	High cost plus specialist maintenance if hydraulic drive. No room for mechanical drive on current Tdi Defender. Rope not contained on winch. Engine must be running.

Table 2. Snapshot data on some Land Rover approved winch types (Superwinch)						
Type	Name	Max line pull	Gearbox type	Brake type	Free spool	Elec/hydraulic power requirements
Electric drum	1. X6 2. X9 3. Husky 4. E10	6000 lb 9000 lb 8500 lb 10000 lb	Planetary Planetary Worm/wheel Planetary	Dynamic In drum Irreversible Disc, wet	Lever Lever Lever Plunger	12v, 390 amps 12v, 435 amps 12v, 360 amps 12v, 360 amps
Hydraulic drum	1. H8 2. H14W	8000 lb 8000 lb	Planetary Worm/wheel	Disc, wet Irreversible	Plunger Plunger	32 litre pump, 2500 psi 32 litre pump, 2500 psi
Mechanical drum	1. H14W	8000 lb	Worm/wheel	Irreversible	Plunger	Power take-off shafts
Mechanical or hydraulic capstan		4000 lb	Worm/wheel	Irreversible	N/A	Power take-off shafts or PTO hydraulic pump

In considering choice of winch, relate your proposed work to existence/type of brake, power requirements and amount of use at a given session.

Terminology
1. Gearbox type. This is an indication of the kind of reduction gear used in the winch. Worm and wheel can be arranged (and is here) to be irreversible hence there is no need for a brake.
2. Free-spool. Free-spooling is the process of disengaging the winch in order to reel out the cable to the item being winched. 'Lever' or 'plunger' indicates the method of activating winch cable release.
3. Brake. Braking is provided for the mid-pull power failure case. Knowledge of brake principle is needed. 'Dynamic' brake is only the running of the winch motor in high-geared reverse as a generator so is a retarder rather than a stop brake. (X6CD has centre drum brake.) Drum and disc brakes activate automatically via one-way clutch in the event of power being lost in mid pull. Worm and wheel gearing is itself irreversible so runaway after power failure is just not possible.

Discovery with Superwinch X6 winch in a low-profile fitting. Protrusions under driving lights indicate 'crush cans'; these establish set deformation rate in collision for airbag deployment. Only approved winch fitments should be used on these vehicles.

an inappropriate winch installation – another reason (see previous spread) for consultation with the vehicle manufacturer before fitting a winch. Factory-fitted installations will take account of this but an incorrect installation could well result in premature triggering of the airbag system. In the case of Land Rover, for example, only approved winches, mounts and crush units are factory-fitted to vehicles with airbags. Being front-mounted, the mountings of these winches will have been engineered for the correct crush-rates compatible with the SRS.

Where a braked wheel would simply slide across slippery earth, ground anchors of this kind will give the winch something to pull against. Weight of the vehicle contributes to bite. Ground anchors like these are very heavy and need proper stowage. Aluminium units are available.

Techniques overview

Accessories. Paradoxically, it is wise to consider the accessories you will need before going firm on your choice of winch since you must envisage the entire operating regime and method of use before you have a clear picture of what is involved. The number of operating crew is a fundamental first consideration since if you are always going to be solo then a mechanical drum winch may not be suitable despite its conceptual appeal. Length of cable is a consideration. Most drum winches are supplied with 30 metres (100 feet) of cable and, whilst this can be attached to extensions, there may be times when a continuous long pull is required and thus a capstan winch would be the best equipment. If this is the case then thought must be given to storage of the rope within the vehicle. It will be bulky and must be kept in good condition. For any winch you are going to need some or all of the following additional ancillary equipment:

Protect trees, by using a strap; people by observing safety rules and keeping clear of ropes and cables. Unless self-recovering, anchor the winch vehicle.

- **D-shackles** – see photo page 5.7. For winching, where line pulls will be higher than for normal vehicle-to-vehicle tow-outs, stronger D-shackles will be needed. A 3/4-inch pin diameter is a good guide.
- **Tree strap.** Usually available from the winch manufacturer, an 8-foot by 4-inch tree strap should be acquired to put round trees to protect them from bark damage that would occur when using a tree as a winching anchor with a bare cable. Always use a tree strap – and as low as possible on the tree.
- **Split pulley block.** Where direction of pull is likely to be off vehicle axis or where a double-line pull is required, a pulley block will be needed to direct or increase the line pull. See photo opposite and diagrams/photo next spread.
- **Ground anchors.** Where high line-pulls are envisaged, possibly on slippery ground, a pair of ground anchors (photo, left) will prevent forward movement of the vehicle during the pull. The right ones will be heavy and cumbersome and take up space and payload in the vehicle.
- **Back-anchor rope.** Where ground anchors are not available or where additional security is required, the winching vehicle can be anchored with rope and tree strap to a tree behind it.
- **Gloves.** Steel cables can have small broken strands along their length; use thick winching gloves to protect your hands. Do not let a steel winch cable slip through your hands even when using gloves. Always pay it in or out hand-over-hand. The same gloves will be useful for the handling of capstan winch ropes too.

The extent of your proposed winching activity will dictate how much of the above you need. It will vary from very little if you are going only to pull a boat out of the water once per weekend, to virtually the whole kit if you are going to be a recovery marshal on an off-road trial or are carrying out logging operations in a forest area. It will all figure in and be part of your eventual choice of winch.

Slope and line pull. Knowledge of your required line pull in various conditions is necessary as the final consideration before choosing a winch.

1. Level ground. For recovering vehicles – or any wheeled object with reasonably large wheels – the pull required to move it varies according to the surface on which it is standing. The pull, as an approximate proportion of its weight, is:

Hard road – 5%
Grass – 15%
Hard/soft wet sand, gravel – 15-20%
Soft dry sand – 25-30%
Shallow mud – 33%
Bog, marsh, clay – 50%.

Thus if the vehicle to be winched is a part-laden Discovery with a total weight of 2300 kg (5060 lb), the line pull to get it out of shallow mud will be just under 759 kg (1700 lb).

2. Sloping ground. If the ground you are winching up is sloping you must *add* an increment to account for this. This is very simply calculated as the slope in degrees, divided by 60, times the total load of the vehicle being towed. Thus going up a 15° slope with the Discovery above would add 15/60 = 1/4 of its 2300 kg total weight to the line pull. So in this example we have:

Terrain component = 759 kg
Slope – 1/4 of 2300 = 575 kg
So total pull is 1334 kg (2935 lb).

Note that the slope component is surprisingly high – and this is assuming an even slope. In real life, of course, ground is uneven and a small local obstacle like a rock or a tree root can put the immediate local slope up to 30 or 40°. Note also that it is the heaviest ground, eg clay, that is likely to get you stuck and in this case the terrain component goes up to 1150 kg and the whole total to 1725 kg.

Margins. Comfortable margins and, probably even more important, a knowledge of how the winch works and whether your usage is to be intermittent or continuous should then be applied in establishing your choice of equipment. Electric winches being hard-working, high revving, hot-running devices that also require the vehicle engine to be running fast are obviously less suited to continuous work than, say a capstan winch running at engine idle speed. Their relative lightness and cheapness, however, would win the day where the occasional winching of a boat or caravan is concerned.

Always use thick leather gloves when handling winch cables. Split pulley is an invaluable 'carry always' accessory to double or direct pull.

Winch cable looped through split pulley block and back to vehicle bumper doubles effective pull of winch – 8500 lb Husky is shown in this mode above (see diagram next spread). Pulley can also be used for indirect pull – photo next page.

Winching is a potentially dangerous procedure. But the danger can be eliminated by care and operator knowledge. Take your time. Take your time.

Photo shows indirect pull electrical winching with cable through a split pulley block – see facing page. Although itself winch-equipped, the stuck vehicle (left) is being winched up a slippery slope by a recovery vehicle (right). Note use of strap to preclude damage to tree bark and that the winching vehicle is square-on to the direction of initial pull.

Safety first. Whilst a clichéd paragraph heading like this will not always do its job, the reminder is nonetheless very necessary since winching is laden with the possibility of accidents if real care is not taken. The good news, however, is that you, as operator, are in charge and there is seldom if ever any rush. Rest assured that thinking ahead, thinking things through, keeping people away from tow ropes and winch ropes, observing the few rules outlined here and *reading the instruction book thoroughly* WILL result in safe winching.

Breaking cables. Breaking cables and ropes are extremely hazardous. Never step over a cable under tension and ensure no-one is close to it when winching is in progress. Wire cables as used on drum winches flail laterally when they break so are particularly dangerous.

Control cable safety. Be particularly careful that electrical cables going to the control unit handset are kept well clear of

the winch wire. Caught up in the winch, a short circuit could make the winch unstoppable without disconnecting the wire.

Radio control. Control cable safety is taken care of if a radio control is used. It also enables the user to get closer to the job when precision is required.

Directing – or doubling – the pull. Unlike the bulk and weight of ground anchors, split pulley blocks (photo, previous spread) are light and small and worth carrying at all times with extra straps and ropes. Be sure its rating is compatible with your winch. They are invaluable as a means of producing an indirect pull (facing photo) and for producing a given pull with half the strain on the winch at half speed (diagram below).

Maintenance, care of cables and ropes. Drum winch cables should spool onto the drum evenly and will do so if the pull is at the correct angle. If there are signs of it not doing so, stop the winching, pay out the cable and spool back onto the drum guiding it by (gloved) hands. Inspect and clean cables and ropes regularly; excessive mud will get into the strands or fibres and cause damage. Extend the cable to full length and

check in detail for damage. Check gearbox oil levels and check for the presence of hydraulic leaks regularly.

Towing attachments – vehicle recovery. As with towed and snatch recovery, the towing attachments on vehicles being recovered must be sound and purpose-built. Attach cables using D-shackles tightened and then backed-off half a turn. NEVER attach cables to axles or steering rods.

Training and practice. Fully absorb the winch instructions, be familiar with the equipment and take time to train and practise before real-life use.

Practise to gain complete familiarity with your equipment before using it on real situations.

Pulley doubles winch maximum 'power' for moving obstacles

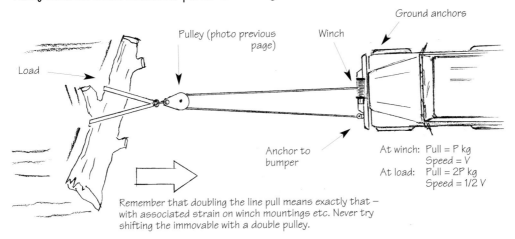

Remember that doubling the line pull means exactly that – with associated strain on winch mountings etc. Never try shifting the immovable with a double pulley.

At winch: Pull = P kg
Speed = V
At load: Pull = 2P kg
Speed = 1/2 V

Pulley reduces line strain – or increases the pull – in self-recovery

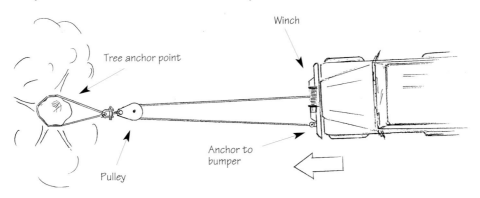

Section 6

Advanced driving

6.1 Non-synchro gearboxes

Main gearbox

Synchromesh? Er ... what? Rumbling into the twenty-first century you could be forgiven for taking synchromesh for granted so don't feel that you would lose credibility by reading what synchro actually does and why it hasn't always been there. If you drive a Series 1 or 2 Land Rover, an old 4x4 truck or any number of other older or commercial vehicles, you may have a gearbox that is not all-synchromesh.

Obviously a gearbox contains wheels and shafts going at different speeds. 'Changing gear' entails, in effect, sliding one gear or shaft into mesh with another. Unless they are going at compatible speeds there will be a 'grinding of the gears' or a huge and solid 'clonk' when the move is made.

What it is. The frictional drag created by the outside of a male cone on one shaft engaging with the inside of a female cone on another co-axial shaft is a means of synchronising their speeds. That is what synchromesh does to one shaft or 'gear' before it actually engages with another.

Although the idea is decades old, synchro was once only fitted to passenger car gearboxes and then usually only the upper two or three gears. So first gear, and maybe second too, was non-synchro and virtually all trucks or working vehicles had no synchro on any gear. Cost was the main reason for keeping synchro out of a lot of gearboxes but all cars now have all-synchro and most trucks do too.

No synchro; what to do. If there is no synchro on a gear (or any gear) in a gearbox you should change gear into that ratio in a different way. To most people who took their driving test on a modern car, changing gear consists of dipping the clutch and moving the gear lever from one position to another. What actually happens (in the gearbox) is that as you move the lever the synchro cones touch, synchronise the speed of the approaching gear wheels or dog-clutch-

es, and then, with the last part of the gear lever movement, the gears are engaged. As you may have already found, even on a synchro box, you can often get a smoother take-up of power by adjusting the throttle a little bit as you engage the next gear to 'cushion the change'.

If you are going down from 3rd to 2nd, for example, blip the throttle slightly to raise the revs while the gear lever is passing neutral. Going up, make sure the engine revs do die off a bit going from 2nd to 3rd. That way, when you let the clutch in again the engine speed will better match the road speed and you will avoid the lurch and transmission snatch that otherwise occurs.

Double de-clutching. In a non-synchro box, without the speed synchronisation of the gear wheels going on, there is still quite a bit we can do with the throttle and clutch to ensure a smooth gear change. It is called 'double de-clutching' and, as its name indicates, it involves de-clutching twice with some rpm adjustment in between with the throttle. It will sound complicated to describe but, like riding a bicycle, after some initial concentration it becomes far easier to do than describe.

It can be summarised as spending a fraction of a second in neutral with the clutch up (ie engaged), before dipping the clutch again and moving the gear lever on to the gear you are about to select. So, specifically:

• *Double de-clutch – down-change.* This is the procedure for a down-change on a gearbox with no synchro, say 3rd to 2nd:

Clutch	Throttle	Gear lever
Dip	–	Move to neutral
Up	BOOST REVS	–
Dip	–	Move, 3rd to 2nd
Up	Resume drive	–

You will get to know the amount by which the throttle needs to be boosted but, if you think about it, you must select the kind of engine revs that would apply at that road speed in the gear you are about to select. Going from 2nd to 1st at any but the very slowest road speed you will find you have to boost the throttle a surprising amount; only do this at about walking speed.

Synchromesh is now so wide-spread you may have to check what it means! Classic outback vehicles – Series 2 Land Rovers, Bedfords have some non-synchro gears.

If you don't double de-clutch on a down-change into a non-synchro gear you will often get a dreadful grinding of gears and the gear may not engage at all. There have been examples of unskilled off-road drivers being so put off by this that they will stall in 2nd gear rather than face trying to engage 1st gear on the move.

• *Double de-clutch – up-change.* This is the procedure for an up-change on a gear-box with no synchro, say 1st to 2nd:

Clutch	Throttle	Gear lever
Dip	–	Move to neutral
Up	FOOT OFF	–
Dip	–	Move, 1st to 2nd
Up	Resume drive	–

If you don't double de-clutch on an up-change you will 'just' get a heavy clonk when the gear goes in. This equates to a small sledge-hammer being applied to the transmission; don't let it happen!

Practise – off-road too. Practise the procedure first with the vehicle stationary in your driveway without the engine even running, just to get familiar with the sequence. Then practise on quiet roads so that you get to know the best speeds and engine rpm boosts suited to change-downs.

Change-ups will be easier. Practise up- and down-changes until a smooth silent change can be made into all gears – including first. The whole thing is tied up with road and engine speeds and vehicle speed decay during the time spent in neutral. This latter, and therefore the whole feel of the gear change will thus be different on-road compared to when on grass, rough terrain or off-road.

The sort of on-road to off-road adjustments to technique to expect would be:

• Down-changes – a little less rev boost.
• Up-changes – a little less rev drop.

Touching third ... . A trick worth knowing, applicable, for example to old Series 2 Land Rovers, is how to avoid that dreadful grinding of gears when engaging a gear to move off from stationary. When moving off get into the habit of 'touching third' before engaging first or reverse. Dip the clutch in the normal way, touch the gear lever into

Ex-military trucks like this one, a natural choice for expeditions, are remarkably agile. But two or more non-synchromesh gears in the gearbox calls for driver agility too. It is well worth getting it right.

third gear (the synchro cones on that gear will calm things in the gearbox) and then, when you engage first or reverse the gear will go in quietly without any noise.

This is a particularly valuable tip when doing any backing and filling – three- or four-point turns getting out of tight spaces. Each time you go from 1st to reverse, or vice versa, touch third gear to still the shafts.

The procedure will apply to any vehicle where you have synchro on an upper gear ratio like third or top and no synchromesh on first or reverse.

Transfer gearbox

As we have seen (p 2.17) although one or two manufacturers are at last addressing the issue, it is rare to get synchro on a transfer box so range changes, in normal 'handbook conditions', have to be made with the vehicle stationary. But see next Section.

Double de-clutching is hard to describe, far easier to do. Remember revs adjustments take place with gear lever in neutral and clutch pedal up. Practise static first.

6.2 Range change on-the-move – manual gearbox

Low range is not just extra-low gearing. It over-laps high range letting you choose best gear-box span. Changing from low to high on the move is well worth learning.

On-the-move range change – the need

Low to high change – when you need it. There are times when it is very useful to be able to start in low range and, while still moving, continue in high – typically, towing a heavy trailer on hard roads (Sec 4.1), tow-ing a trailer off-road (Sec 6.5) or just starting the vehicle in marginal traction conditions such as soft sand or mud where it would be risky, once moving, to stop in order to re-select high range – photo opposite.

The problems. Few manufacturers have designed their drivelines to enable an on-the-move range changes to be executed easi-ly – or at all. Push-button range change selection often has an electronic lockout built in to actually prevent an on-the-move change and where the change is by lever, synchro in the transfer box would make life a lot easier but is seldom provided. The pro-cedure opposite, however, can work with-out synchro in the transfer gearbox.

Speeds in the gears. If you study your gear ratios data – and the diagram below – you will see that there is inevitably an over-lap between low range and high range – for example 4th or 5th gear low is roughly

equivalent to 2nd gear high so that a given piece of ground could be covered equally well in either and at roughly the same engine rpm. Often, where there is a choice, being in low range rather than the high will give you the ability to tackle sudden track deteriorations such as road washouts or obstacles, without having to carry out a range change. So being in low range – and wanting the capability to move to high easi-ly – is a fairly normal scenario. (See also 'Low range – when and how', Sec 2.4.)

On-the-move range change – manual

Low/high change – what gear, what speed. A change across from low to high is usually possible on vehicles having a lever range change. In practice it is best to get the vehicle properly moving first – say 25-30 mph. That way, momentum will keep you going whilst you execute the change. Before contemplating a change from low range to high you should also be sure that conditions are suitable for sustained travel in high range since to change back again from high to low range you will usually have to stop.

No clunks or grinding gears please. The procedure outlined here should only be done if you can *execute it without heavy clonks or*

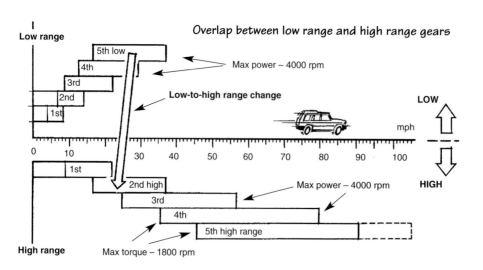

Bars represent speed in that gear between max torque (c.1800 rpm) and max power (c. 4000 rpm). Land Rover Tdi diesel engine shown but values for many engines are similar. Best change point for low to high on the move is 25-30 mph – 5th low to 2nd high. Don't just move the transfer lever on its own.

Overlap between low range and high range gears

Low range
5th low
4th
3rd
2nd
1st
Max power – 4000 rpm
Low-to-high range change
LOW
mph
0   10   30   40   50   60   70   80   90   100
HIGH
1st
2nd high
3rd
4th
Max power – 4000 rpm
5th high range
High range
Max torque – 1800 rpm

grinding gears in the transmission. It is a way of getting round the absence of synchro on most transfer boxes. Currently, the Mercedes G-Wagen and one or two of the more recent Land Rovers are some of the few cleared by the manufacturer for on-the-move (synchro) transfer ratio change.

4th/5th low to 2nd high on the move – procedure – manual gearbox. With no transfer box synchro, try this (diag right):

1. In low range, accelerate through the gears to 25-30 mph.

2. With the main gear lever still in 5th, depress the clutch and move the transfer lever into neutral. (Note, this will need a short, sharp action with a *definite halt at the neutral position.*) Keep the clutch depressed. Then move the main gear lever from 5th into 2nd gear. Main gearbox synchro will make this quiet.

3. Clutch foot up then down again – performing a kind of double-de-clutch operation – then move the transfer lever from neutral to 'H'.

4. As the engine was losing rpm whilst you moved the transfer lever, you will need a blip of throttle to raise engine revs to the right level for 2nd gear, high range at 25 mph. (since vehicle speed will have dropped to that from the 25-30 mph at 1.) Gently up with the clutch pedal and accelerate away.

Push-button range change ... ?. With one or two exceptions – see mention of Discover 3, next spread – none of the above is usually possible with a push-button range change since there are often electrical inhibits and no neutral position between low and high is selectable.

High to low on the move ... ? This can be done under certain conditions to demonstrate driving skill but there is little practical application. Deteriorating heavy going is when you might need this change and here the time taken to execute it will be enough for the vehicle's speed to have decayed to nothing. Make life easy; change to low range when stationary. Discovery 3, however, has a synchro transfer box and is cleared for hi-to-lo changes on manual.

Low to high range on the move – manual

Manual transmission, no transfer synchro
Lever range change, with neutral

1.
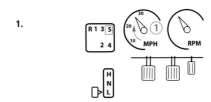

2.
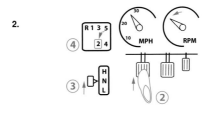

3.
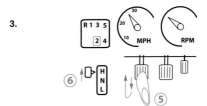

4.
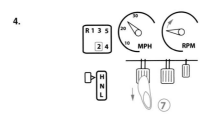

Low to high – do it from 30 mph in 4th/5th low. Complex to read but simple to do. Practise it first on hard roads, then off-road where speed decay will be different.

Classic situation for low-to-high change on the move – soft-ish sand, hard to start in but which, moving, you can take in high range. More usual example is heavy trailer towing – hill starts or moving off from traffic lights. Get it going in low range, then change to high.

6.3 Range change on-the-move – automatic gearbox

Large-throw transfer box lever makes on an-the-move range change easier since the all-important neutral is easier to locate. Jeep's Grand Cherokee now has switch selection with a neutral only available (usefully) for towing.

Do use low range in auto

Don't overheat the transmission. First a reminder. Just because it will often work, don't be tempted to use high range in auto transmissions in conditions that demand low range (see p 2.25). Serious overheating of the transmission fluid can result. Once in low range, you will need to go back to high range eventually, and doing it on the move can be very useful – at times essential.

Low to high – moving (auto)

Just because automatic transmission is so accommodating, don't omit to use the low range gears. Using high range inappropriately will overheat transmission.

Generic method. Using the procedures shown here this is possible – but *check, if necessary, with the vehicle manufacturer* that there are not special design features making it inadvisable with your particular vehicle.

Where an electric button/switch selection is involved, speed sensors may prevent range change unless the vehicle is stationary and the main gear selector is in neutral. However, since there are a number of different techniques that can effect an on-the-move range change with an automatic transmission here are some general principles:

• Get up to 25-30 mph in the low range.
• Get the main transmission lever into 'N' before moving the transfer lever/button.
• With or without synchro on the transfer box match the rpm to the road speed and gear before the final move.

Lever range change, with a neutral. So, following the diagram (below):
1. Accelerate to 25-30 mph in low.
2. Main lever to 'N', then range to 'N'.
3. Allow rpm to drop.
4. Match rpm to road speed, range lever to 'H', then main lever to 'D'. Drive on.

Low to high range on the move – auto

Automatic transmission
Lever range change, with a neutral position

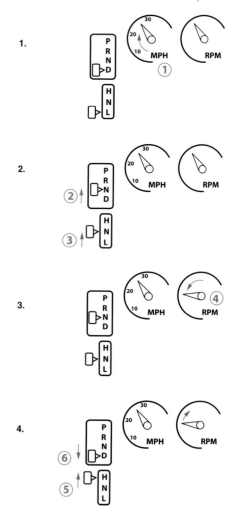

Button/switch range change, no neutral. When the range change of the transfer gears is selected electrically via a button or switch there is often an inhibit built into the system that precludes execution until the vehicle is stationary. But the value of an on-the-move change is at last being recognised by some manufacturers – Land Rover were among the first, on the Discovery 3 and Range Rover in 2005, to follow the Mercedes G-Wagen's 25 year lead in providing synchro on the transfer gearbox.

Manufacturer's OK. The procedure for the Discovery 3, for example, is shown on the right.

1. Accelerate to 25-30 mph in low range though the system will allow changes at up to nearly 40 mph.

2. Main transmission lever to 'N'.

3. Allow rpm to drop. Match rpm, move transfer gear lever to 'H'.

4. Move main transmission lever to 'D'. Drive on in high range.

Refreshingly, this procedure is not only approved by the manufacturer but covered in detail in the driver's handbook for both the automatic and manual transmission.

High to low on the move. Less frequently required but still useful – and applicable to the case when difficult terrain ahead looms – the drivelines on the G-Wagen, Discovery 3 and Range Rover enable a change from high to low range gears to be made without stopping. This is less often needed in day to day off-road operation – since in deteriorating going since the vehicle's speed will decay so quickly while the change sequence is undertaken that a stationary engagement is rarely that much of an inconvenience. It is nevertheless a valuable facility to have at the driver's disposal.

High to low, no synchro. Without synchro on the transfer gears this high to low change has usually to be made at under five mph – main gear selector to neutral first, boost engine rpm, then move the range change lever or switch (in the absence of an electric lockout) to low.

Low to high range on the move - auto

Automatic transmission, transfer synchro
Switch range change, no neutral

1.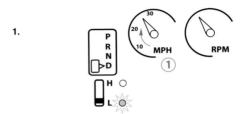

2.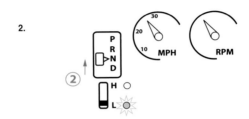

Unlike manual transmission, high to low with auto can – occasionally – be a useful technique in certain cases.

3.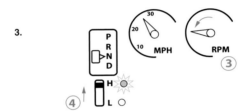

4.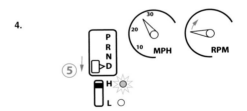

Range change, mobile. It is definitely worth practise before using this capability in real conditions – confidence is all! Where a transfer lever, as opposed to a switch or button is involved, short, crisp movement is usually required and the tendency to overshoot without stopping in neutral must be avoided.

6.4 Down-slopes

Emergency sequence

Steep initial section, you find you have too low a gear; wheels are sliding ....

Engine braking

Engine braking recommended...but.
Read this section after reading Section 4.5. Engine braking is the safe way to keep speed in check – especially on steep off-road slopes. On long hills – classically, on-road Alpine pass descents – use engine braking to avoid overheating the brakes. Even today's disc brakes can suffer from a degree of 'fade' (reduced efficiency) when they get very hot. All this is a well accepted part of our armoury of safe driving techniques.

Old wives' tales and delicate braking.
But it is also something of a relic of the days of poor brakes. Indeed, on a two-wheel drive car, engine braking derives retardation through only one pair of wheels on the driven axle whilst sensitive and delicate use of the foot brake uses all four. The same retardation spread between four wheels instead of two reduces the risk of wheel locking.

There is thus a place for sensitive and delicate braking in many situations, certainly the short off-road ones, in which we have learned to leave the brakes alone. ABS and cadence braking (see Section 3.2, 'Gentle right foot') are especially relevant here. What we are really trying to avoid is sliding wheels – whatever their cause.

Bedrock tenets. Engine braking (especially on a 4x4) and readiness to use cadence braking are bedrock tenets of safe descent of steep slippery off-road slopes and must never be forgotten.

ABS, HDC, DAC, etc. But now there is more. There is ABS to do the cadence braking for you should it be required – but be certain whether your system is cleared for off-road use. And we are starting to see ingenious, logic-controlled systems emerge that will automate it further. If you have one of the iterations of automated steep-down-slope auto pilots such as Land Rover's Hill Descent Control (HDC) or Toyota's Downhill Assist Control (DAC) then these

Just as excessive braking can cause wheel slide, so can excessive engine braking – 1st gear low range on a very steep, long, slippery slope. Remember cadence braking.

will get you safely down extreme descents. Land Rover pioneered the concept with HDC which keeps the vehicle at or below a target slow descent speed by use of various sensors and the ABS braking.

Some may say that you must be able to recognise a challenging descent in order to use the system – ie, know when to select HDC, low range and a low gear. And that if you have the experience to do that you will be aware of the bedrock tenets mentioned in the previous column and will thus not need the system anyway.

But there will be an experience level where knowing is one thing and doing is another and an automated, flexible concept like HDC is a comforting fall-back.

Manual procedures

Beware sliding wheels. If you have selectable four-wheel drive ('Type 2' on page 2.2) then you must, of course, be in 4x4 before tackling any really steep down-slopes. With or without automated descent control, however, you must still be aware of the risk of selecting *too low* a gear on steep and slippery slopes. Just as excessive use of the brakes can cause lock-up and discontinuity of rolling contact between the wheels and the ground (page 3.4), so tackling a really steep *slippery* slope using 1st gear low range can sometimes amount to excessive engine braking and also result in wheel slide.

Accelerate. Be ready to use the accelerator. Or it will likely be better to use a higher gear such as 2nd – even 3rd sometimes. (See photo above.)

... add throttle. Delicate application of brake; quit at the first suspicion of lock-up.

If, in gear, wheels just cannot keep up with speed increase, de-clutch and use cadence braking. Keep front wheels pointing straight down slope.

Select a higher gear once the problem is over, boost the revs as you engage clutch and resume engine braking.

A matter of judgement. If it is this steep you want retardation but too low a gear when it is slippery or loose will give you slide. 2nd low, rather than 1st, would be best if it were muddy earth. In the special case of this high sand dune you need to go higher still – 3rd or 4th low or even 1st high range – to prevent the vehicle nosing into the sand. (In this context see also Glossary 'Castor angle', and 'Steering feel', Section 9.1.)

What to do. Firstly remember that some ABS systems do not work properly off-road or the system may have auto-disabled when you select 4x4. There are two classic cases of extreme down-slope slide to consider – which off-road-capable ABS brakes will make very much simpler:

1. Almost the right gear, brake assistance. Take the case of an initially steep, long slippery down-slope with a loose surface. You judge that 1st low would result in slide and that 2nd low is appropriate. But the initial section is so steep that the vehicle gains speed faster than you anticipated. Clearly it is inadvisable to attempt to change down at this critical stage (even an automatic will not always change down to 1st in these conditions, see page 2.19) so a gentle and intermittent use of the brake pedal – gentle cadence braking (or ABS) – can be used to slow to the limits of the available grip. Don't let the wheels lock; and if they do, release the brakes altogether, immediately.

2. Wrong gear, cadence braking takeover. Take the same steep, long, slippery down-slope. Starting down it in 1st gear low box may result in wheel slide because in such a low gear – even with

the engine revving hard – the wheels will not be able to turn fast enough to maintain rolling contact with the ground. You realise too late that you have got the wrong gear so, after using all the throttle you can, you must undertake a rescue operation. De-clutch so that the wheels can regain rolling contact with the ground, then with great sensitivity carry out cadence braking – *rapid gentle jabs at the brake pedal that never permit the wheels to lock* but which give you the best retardation the circumstances allow. This is a rare scenario but keep it in the back of your mind rather than slide out of control, throttle wide, in 1st.

Emergency procedure: really sensitive use of the brakes, releasing them the instant they lock the wheels – or cadence braking.

6.5 Towing off-road

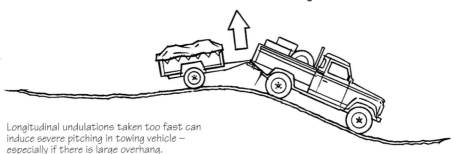

Longitudinal undulations

Longitudinal undulations taken too fast can induce severe pitching in towing vehicle – especially if there is large overhang.

Potential problems

Heavy trailer off-road – or light trailer driven briskly – will feed back considerable inertia loads to tug.

Greater trailer feedback. (Read Section 4.1, 'Towing – on-road', first, noting the typical maximum off-road towing weights shown in the table.) Using trailers off-road requires even greater anticipation and care. Feedback effect to the towing vehicle is much more noticeable than on hard road. Inertia fed into the trailer by the tug has to be arrested at every change in direction. For

example, traversing undulations too fast can cause interactive responses between vehicle and trailer. Specifically, the trailer can cause considerable pitch in the towing vehicle as it swoops into and out of a dip. This can be bad enough in extreme cases to lift the rear end of the vehicle momentarily off the ground, especially if there is a long tail overhang in the towing vehicle.

Trailer inertia – drag and push. Off-road trailer drag over uneven ground and 'trailer-push' down steep slopes will be

Gently does it. Bulky body, light construction, small wheels and minimal underbody clearance make this trailer far less capable off-road than the tug.

High-density industrial plant trailers need treating with more than expected care off-road – mainly due to very high inertia, feedback to the tug and limitations of trailer suspension. Often wheels are small and the unit is designed for simple site mobility, not for extended off-road towing.

more pronounced – with braking correspondingly more difficult and liable, in extreme cases, to provoke the trailer to try to overtake the vehicle in a form of jack-knifing.

Lateral roll. Off-road there is also a surprising susceptibility to lateral roll by the trailer. Trailer suspension is seldom damped sufficiently in the laden condition compared to that of the towing vehicle, often compounded by a degree of roll-steer due to crude axle location geometry on the trailer. Lateral roll over an uneven track which the tug suspension will cope with easily can result in alarming roll angles on the trailer – sometimes resulting in capsizing. (See next spread, revolving tow hooks.)

Centre of gravity position vital. This background and the aspects of trailer dynamics covered at Section 4.1 emphasise the vital importance of low, and forward

centre of gravity (giving appropriate nose-weight) when off-road towing. Remember to take twice the trailer nose-weight out of the available vehicle payload.

Beware especially of under-damped lateral roll of trailer on poor tracks.

Trailer push under braking

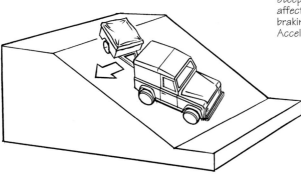

Trailer influence is especially noticeable on steep slippery down-slopes – adversely affected rear wheel adhesion and, under braking, promoting a tendency to jack-knife. Accelerate out of it.

Keep trailer light compared to the tug – well done here, albeit trailer load of luggage and camping gear will be high density. Small wheels and tyres at high pressure on trailer will put it at disadvantage on softer going and the prodigious traction of the Unimog may be needed. Compare this with the desert optimised combination shown opposite. Unimog's short rear overhang is good. Its long wheelbase compared with the trailer towing arm length will make reversing difficult.

Checks and procedures

Trailers can be used to avoid a vehicle overload situation in expeditions. Large tyres enhance flotation. Manpower needed to manhandle the trailer when stuck.

Overload solution: provisos. For over-landing expeditions, use of a really robust trailer can be quite an elegant solution to the problem of having a payload requirement in excess of that shown as the maximum for your vehicle on its own. Spreading the load over six wheels is better than the unacceptable alternative of overloading the vehicle's four. The prolonged stress of an overland trip is perhaps an extreme case but it encapsulates the potential problems of all off-road towing so is worth examining. Four provisos should be remembered for sustained off-road trailer operation:

1. Weight. Minimise the weight of the trailer and load to give the vehicle the best working conditions off-road – see photo caption page 4.2. An ex-military 750 kg trailer with overrun brakes, loaded to no more than 500 kg gross provides a sensible margin of strength and is in roughly the right category for a medium 4x4 towing vehicle – photo facing page.

2. Tyres. The same rationale mentioned earlier about big wheels applies to trailers and is arguably even more important since the trailer wheels are following in

ground already cut up by the towing vehicle. Trailer axle loads of the order indicated above will enable trailer tyre pressures to be lower (see Section 8.2) than those of the tug, enhancing flotation in the wake of the towing vehicle. Note that off-road a trailer needs the best combination of low rolling resistance and flotation (mainly the latter), not traction, so in absolute terms its tyre requirements will be unique. However, in practice it is sensible to use the same wheels and tyres on the trailer as you have fitted to the towing vehicle; this is right functionally and has the additional advantage that the same spare wheel will fit trailer and towing vehicle. As noted, flotation can be optimised and drag minimised by the use of lower pressures on the trailer.

3. Personnel. There will be times, off-road and overlanding, when the trailer has to be detached and manhandled. It will be necessary to have at least two people to do this; three or four will be better still.

4. Towing hitch. Every manufacturer will have their own approach to towing problems and accessories. The standard

50 mm ball hitch is widely used in the UK and Europe but on Land Rover products, for example, it is suitable for a maximum gross trailer weight of 1000 kg off-road. The European specification ball hitch (Part no RTC9565) is stronger than the standard UK item. Note also the ratings of the 2-bolt and 4-bolt Land Rover Parts combined ball/pin hitches shown at Section 4.1. Because of problems of trailer lateral stability in extreme off-road conditions as noted on the previous spread, be sure your trailer has an EC-standard hitch that can rotate at the trailer since a trailer that has tipped would not then affect the towing vehicle.

Low range start. As with heavy trailers on hard roads (see Section 4.1) there will be many occasions off-road when it will make for a smoother start to move off in low range 2nd gear, continue up the low ratio gears and change into high range on the move using the techniques outlined in Sections 6.2 and 6.3. For off-road towing, low range is sometimes the better choice to stay in.

Pay meticulous attention to condition of towing hitch, bolts and attachment areas. Starting in low range with an on-the-move change to high ratio is useful off-road.

Classic demonstration (below) of the benefits of trailer tyres being larger than those of the towing vehicle and thus able to run on lower pressures; better flotation, less sinkage, less drag. Beware, however, since low trailer tyre pressures can cause weaving at speed. Trailer here is deliberately and beneficially running at well under rated payload. Fore and aft motion of loose fitting towing eye over long off-road distance caused considerable wear (left).

Section 7

Expedition basics

7.1 The call of the wild

Freeing the spirit

Examining the operating envelope. The pace of everyday life often constrains us to under-utilise what we have – be it our own skills, the potential of our hobbies or the potential of our four-wheel drive vehicle. Our early plans, made at the time of purchase, may not have been realised and we may be left with a gnawing urge to utilise more of the latent capability of our 4x4, to use it for some of the more adventurous projects for which we bought it. With a machine of such potential in your possession it would perhaps be the more unusual *not* to want to stretch its operating envelope. Without any doubt at all, there is little to compare with the feeling of being in the world's wilder places with a well-equipped and well-trained expedition savouring the space, the beauty, the feeling of being self-sufficient.

Entrepreneurs too. Whilst this Section is inevitably aimed, primarily, at private recreational use it is hoped that it will also be of interest to commercial operators, perhaps in tourist-related or leisure pursuits, where operation of a vehicle in complete safety away from its home territory may form part of a package or proposal.

'Expeditions' – a day in the hills or a major overseas project – hugely enhance enjoyment of your vehicle. But you have just stepped into careful-planning territory.

Basics only. Note, right from the start, however, that the whole of Section 7 is entitled 'Expedition basics' and it claims to be no more than that. An 'expedition' can be a half-day trip to the hills or a major three-month overseas project. They will have in common the importance of infallible preparation – an examination of all the 'what-if?' situations – but there will be in the major projects less margin for error and the need for very precise logistic control. This Section is an introduction to the subject and aims to help you prepare to broaden your enjoyment of your off-roader in relatively short trips. More demanding projects including the planning of overseas expeditions that may include a scientific project are covered in the book *Vehicle-dependent Expedition Guide*, also published by Desert Winds. The book also contains considerable extra detail on vehicle preparation, modifications, navigation, equipment, communications, clothing and emergency procedures.

Day trip or major expedition?

The methodical approach – again. We are not all able to respond unquestioningly to the call of the wild since time, cost and other responsibilities will influence where we are able to go. What is certain, however, is the importance of how we tackle what we propose to do, however 'big' or 'small' it may be. As has been observed about that most unforgiving of all environments, the

One step at a time. Start with off-road tuition, then practise on your own. Get completely comfortable with your own and your vehicle's limitations. Unless you are, you will not enjoy the huge sense of freedom an off-road outing can confer.

Safely operated, a 4x4 epitomises – and realises – the need to seek the earth's wild places. Allow time. Never be in a hurry, Enjoyable as a 4x4 is to drive, don't turn your journey into a mile-eating marathon.

Sahara desert, you can die pinned under a capsized motorcycle behind a knoll a kilometre from the track just as easily as if you did the same thing 500 kilometres farther out in the desert. A sombre example that nevertheless makes the point admirably regarding the differences between everyday on-road operations where the swish of passing traffic is your assurance of some help, and being only a few miles up a mountain track with what is becoming more than a minor problem on your hands.

One step at a time equals confidence. Although a gentle progression up the scale of challenge is the natural way to do things, the importance of taking things a step at a time cannot too strongly be emphasised. Going hand in hand with this – importantly and almost inevitably – will be the growth in your confidence. Confidence begets early recognition of, thus avoidance of, and measured response to – problems. Confidence – well-founded confidence, not over-confidence or cockiness – further begets the ability, comfortably, to say 'no' and turn back before getting into trouble.

Savour but beware the feeling of amazement and invincibility you may have experienced on your first competent off-road demonstration of your (or your dealer's) off-roader. The feeling of unstoppability is very strong but, as has been emphasised through-

out this book, all vehicles have their limitations and in most demonstration you will have been shown what *can* be done, not what happens when you get it wrong. A significant omission.

So, assuming you are just making a start, the answer to the 'day-trip-or-major-expedition' question is clearly 'day-trip' – and then only after planning and training. If you are already thinking that actually it was release you were after and not another career development project, be of good cheer; the training and practice is great fun – putting into effect what you have read in the other Sections of this book. And during training there is someone to help when you get into trouble. There is also a hot shower to go home to afterwards.

Planning

The aim. Paradoxically, despite the emphasis on planning, it will not be easy to plan in a 'capability vacuum'. In other words, until you know a little of what you individually can do with your vehicle it will be hard to make a realistic plan for an expedition. It is likely, however, that you may want to explore some unsurfaced tracks you have seen on the map as part of a weekend break you may be taking in the mountains. The aim can be as general as this for the time being.

Take your projects a step at a time. Confidence and competence will then build on a sound foundation.

Maps, research – the UK example.

Small, 'white-roads' trailing off into areas of close contours or wide-open space on the map, together with a ford or two and linking up – still in the context of UK Ordnance Survey maps – with another 'white' or 'yellow' road away from all the traffic can have an irresistible appeal. It is worth, at this stage, rereading the Foreword to this book to remind yourself that ownership of a 4x4 brings considerable responsibilities in regard to environmental care, the obligation to set an example and accept the often complex matter of rights of access. This latter will be different in every country and must be individually checked.

Know first what you and your vehicle can do – train; see Sec 7.3. Be sure about rights of land access for off-road vehicles – sensitive in developed countries.

The rising general population of 4x4 vehicles has regrettably brought with it a small element of irresponsible users and a corresponding tightening of access rules. Awareness of these rules is therefore essential. Quoting a summary of those applicable in the UK will give an idea of what to expect in 'developed' countries – countries with relatively high populations and a legislature steeped in historical evolution. The UK situation is at once knocked slightly off-balance by the fact that a new system of classification is *being* introduced and is not yet reflected on all maps. The maps to use are the excellent 1:50,000 Ordnance Survey Land Ranger maps, backed, where possible, by the 1:25,000 series. You will find:

- Public footpaths – no vehicles.
- Public bridleways – no vehicles.
- BOATs (Byway Open to All Traffic) – vehicles are permitted.
- RUPPs (Road Used as a Public Path) – will cease to exist soon and a new category of Right of Way will come into being. (See below Restricted Byways). The change is part of the Countryside and Rights of Way Act 2000, section 47.
- Restricted Byways will carry a right of way for those on foot, for horses, but not for mechanically propelled vehicles. They will replace all RUPPs recorded on the Definitive Map prior to a (still – mid 2006 – unspecified) date. Vehicles allowed only if historical precedent permits re-classification to BOAT.
- UCRs (Unclassified County Roads) – minor roads or lanes, with a sealed surface, others comprising only rough stone. These may be driven by vehicles.

Thus the indication of a road on a map does not automatically confer a right of way. At the County Council offices you'll find the Definitive Map which will indicate the current legal access status of every road in the county. Asking permission from the local landowner, if you can ascertain who it is, will always be a safe alternative. A catch-all and usually temporary TRO (Traffic Regulation Order) can, however, be issued at the discretion of the Highway Authority on given routes in relation to given types of vehicles to cover the case, for example, of local overuse causing damage – a reasonable enough concept despite the further confusion factor.

Navigation. It goes without saying that close attention must be paid to map-reading and navigation in order that you may, at any time, be able to pinpoint your position on the map and know where the next track-junction or other waypoint may be.

Navigation is about maps, headings, distances – satellite images, even. Wherever you are, GPS (opposite: basic marine and early 'outdoor' units shown) will pinpoint position – but GPS is only as good as the maps you use it with. See also photo on page 7.18.

Ascertaining heading in a vehicle with a magnetic compass is virtually impossible since the internal magnetic field is strong, variable and virtually uncorrectable for a normally mounted magnetic compass. Use a hand-held compass outside the vehicle and about five metres from it.

'Sat-nav'. Nowhere is satellite navigation more useful than on vehicle expeditions – local or major. GPS (Global Positioning System – a constellation of 24 satellites from which 3D position, speed and heading may be derived) is invariably at the core of all satnavs. Though GPS is central to them, all satnavs are not the same. GPS is just that: a system that gives position on a conceptual grid – latitude and longitude or national grid covering the earth. It is thus only as good as the maps (also grid-based) it is used with. 'Consumer' satnavs as fitted to many cars are already internally integrated with an on-board digital map. At the other end of the scale, basic marine units may just give lat/long position and leave the user to apply that to his own map.

Most consumer car satnavs do a staggeringly impressive job navigating, turn-by-turn to street destinations or post codes in the country for which they are designed, but have not been programmed to give lat/long positions, create lat/long or grid waypoints or operate independent of their own mapping. As an exception, Land Rover's Discovery 3 has a factory-fit satnav that can cope with street nav and also switch to off-road navigation for use with external maps.

This latter is a facility that will be essential if you are operating overseas or in remote areas so be sure to fit a satnav with this capability. Lowrance in the US (lowrance.com) make an exceptionally wide range of equipments categorised as marine, aviation, automotive or 'outdoor'. This latter category , usually also capable of accepting an MMC card digital map suite, will be best for expeditions – up to and including the most demanding off-piste African exploration using such paper maps as exist. Large-display units, hard-wired, with an external antenna will be best for

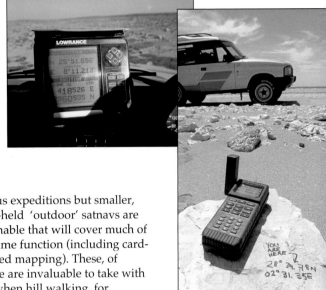

serious expeditions but smaller, hand-held 'outdoor' satnavs are obtainable that will cover much of the same function (including card-sourced mapping). These, of course are invaluable to take with you when hill walking, for instance, so you can locate your vehicle should the weather turn bad, but the disadvantage is a smaller display, less practical for driving, and an internal antenna. See also photo and caption on page7.18.

Second vehicle, safety message. Two vehicles driven in sensibly-spaced convoy is a wise precaution on most routes off the tarmac and certainly when off-road. If one vehicle gets stuck in mud the other (long tow-rope) will be able to tow it free, or go for help if mechanical damage has occurred. It is well appreciated, however, that the whole point of some trips will be to 'get away' in a single vehicle. It behoves you for such excursions to take a mobile phone, recovery equipment and inform people where you are going. Train (next spread) with schools organising safaris to understand the terrain and safety requirements.

Expeditions book

The full monty. The whole of Section 7 can only cover a tiny proportion of what has to be planned into a major expedition. This is covered comprehensively on a wide range of subjects in *Vehicle-dependent Expedition Guide* published by Desert Winds.

As with expedition projects, develop your navigation skills a step at a time. Take a second vehicle for safety unless you are certain about a particular route.

7.2 Training for the trip

Before planning your own expedition, establish and hone your driving skills – first with dealer-day demonstrations, then professional tuition. An off-road site day-pass lets you practise on your own – an essential to develop confidence.

Developing the skills

Learn first. 'Training for the trip' may initially sound a forbidding concept when many 'expeditions' are no more than recreational excursions. But you would not go rock climbing without knowing how to do it and having the equipment and you would not go canoeing without being instructed on how to control the canoe and observe the correct safety precautions. To do any of these things without proper preparation would be foolhardy; and that applies to vehicle-based expeditions as well.

Off-road training. Use one of the many off-road driving schools to become familiar with your vehicle away from tarmac and in the low-range transfer gears. Many dealers run introductory off-road demonstration days. Start with these; they will be invaluable and are usually free. Initially it may be no more than a sedate trundle round without the need even for gear changes but you will find it easy and that, at first, is the important bit. You will start to see what the vehicle can do.

If you have read this book you will have the advantage of having absorbed the theory – and the written practice – but it is essen-

Learn the full spectrum of your vehicle's and your own capabilities before planning a trip.

tial that you try it yourself and become completely comfortable with your own and your vehicle's behaviour in demanding conditions before going out on an expedition, however 'small'. Taking on board the message is a very significant first step.

Practise on your own

Consolidation. Going to a dealer demonstration you will have experienced the dynamics of off-road driving and the significance of the gentle right foot but you will need a lot more practice and for this you should go to a local school for consolidating tuition and, most important of all, a day-pass access to their off-road site which will enable you to 'play' in your own time and practise the techniques you have been taught. Take your time, read this book, know and analyse what you are doing. Being on a driving school site you will do so in the knowledge that should you get stuck, help will be on hand to tow you free. Such sites, additionally, are designated for off-road practice and you will not have the worry of seeking special permission for where you go. A considerable number of such schools advertise in the off-road magazines; go for the ones that emphasise thorough briefing and care for the vehicle. Do not be rushed into precipitate driving methods; you are paying the bill and it is your vehicle.

Safari. A number of schools also organise 'safaris' lasting one to three days in which a small group of owner-driven-vehicles is led along pre-chosen routes which incorporate a variety of demanding driving conditions – and usually some exhilarating scenery. The experience is enjoyable in itself and valuable in a hundred ways for learning driving techniques. Choose a safari school that operates under similar terrain conditions to those you wish to travel later.

Fitness. Your off-road driver training and the physical effort required to push, jack, lay sand channels or dig out a stuck vehicle will be a reminder that your own fitness is no less important than that of your vehicle. In a perfect world your training will have conferred such skill and judgement that you never get your vehicle into a condition warranting the undignified description of 'being stuck'. Few will need reminding of the world's imperfections and from the fitness point of view it is wise and prudent to be prepared ... !

Mechanic?

Skill with the spanners. This far into the book the importance of mechanical sympathy and not damaging the vehicle in off-road jaunts hardly needs further emphasis. Modern vehicles are very reliable but overseas, and really far from the beaten track, pre-trip training must have included a thorough knowledge of the vehicle and – within feasible limits applicable to electro-fest 21st century vehicles – how to maintain it. Read that again.

Initial impressions of your vehicle's off-road performance will be dazzling; but learn the demarcation between what it can and cannot do. then practise on your own.

Could you maintain this in the field? In truly remote areas you must be able to rely 110% on a vehicle or be able to maintain complex electronics using equally complex test equipment. Professionally run group safaris make an excellent start.

7.3 Vehicle preparation

Re-familiarise yourself with routine owner maintenance tasks. Jacking the rear is a long reach; groundsheet, wood block help.

What preparation?

Off-road requirements. Just a few 4x4s can be driven straight from the showroom and turn in a competent off-road performance. Most vehicles, however will need further preparation. Tyres are usually the most obvious item requiring attention – see below. On-road accessories and equipment like front spoilers, side step-cum-running boards and low-set towhooks, however, all affect real-life off-road agility. You will have to accept the limitations they incur or, as part of your off-road preparation, consider their removal.

Payload, securing the load, recovery equipment, mobile phones or other rescue aids are further aspects to bear in mind. Naturally you must ensure that your vehicle has been properly maintained, at least to manufacturer's servicing schedules, and is thus on the top line mechanically. 'Up there' on the hills is no place to be breaking down for the want of proper servicing.

Vehicle knowledge. Your training sessions should have refreshed your knowledge of the traction enhancement facilities such as low range and the applicability for your vehicle of differential locks, stability control systems, ABS brakes, traction con-

Initial preparation will be mundane – simple things like knowing the driver's manual, jacking. Tyres are fundamental to defining your expedition capability.

trol. Some vehicles – like the Touareg, later Discovery and Range Rover – have extra under-belly clearance available where air suspension has been specified.

Tyres

Compromises. Tyres can usually only be optimised for one set of conditions. Other conditions, for those tyres, will involve a degree of performance compromise. Quiet-running tyres with treads designed for on-road wet grip need a cool objective assessment if you are going off tracks – the point has already been made that particular tyres perform best in one set of conditions only. This applies to wheels also. Following fashion rather than (as you might hope in a 4x4) function, some vehicles are bought with large diameter rims fitted with low profile tyres. Both are fundamentally unsuitable for any off-tarmac activity.

Types. Study the detail on tyre types, axle loads and pressures, pressure reductions for tracks and emergency conditions, Load Index and Speed Symbol, in Section 8.2. You will likely find your vehicle fitted with road-oriented or M+S tyres when you buy it and you would be wise to adjust the demands of your first expedition to be within their still considerable capabilities before going to the expense of buying others.

As if to invalidate the mantra of tyres having to be selected for defined conditions, some 'all terrain' tyres – specifically the BF Goodrich All Terrain – are remarkably versatile. In temperate zones such as Europe you will find the main compromise with these tyres is reduced performance in mud/clay mixtures due to the treads filling up. Where the best performance in mud is required, such tyres as the Michelin XZL or BFG Mud Terrain will provide it.

Remember that one aspect of a mud tyre's effectiveness derives from a carefully judged width – or narrowness – that enables it, together with an equally deliberate tread design, to cut through slippery upper layers of soft mud and into the grippier ground beneath – see page 4.27.

Fat tyres not always best. Thus the

Wide tyres, per se, are not always 'best'. Road-oriented tyres (near right), however fat, will fill with mud off-road. These BFGoodrich Mud-Terrains (far right) will do far better but will be less grippy on-road. They say "there's no such thing as an all-purpose tyre" but BFG's AllTerrain is very impressive (see Sec 8.2).

extra-wide after-market tyres frequently seen on recreational vehicles will usually yield poorer traction on wet grass and mud than will standard items. Certainly they will be less effective than the mud tyres mentioned above.

Jacking. Tyre reliability these days is such that few of us get experience even in fitting the spare wheel, much less repairing a flat. An off-road expedition may result in sidewall damage and a flat if you are not sufficiently vigilant – see Section 3.4 on Marshalling. Check the handbook procedures; practise choc-ing the wheels, positioning and operating the jack (take the main tightness off the wheel nuts with the wheel still in contact with the ground). You will find it quite a stretch positioning the jack under a rear axle; keep a set of overalls for this job. Be sure you can undo and properly tighten the wheel nuts.

If you have to jack on soft ground you will need a small wood baulk as a load spreader – about 45-50 mm thick and the size of this book; keep it in the vehicle. A second jack and wood block is useful where the ground is really soft and you may have to jack up a stage at a time.

Tidiness – inside and out

Ground clearance. The obvious hang-downs that affect front-end, rear end and side clearance have already been mentioned. But it is worth re-familiarising yourself with the under-belly clearance of your vehicle and the 'what will touch first' parameter. Whilst many off-roaders do have vulnerable items like silencers, neatly tucked away underneath, getting down on your hands

and knees before a trip will show that others do not! There will be items underneath that should definitely not be run into rocks. Check page 3.7 for a refresher.

Tie-downs, internal stowage. Similarly, aim to keep the inside tidy too by ensuring the cargo stays where it is put. As mentioned in Sec 8.1, there is much to recommend the fitting of tie-downs in your vehicle if it is to operate over rough ground.

Manufacturers are at last waking up to the uses of tie-downs and fitting them as standard. Used for really heavy items such as jacks and with modular containers like lidded plastic storage boxes, equipment such as wet-weather gear, camping equipment, recovery items, and refreshments can be strapped-down so that they do not slide around the vehicle on uneven tracks or off-road.

This is part of the basic philosophy of eliminating loose articles so that not only does equipment avoid damage but the vehicle itself, as a result, is free from rattles and other internal noise. Few aspects of off-road driving can be so nerve-jangling as boxes and loose items sliding about in the back of a vehicle. It is a curious but repeatedly observed fact but you will find that vehicles that are tight and rattle-free are driven better and more sympathetically than those full of randomly noisy avalanches of equipment.

Modifications. Further vehicle modifications for more demanding trips are covered on page 7.18.

Think ground clearance. Does spoiler or tow-hook have to be removed to enhance approach and departure angle? Plan, containerise and secure the load.

7.4 Equipment

A second vehicle and a long tow rope are two of the most comforting items of out-back equipment. Choose footwear with care (right). The brown Clarks Rock Inlet is low-cut at the heel for driving, ankle-sup-portive, Goretex lined, flexible, grippy, multi-role. Berghaus Expedition walking boot (gtx too) more robust, excellent but not for driving. Cheap deck shoes are bliss for camp relaxing. Typical cold/wet layers (far right): fleece or fibrepile inner, Goretex trousers and hooded jacket (NOT waxed cotton!)

Influencing criteria

What if ... ? Television news bulletins continually remind us of how easily a short recreational excursion can turn into a life-threatening drama. Common to many of these news items is how simple were the precautions that could have avoided trouble. Occasionally, this is proven when some-one, well prepared, has survived cheerfully by digging a snow-hole or taking appropri-ate action that has enabled them to ride out the storm or assist rescue teams to find them when things have gone wrong. European weather systems, especially in the regions attractive to outdoor or adventurous people are notorious for their changeability and the suddenness with which conditions can become threatening. Some of the 'what-if' questions that must be asked in deciding what equipment to take on even a minor, 'day-trip', expedition are:

- **Weather.** If the weather turns from to-day's fine sunny conditions to 'snow-on-high-ground', zero visibility or a down-pour, am I appropriately equipped?
- **Track condition.** Can I self-recover a

Simple problems can develop into emergencies when no help is at hand. Don't be self-conscious about taking sensible safety measures.

vehicle brought to a wheelspinning halt in mud?
- **Off-road.** If my vehicle bellies-out on a ridge can I recover it?
- **Overnighting.** If my recovery prob-lems take so long that we are overtaken by darkness or sudden bad weather, have we food, drinks and warmth enough to overnight in the vehicle and resume operations in the morning?
- **Going for help.** If I get myself into such deep trouble off-road that I am unable to recover, how far is it to help? Can I walk it with the equipment I have?
- **Emergency equipment.** Do I have any means of attracting attention or calling for help?

(These are questions that will also influ-ence your taking along a second vehicle and that all-important *long* tow-rope.)

Protective clothing

Plan for the worst. Most often you will be protecting against cold and wet. On any expedition, even a short drive on mountain tracks, you will not wish to – and certainly not be able to – remain in the vehicle with the heater on all the time. Assume, as a matter of course and whatever the weather at the start of your trip, that it will rain, get cold and blow a gale. Assume also that you will find it necessary to wade up to your knees in mud or water and/or walk a number of kilometres on rough ground. Equip yourself with appropriate clothing and add overalls and a groundsheet to lie on when you have to dig under your vehicle or change a wheel.

If you have not got recent (or any) experience of hill walking or similar outdoor pursuits, consult one of the many outdoor centres or camping gear shops for advice on the latest clothing. Some (eg Field and Trek in the UK) issue comprehensive catalogues (more informative than their website) containing full information on equipment. Standards of design and materials technology have never been higher – Goretex and many other breathable water/windproof membrane, windproof fleeces and Thinsulate insulation being developments that have made considerable impact on the design and effectiveness of outdoor clothing. Do your own study, adopt the layering principle – several layers of garments rather than a single very thick/warm one. The following will act as a guide:

• **Footwear.** Versatile, new-generation, Goretex-lined boots from Clarks high-street shops, low at the heel for ankle-flexing driving are a hugely comfortable and practical multi-role proposition. Hill-walking boots will be little more robust but, high on the Achilles tendon will not do for driving. Gumboots are for wading emergencies – you would not wish to walk far in gumboots nor carry out a reconnaissance wade-through of a stream in walking boots. Stow them in a boot-bag or plastic sack to keep the inside of the vehicle clean.

• **Outer layer.** Fabric and Goretex overtrousers and a roomy-fit hooded anorak of similar material with drawcords at hood, waist and hem. Waxed cotton, which has an inexplicable following, is a disaster. Its stickiness holds dirt, spoils seats, cannot be machine-washed, does not breathe and needs regular re-proofing. Woolly hat or similar to prevent heat-loss from the head. Two pairs of gloves – thin leather for driving, another set for mucky outside work.

Most problems are climatic – too cold or too hot. Be properly equipped. Breakdown or bad bogging involve prolonged work or walking; plan for it.

The satisfaction of being properly clad against the elements is complementary to that of being the master of difficult terrain in a 4x4.

• **Inner layers.** As experience demands. Fleece (Polartec *et al*) or fibre-pile jackets are excellent for warmth and wicking of perspiration vapour; use as an either/or (or additional to) a Thinsulate zip-in liner to your anorak. Often a boiler-suit or overalls of generous cut can make a very practical inner layer over your day clothes when not wearing the wind/water-proof outer layers.

• **Other.** Groundsheet, as mentioned above, for under-vehicle access or digging.

• **Emergency.** Take a sleeping bag for emergency use in case you are overtaken by night or storm when stuck. It seems to be a rule of nature that all serious boggings take place just as the sun is going down.

• **Vehicle heater.** Remember, if you run the engine to keep the vehicle heater effective in snow, to be sure the exhaust pipe is clear of drifting snow that could prevent escape of poisonous exhaust fumes.

Recovery gear

Causes. Getting stuck with a greater or lesser degree of permanence will the be result of a temporary mismatch of your driving skills, assessment of the ground, capability of the vehicle and what the ground is actually like. More direct and specific causes will be:

• Soft ground.
• Slippery ground.
• Limit of articulation limit.

Commonly a combination of all three is what will halt you. Note the exclusion of gradient as a cause of getting stuck. A vehicle capable of a nearly one-in-one climb on dry concrete is unlikely to be halted by any sensible gradient.

Don't hazard your enjoyment of scenery like this by cutting down on safety equipment. The same applies in 'green and pleasant lands' as in harsher climates.

A selection of recovery gear (see Sec 5) – winch (with tree straps), load spreaders (PSP, even the alloy type here is crude and awkward to stow), <u>long</u> tow rope, shovels, fire extinguisher, first aid kit. EPIRB is a marine-type Emergency Position-Indicating-Radio Beacon; sensible for really remote regions. Thuraya satellite/GSM phone is worth its weight in diamonds.

What to take, what to do. Getting close to the specifics like this will again emphasise the value of a second vehicle in the convoy. Re-read Section 5 (and 4!) and take:

- Two shovels (pointed ends, not spades); fold-away type will do.
- Long towrope, 7-tonne breaking strain minimum, not less than 25 metres long, with soft spliced-in eyes and U-bolt shackles (see p 5.8).
- Standard hydraulic axle jack as supplied, wood baulk load spreader as above, plus second jack and baulk.
- Aluminium sand ladder. PSP or Barong grip/load spreaders to put under the wheels.

Rescue aids

Use the technology. Though you may be on your trip to get some peace and quiet, the potential of the dreaded mobile phone as a safety life-line in areas served by appropriate networks makes it essential emergency equipment. Used with GPS (page 7.5) to also transmit your actual position in Ordnance Survey grid or latitude/longitude, it would be invaluable. A simple and sensible set of rescue aids would thus be:

- Mobile phone and GPS. The Iridium satellite network will work from anywhere on the planet. Thuraya covers Europe, Middle East, Gulf and also works in-country GSM networks.
- Mini-flares. Commonly carried by boat people, a pack of six or eight is not much bigger than a spectacles case.
- Beacon. For major expeditions overseas a satellite emergency beacon triggering a transmission on 121.5 Mhz or 406 Mhz is a life saver. Again, quiz the yacht chandlers.

Sound recovery gear need not be complex. Shovels, long tow ropes with shackles, jacks and load spreaders – reread Section 5.

7.5 Logistics, vehicle choice

*Match your
vehicle to your
trip – or vice
versa. Distance
between replen-
ishment points,
load you need to
carry and kind
of terrain dictate
the vehicle.*

Strategic thinking

The broad view. Sections 7.1 to 7.4 have assumed introductory expeditions probably carried out with your own existing vehicle. If you are planning something a little more ambitious – going to the full extent of your 4x4's capabilities or considering a team of vehicles that could fulfil a particular expedition project – then it is well to have a feel for the kind of strategic thinking involved. This concerns, mainly:

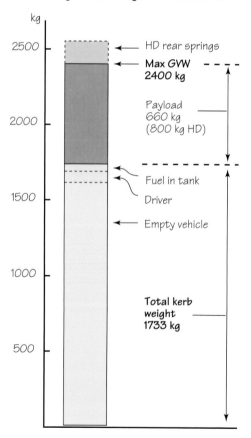

Gross weight, kerb weight – Defender 90

• Payload/range – how far you can go with what payload. The two parameters are interdependent: the more payload you carry, the less capability you have to carry fuel, water and supplies. The more fuel and water you take, the less capacity you have for payload. The unbreakable rule here is the maximum gross vehicle weight – GVW: *never* exceed it.
• If the above sums do not come out the way you want them and you have to select special vehicles for a project, what are the criteria?

Preliminary criteria, payload/range

Preliminary criteria. If you are already wondering why there is so much talk about weight, the philosophy of sound expedition planning revolves around taking care of the life-blood of the trip – the vehicle. It will already have enough to cope with on a demanding expedition and these are the very conditions in which a breakdown is unacceptable. So preliminary criteria before even thinking about an expedition are:
• Vehicle in top class condition.
• Thorough overhaul and service.
• Impeccable driving.
• Vehicle operating within design limits.
And this latter includes the most often abused aspect of vehicle operation on expeditions – the weight of the payload. It is the most often abused because it seems to be the item that most often catches people out.

Gross weight, kerb weight. Never, ever, overload a vehicle on a trip. It is easy enough to avoid. The diagram on the left shows a typical expedition vehicle and how its kerb weight (its 'empty weight') and its gross weight are made up.

Long-range trips. Since most expeditions involve going long distances and subsisting there on supplies brought with you it is instructive to look at the interplay of payload and range quantitatively. The diagram opposite and its caption show how the fur-

Logistics – spare payload dwindles with range. V8 Defender 90 example

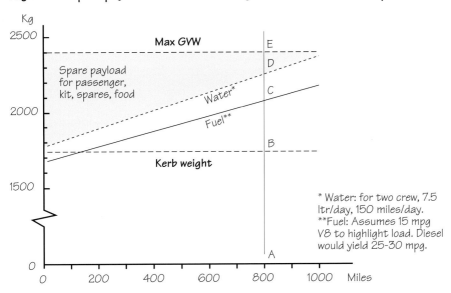

* Water: for two crew, 7.5 ltr/day, 150 miles/day.
**Fuel: Assumes 15 mpg V8 to highlight load. Diesel would yield 25-30 mpg.

ther you have to go, the less the payload you can take. Again, a typical expedition vehicle is used, albeit here it is fitted with an inappropriate and thirsty engine to emphasise the effect of fuel supply weight. Diesels are invariably the best for expeditions.

Jimny or Unimog. All off-roaders will have weight maxima that beget graphs of the kind shown here. In general, bigger ones, all the way up to medium or heavy trucks, can carry more and go further than

Rough sums will do just as well but graph shows vividly how the distance between replenishment points erodes spare payload. In a fairly extreme case, on an 800 mile leg, A-B is kerb weight, B-C is fuel load, C-D is water required, only leaving 150 kg (D-E) for a 75 kg passenger and remaining kit. In real life you'd go diesel, shorten legs and/or get bigger vehicle like Defender 110 or a robust 4x4 pickup like a Toyota Hilux. Fuel calculations assume reserve. Fuel formula: distance plus 100 miles plus 25% at worst mpg. Bigger vehicle equals more payload but less power/weight ratio. (Diagram below left.)

The size trade-offs

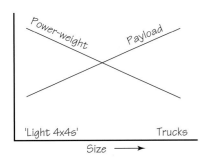

little ones – albeit at the expense of agility and power-to-weight ratio. The size trade-offs diagram (left) shows the trend. The real significance of the table all the way back on page 1.6 is now clear. Luxury vehicles tend to have low spare payload (in order that springs can give a better ride – see unsprung weight, page 1.4. 'Working' vehicles carry a lot more – classic examples are pickups, hard-tops (van bodies) and light-bodied vehicles like the Land Rover Defender.

For long trips in remote areas the correlation between fuel point spacing, payload and vehicle size/type is absolute. Don't fudge it. Same mind-set applies locally.

It would be hard to find a more expedition-oriented mount than Toyota's Land Cruiser 78 (near left) – permanent 4x4, standard limited slip diff, optional front and rear diff locks, 1000 kg payload, 180 litre fuel tanks, lazy 4.2 litre turbo diesel also available as an ultra-low-tech non-turbo, raised intake, 7.50x16 tyres (many options) – but alas not normally available in Europe. Land Rover's 110 Defender (far left) comes a close practical second historically, but offers no in-house axle diff locks, has less payload, smaller fuel tank – though more power from 2007.

The criteria

Ingredients. How is an expedition vehicle made up? How is any 4x4 made up? If you are wondering what vehicle to buy next and want to identify criteria a little more incisive than the average brochure-writer's obsession with cup-holders and interior trim then look at the list opposite. If the size and scope of your planned expedition or other project demand that you consider what vehicles you need, do likewise.

The evolutionary chain. These are criteria that chart a vehicle's growth from a basic two-wheel drive pickup through to an exceptionally capable off-roader. Beware the trap of equating *all* upmarket vehicles with flabby, dilettante incompetence. Some. certainly, are like that. Others, even in deluxe trim – the Range Rover of course jumps to mind – are very capable even though their payload may not be as high as a stripped-out pickup.

Legislation-driven vehicle design leads to complexity, acceptable on short trips in reach of assistance but needs careful thought for long trips in remote areas.

New-fangled stuff

Simplicity, reliability? What cannot be covered here is individual brand reliability. Whilst in general an expedition vehicle should be a simple one, easy to service in the field and less likely to go wrong anyway, designers and engineers entering the 21st century are confronted with wholly laudable emissions regulations which nevertheless force them to electronic solutions and thus the need for complex and expensive test gear for checking systems. If you are going to truly remote areas you have to face this problem head-on.

- Can I be absolutely certain that this complex vehicle will be 100% reliable?
- And have I the knowledge, special tools and equipment to fix if it is not?
- If not, is there a sufficiently simple vehicle maintainable in the field by me or by local mechanics? Toyota, catering to a world market, address this by offering 'non-electronic' simple-spec vehicles for remote area markets.

Luddite reaction? In comparison to vehicles even 20 years ago, present-day cars are – despite the increased complexity that regulations demand – enormously reliable. But failures on a Spanish mountain track can be bad news. Even worse in the Sahara.

Under-axle clearance – portal axle

See also page 3.7 for beam axles and independent suspension clearances

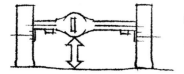

High ground clearance but high CG and cost

EXPEDITION VEHICLE ATTRIBUTES – IN ORDER OF PROGRESSION FROM SIMPLE 4X2 PICKUP

Feature	Benefits	Disadvantages
Leaf-springs	Low cost, simplicity, easy replacement. Springs act as means of locating axles.	Inter-leaf friction gives stiff ride, poor traction; limited wheel movt. Long springs are best – see Nissan Navara, p 3.8.
Large diameter wheels (ie 16" not 15")	Improved under-axle ground clearance. Goes *over* pot-holes rather than into them.	No functional disadvantage, provided low profile tyres not fitted on eg, 18-22" rims.
Torsion-bar front springs	Smoother ride than leaf-springs. Better traction and braking. More wheel movement?	Usually associated with independent front suspension so less ground clearance.
Beam axles	Good under-axle clearance, wheels always perpendicular to ground.	Clearance above axle needed for wheel movement makes vehicle tall. High unsprung weight difficult to damp.
Coil springs all round	Smoother ride than leaf-springs. Better traction and braking. On beam axles more wheel movement than leaf springs so best traction on uneven ground.	More expensive than leaf-springs due to need for alternative axle location links. If too short and stiff, ride is still poor.
No anti-roll bars (See p 2.6)	Permits full axle articulation – twist relative to body – off-road wheel movement enhanced.	Body roll. Designer's nightmare to balance on- and off-road performance.
Short wheelbase	Improved off-road capability but only noticeable in extreme conditions.	Lower max payload than long wheelbase versions. Pitching, lumpy ride.
Large approach, departure, ramp angles, 'high stance' (See p 3.6)	Off-road agility without danger of grounding body parts. Short tail overhang specially valuable exiting ditches.	High centre of gravity can cause body roll.
High payload	Obvious advantage when there are long distances between provisioning points.	Less pliant ride, lower power/weight ratio. Classic division between luxury/working.
Automatic transmission (See p 2.24 and 6.6)	Helps driver. Smoothest gear changes safeguard driveshafts, precludes lost traction through jerkiness. Very good indeed.	Cost mainly, some weight. In some cases if it breaks down, prop shaft removal for towing.
Auto-engage 4x4. (See p 2.2)	Better than 4x2 on- and off-road. Zero driver input required. Some do have 4x4 select override (eg X-Trail) which is good.	Not suitable for sustained off-roading. Front/rear speed axle differences have to be sensed before 4x4 is engaged.
Selectable 4x4 (See p 2.2)	Huge improvement over two-wheel drive (4x2) in all off-road conditions. Simplicity. Low cost.	Compared with 4x2, cost. Must be selected when needed and de-selected on hard surfaces. Full-time 4x4 better.
2-speed transfer box (See p 1.11 and 2.20)	In effect a 2nd set of extra-low gears for off-road use. Essential for expeditions.	Cost and complexity but a must-have for any serious expedition.
On-the-move range change (Lo to Hi range) (See pp 2.17 and 6.2-6.7)	Invaluable if you start in Lo and need to change to Hi without stopping. Can't be done with most 'electronic' range changes.	No real disadvantage except some skill / technique required to do it on most vehicles
Permanent ('full time') 4x4 with centre differential (See p 2.2 and 2.6)	The best. Better than part-time 4x4 or auto-engage 4x4 because it is there all the time. Best kind has lockable centre differential.	Compared with part-time 4x4, more cost since centre differential needed.
Locking axle differentials (See p 2.19)	Overcomes those 'one spinning wheel' situations superbly to preclude getting stuck.	Cost. Risk to half-shafts if not properly engineered. Must remember to de-select.
Traction control (See p 2.6)	Foolproof way round wheelspin. Automatic.	Electronic-dependent, brake heat, wear. Not as good as manual-select diff-locks.
Portal axles (See diagram opposite)	Dramatic increase in under-axle clearance for rough ground and deep ruts. Used in Hummer H1 and the unstoppable Mercedes-Benz Unimog.	Very expensive to produce, high centre of gravity, higher unsprung weight.

Know the progression of features that take a vehicle from a boulvardier to an expedition star. All the time try to match this to known terrain and requirements.

Expedition modifications. GPS is invaluable. Turn-by-turn units for street address-finding rarely have geo-referencing or a lat/long 'waypoint create' facility to give bearing and distance to waypoint for outback use. Lowrance 3500c marine unit (left) with external antenna also takes MMC card for local mapping but not turn-by-turn direction. Overhead 'eyeballs' duct fresh ambient air from external scoop: aircon takes power. Outside temp and GMT shown on silver item to right of steering wheel.

Modifications?

Why modify? There is a blur between preparation (page 7.8) and modification. Many vehicles can lope through a dozen outings of a fairly routine nature just as they left the showroom. Anything more focused – say, overseas, with a lot of cargo and a lot of camping and demanding off-road terrain may call for some 'optimisation'.

The hazards ahead. Cargo tie-downs, compartments, racks, and a bit more light are the usual starting points for modifications. Think in any depth and you quickly come up with a list of issues that may need to be addressed:

Not all vehicles or expeditions require modifications to be done. But matching your specification to your needs brings benefits to safety and capability.

Moths and insects attracted by the interior light in the evenings can be kept out and your sanity saved by simple slip-over window nets with Velcro and elastics at the bottom – windows still down for air.

Dust
Extreme heat
Extreme cold
Getting stuck
Tracks with deep ruts
Cargo bumping around
Deep wading
Animals, insects

Modifications – the spectrum

The categories. Having regard to what is designed-in already, most modifications fall into three categories. Not all of the following are 'do' mods; some are 'don't do' or 'think very hard first' headings.

1. Vehicle function – engine and electrics.

• *Engine and fuel system*
Fuel filler extension for jerry cans
High level air intake (dust, wading)
Tachometer (old vehicles)
Long-range fuel tank – but see p 8.6
Fuel sedimenter / filter
Fuel system / block heaters
Electronic contact breakers (old vehicles)
Oil temp gauge, oil cooler (old vehicles)
(NB Most modern vehicles are type-tested in ambients up to 50°C so extra oil cooling may not be necessary. Axle and gearbox oils often get hotter anyway.)

• *Electrical system*
HD or 2nd battery, split charge system
Battery master switches
Extra interior lighting (fluorescent)
Accessory power points
Courtesy lights – deactivate / switchable
Battery warmer (mains powered)

• *Vehicle security alarm*
• *Navigation system*

2. General and expedition function. Special fitments related to the role of the expedition.

Tyres – mud, desert, winter (see Sections 4.7, 4.8, 4.11)
GPS installation (p 7.5 and photo above)
Rear seats out for cargo space
Internal tie-downs
Special equipment mountings
Sand ladder and shovel racks
Tow hooks and rings
Roof tent

Good interior lighting is essential – cooking, writing-up logs and planning the next day's navigation. Fluorescent tubes give more light per amp used. Boxed duplicate battery for accessories, with split charge system (below, between front seats in G-Wagen) ensures you can always start the engine in the morning. It's also a direct substitute for the main battery should that fail.

Belly protection
Jack sockets
Winch
Rollover cage

3. Crew function.
Modifications that affect crew comfort:

Insect nets for windows
Seat upholstery – cloth best
Extra ventilation ducts
Roof, body-side, floor insulation
Side window in 'van' bodies
Audio, MP3/iPod plug-in facility

Priorities

Fit for purpose. Every proposed modification should be carefully considered before being undertaken but the most common need is beefed-up electrics – the ability to run lighting and accessories and still be sure of starting the engine in the morning. A second battery, with a split-charge system and accessories coming off that battery should be the aim. Caravan users will be familiar with such a set-up.

Next in importance, as already hinted in Section 7.3, is organising the load, not only to strap it down but to render things more accessible and easy to locate. Secure location of heavy items like fuel and water cans is extremely important; when tied down they should be all but impossible to budge by hand. Force yourself to consider the consequences of such heavy items, loose, in the event of an accident or roll-over.

No roof rack. Roof racks and the explorer image seem, alas, to go hand in hand, but, as covered in Section 8.1, avoid roof racks in off-road vehicles if at all possible. If you do have a major storage problem, use roofracks only for featherweight items like sleeping bags, tents and the like; *not for heavy items like fuel cans* (see below). Limit the roof load to a maximum of 75-100 kilos (see p 8.4).

Tyres, tie-downs, stowages and a fully capable GPS systems are probably the most important mods. Keep away from roof racks if you possibly can.

Compact. lightweight roof tent (left). Overloaded roof rack (right and see page 8.4) is bad for vehicle stability but here at least has been structurally integrated with internal roll-cage.

7.6 Fuels

Fuels – petrol engines

Octanes, lead – summary only. Using the right fuel for your engine, or, in some cases, matching your vehicle and engine to what fuel is available, is extremely important. Running an engine on fuel it is not designed for can ruin it. In western Europe engines are generally high compression (9.5:1 or higher) and thus require high octane fuels to run on – the graph below gives a guide. If going to an area where only low octane fuel is available a low compression engine should be used – or a limited amount can be done by:

- Richening the mixture (if possible)
- Retarding the ignition
- Fitting low compression pistons.

Even this requires expert knowledge – especially if your engine has fuel injection and an engine management system. The parameters for this are not easy to change. Modern engines will have been designed to

Sustained knock kills petrol engines. Modern engines are less easy to tune for low octane fuels so be sure you know the fuel available where you are going.

run on unleaded fuels for emissions reasons and likely have a catalytic converter in the exhaust system – a very expensive item that can be ruined by using leaded fuel. And running an older engine on unleaded fuel can damage the valve seats. See table and Note on page 7.22.

Study this carefully. Also the table opposite: this a summary based on CONCAWE's invaluable world survey of fuels, 2003. Things may have got better – or not; double-check with the oil companies operating there. Manufacturer's Customer Service department should be able to help. Likely advice: Go diesel.

Go diesel. In most cases, the only sensible solution to expeditioning abroad is to go diesel – better mpg, greater flexibility, usually greater durability and simplicity.

Moving target. The updated fuels overview here will be mainly of interest to those taking their vehicles overseas on expedition or civil aid or engineering projects. The oil update on p 7.24 – galloping on as ever – applies wherever you are. Oils get smarter and more supportive of longer engine life, longer oil change intervals and, rightly, lower emissions.

Compression ratio vs minimum required fuel octane – conceptual guidance only

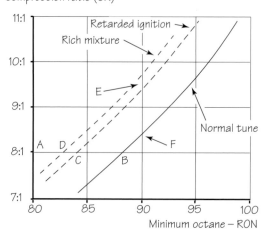

Examples:

1. Engine with 8:1 CR (A) in normal tune requires 88 RON fuel (B). With retarded ignition it can make do on 84 RON (C). If mixture can be richened it will run on 83 RON (D).

2. Or, if your engine has 9.5:1 CR (E), and you'll only have 90 RON fuel, then low compression pistons to achieve 8.4:1 CR (F) will be needed – or max retard and richening.

Note: This is conceptual only. Take the manufacturer's advice. Engines vary a lot and CRs of 10:1 or 11:1 routinely use 95 RON. At the lower end, however, poorer fuels do demand lower compression ratios.

GASOLINE ENGINES: HIGH OCTANE, LOW OCTANE, LOW GRADE LEADED FUELS

Engine type (CR = compression ratio)	Run on high octane petrol? ('4-star', 'premium', 'super', RON 95-97)	Run on low octane petrol? ('2-star', 'regular', 'normal', RON 91-92)	Run on low grade petrol? (RON below 90, down to 80 or lower)
1. Low compression engine (CR = around 8.5 or less)	Yes but needless expense. No damage.	Yes	Often yes, but if knocking retard ignition. See para opposite.
2. High compression engine (CR = 8.5 to around 10)	Yes	Rarely. If knocking retard ignition. See para opposite.	Almost certainly no.

Note:
1. Retarding ignition alone can only accommodate lower grade fuels to a certain extent. Fitting low compression pistons would be the next step – a major job that can be very expensive. Don't do this randomly or lightly; manufacturer's advice and approval should be sought first, then that of specialist engineers. JE Engineering Ltd of Coventry, tel 01203 305018, well known for extra-power tuning of Rover engines is one company that could undertake such work in the UK.
2. See next table for countries with low grade fuels and how to obtain latest information.

Unleaded gasoline – who has it

Reg'lr/premium RON shown if known.(CONCAWE 2003)

<u>Unleaded petrol</u> is available in addition to that below in:
Argentina 83/93, Bangladesh 80/95, Iran 87/95, Jordan -/95, Mexico 87/-, Oman/UAE 90/97, Pakistan 80/97, Syria -/90, Venezuela -/95.

<u>ONLY unleaded petrol</u> is available in:
Australia 91/95, Brazil -/87, China 90/95, Colombia, Equador, Guatemala, India, Indonesia 88/91(?), Kuwait 93/96, Malaysia 92/97, New Zealand 91/97, Phillipines -/93, Saudi Arabia -/95, Singapore 92/97, South Korea 91/96, Thailand 87/95, Vietnam.

Leaded petrol – availability (Africa, Mid East)

Countries where *'normal/regular' petrol is under 90 RON* but another higher grade is available (CONCAWE, 2003). * = 1997 data where no other is available.

Country	RON of regular	RON of premium
Africa		
Algeria	89	96
Benin	*83	95
*Botswana	87	93
Burkina Faso	87	93
Cameroon	85	95
*Central African Republic	83	95
*Chad	83-85	93-95
*Djibuti	83	95
Egypt	81-83	90
Gabon	85	93
Ivory Coast	87	95
Kenya	87	93
Madagascar	87	95
*Mali	87-88	95-97
Mauritania	88	92
Morocco	87	95
Namibia	83	93

Nigeria	90	90
Senegal	87	95
*Sierra Leone	83-86	95
South Africa	*87	93-97
Tanzania	83	93
Togo	87	93
*Uganda	83	93
Zambia	87	93
Middle East		
*Iran	82	95
Iraq	88	91
Jordan	88	96
Syria	-	90
UAE and Oman	90	97
Yemen	83	93

Countries where there is <u>no petrol of 90 RON</u> or over

*Afghanistan	80	87
Equatorial Guinea	*87	93
*Ethiopia	80	-
*Somalia	79	-
*Sudan	78-84	87
*Western Sahara	83	-

For detailed and accurate information on fuels contact the oil company that operates where you are going or the vehicle maker's export department. Do this very early in the planning stage

Asking the attendant – if you can find one – is unlikely to yield fuel specification! Get information from the oil companies and vehicle manufacturer way in advance so that any tweaking of the engine can be done. Probably not feasible on modern petrol engines.

WHAT WILL RUN ON WHAT – PETROL ENGINES: LEADED AND UNLEADED FUELS

Engine	Run it on leaded fuels? (2-star, 4-star etc)	Run it on unleaded fuels?
1. Older engine designed for leaded fuels – (2-star, 4-star etc)	Yes	Normally no; valve seat damage likely – but see note below.
2. Modern engine designed for unleaded fuel. Simple exhaust	Possible. May damage oxygen sensor in engine management system	Yes
3. Modern unleaded fuel engine but with CAT (catalytic converter in exhaust system)	Possible but will damage the CAT and may harm oxygen sensor	Yes

Note. Modern engines, designed for unleaded gasoline have 'hard' valve seats to cope with the absence of tetra-ethyl lead in the fuel. Engines designed for leaded fuels will suffer VSR (valve seat recession) if run on unleaded gasoline. This can be overcome by:
   1. Using an LRG – lead replacement gasoline – where different, non-lead, additives have been used in bulk, or
   2. Putting in an aftermarket additive yourself such as Octel's Valvemaster. This product has been used in both roles, or
   3. Buying a reconditioned cylinder head having special 'hard' valve-seat inserts.
Don't use LRG or VSR additives in a CAT-equipped engine as it may damage the CAT.

Octane fixes – how satisfactory? The octane fixes mentioned on the previous spread should at best be regarded as only temporary – for example if you are transiting one country and know that lower grade fuel will have to be used. Retarding the ignition may be good for 3-4 octane numbers. Richening the fuel/air mixture (if you can do it – it's best not to meddle), another one.

Diesel – the answer to it all?

Usually yes ... but. Diesel engines are far more tolerant of variations in national fuel import or production variations. In general and in 'normal' climatic conditions, a diesel engine will run on pretty much anything labelled 'diesel'. But when planning an expedition or a project that will entail taking your vehicle(s) to a distant land it is very much in your interest to check on the kind of diesel available at your destination.

The variables. Just like gasoline, there are specification variables in diesel fuel:
   • Cetane number – starting, power.
   • Sulphur content – lubricity of the fuel, engine lubricant contamination.
   • Cloud point – susceptibility to waxing in cold climates.
Cetane. Cetane influences the readiness of a fuel to ignite under compression so affects starting, smooth running and power. Unlike octane in petrol it is not 'first

Petrol engines are designed exclusively for leaded or for unleaded petrol with only a small overlap. Know the table above or expect damage.

world/third world' related and the 'around 50 cetane' required by most vehicle diesels is easy to find. Brazil and Canada (both 40) and India (42) are among those with under-45 cetane diesel in the pumps. Marine diesel is very low cetane so don't be tempted to use that if it comes your way.

Sulphur content. Sulphur content is much more important (table facing page) and foreknowledge can be useful:
   • *Too little.* Strangely, when low-sulphur diesel fuels (0.05%) were first introduced into Europe, they were found wanting in lubricity and injector pumps, which rely on the lubricity of the fuel, were getting damaged. This has now been addressed by the fuel companies but if you suspect the fuel – eg really old stock in some far northern Swedish village – add a tablespoonful of ordinary lubricating oil for every 50 litres of fuel.
   • *Too much.* High sulphur is a far more common problem with diesel fuels. It is cheaper to make and in countries without strict emission laws it is what is on sale. If you are asking if this is your concern, the answer is yes because high sulphur levels lead to contamination of engine lubrication oils. This takes the form of sulphuric acid and can cause engine corrosion and eventual breakdown of the lubricant as well since it

When taking expeditions – large or small – overseas, check specs of en route fuels. Relating petrol octane to your engine's compression ratio and exhaust system (catalytic converters) is fundamental. Diesels are usually more tolerant but high sulphur will damage engines without the right lubricating oil. The wrong cloud point will stop you dead in very cold conditions.

shortens the life of the additives. It matters – and is taken very seriously by people such as Caterpillar who watch over world-wide fleets of very expensive and hard working diesel equipment.

High sulphur – what to do? Two things can be done to safeguard your engine by you as vehicle operator:

• Use an engine oil with a high TBN (see table, page 7.25): 20x sulphur content for indirect-injection engines; 10x sulphur level for direct injection. (So an indirect injection engine in Turkey – 0.70% sulphur – needs oil of at least TBN 14.)

• Reduce oil change interval – page 7.27.

Diesel fuel waxing. You will be aware of this in severe European or Canadian winters. Fuel supplied by the oil companies varies in formulation for summer and winter; the cloud point (waxing threshold) of the diesel at the pumps is higher in summer and lower in winter. Invariably, local supplies, wherever 'local' may be, will take account of this. Should you get exceptionally cold conditions, or find yourself using last summer's stock, adding kerosene to diesel will lower the cloud point; 25% kerosene (or 'Jet A' aviation fuel) will drop the cloud point 5°C. Up to 50% can be added to obtain a 10°C drop but, over 25%, add lube-oil as at left for low sulphur fuels.

Some modern diesels, like Land Rover's TD5 using an in-head fuel gallery, warm the fuel and circulate it back to the tank. Not an anti-waxing move but a neat spin off.

HIGH SULPHUR DIESEL FUELS

Where is it? Is it relevant? What to do. High sulphur diesel harms the environment, the population (particulates) and your engine. Only national legislation can tackle the first two but there is something you can do about preserving your engine – a carefully chosen oil, with a high TBN (value c.10-16, see opposite and main book glossary p.9.12). Meantime, here is where high sulphur diesel is, or is not a problem. Anything above 0.5% is specially bad news. (Data: Courtesy CONCAWE, 2003)

Country	% sulphur	Country	% sulphur
Africa		Ecuador	0.05
Algeria	0.25	Mexico (capital,	
Cameroon	1.00	main towns)	0.05
Egypt	0.3-0.9	Mexico (rural)	0.50
Gabon	0.80	Venezuela	1.00
Ghana	0.12		
Malawi	0.55	Asia, Australasia	
Mauritius	1.00	Australia	0.05
Morocco	1.00	China	1.00
Mozambique	0.55	India (cities)	0.05
South Africa	0.3-0.05	India (rural)	0.25
Tunisia	0.20	Indonesia	0.50
Zaire	1.00	Malaysia	0.20
Zimbabwe	0.55	Malaysia, new?	0.05
		New Zealand	
Middle East		(N island)	0.14
Bahrain	0.50	New Zealand	
Iran	0.7-0.8	(remainder)	0.30
Israel	0.035	Pakistan	1.00
Jordan	1.20	Singapore	0.05
Kuwait	0.50	South Korea	0.05
Saudi Arabia	1.00	Thailand	0.05
Syria	0.70		
UAE 1	0.50	**Other data – 1995**	
UAE 2	0.05	No updates available	
Yemen	1.00		
		Turkey	0.70
Cent and South America		Tanzania	1.00
Argentina	0.25	Zambia D2	1.00
Brazil grade B	0.50	Bangladesh	1.00
Brazil grade D	0.20	Sri Lanka	1.10
Chile A1 (cities)	0.05	Vietnam D2	1.00
Chile B1 (rural)	0.10	El Salvador	0.90
Colombia	0.40	Uruguay	0.75

High sulphur diesel causes engine lubricant contamination. Use high TBN oil or reduce change intervals. Low sulphur fuels used to cause lubricity problems ...

7.7 Engine oils

Engine oils – the broad picture

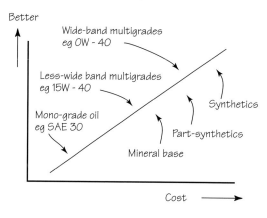

Engine oils

Good, better, best. Highly relevant to expeditions where total reliability and the welfare of your engine in literally vital, this section also applies to the everyday running of your 4x4. So first be clear about the engine lubricant hierarchy indicated above.:

- Mineral oils: good
- Semi-synthetic: better
- Full synthetic: best.

For *any* engine, once it is run-in. Not surprisingly it's a 'get what you pay for' situation; the best is the best – much longer *potential* life (see below), better engine protection from wear and oil contamination – and thus more expensive. Remember too there's a lot more to defining an oil than just the maker's name, viscosity and base oil. There are essential oil performance parameters as defined by Service Categories – the 'API' and 'ACEA' notations on the back of the can, sometimes also with 'ILSAC'. And, coming soon to a dealership near you, 'Global DHD'. Once on a simple ascending scale, even the long established API and ACEA categories now need special attention. But first ... .

Expedition usage is niche in oil market. Seek the most advanced grades capable of also dealing with the worst climates, stress and fuels. Look first at the service category.

Beware those marketing people – again. As with all the fancy trade names for simple 4x4 concepts (remember 'SupaTork', 'Auto-Drive', 'UltraGrip' and the like? See p 2.2), so with oils. Flashy packaging, glossy tell-you-nothing leaflets, dinky catch-phrases, the compulsion to portray every product as three times better than something else (ill defined) and associate full synthetics only with 'racing' or 'max power' ... all this, thanks to the marketeers who do a major disservice to their own research departments, obscures the basic information you need to make a mature decision on what engine oil to use. Does it matter? Yes, it matters if you value your engine.

Check some of the web sites. Most are over the top and unbalanced. Others try but don't really set the scene overall. Some can't be bothered and refer you somewhere else through URLs that take five minutes to transcribe. Toes will start to uncurl, though, with the US Mobil pages – (www.mobiloil.com) alas, with brands available only in the USA. But clarity and a sense of the real-world, price- and spec-related oil-archy is conveyed: 'Mobil 1 Extended Performance' (for 15000 miles oil changes), 'Mobil Clean 7500' (7500), 'Mobil Clean 5000' (5000), plus 'Mobil 1' and an oil for engines over 75000 miles. Full synthetic, synthetic blend or conventional (mineral) base-stock is clearly stated. You start to know where you are.

UK motor accessories factors Halfords, however, set a good example with their plain oils packaging, clearly labelled as one of the three oil types above; colour coded containers with viscosity and the Service Categories on the front.

And the drivers' handbooks too. Rare to the point of suspected non-existence is the drivers handbook that even acknowledges the existence of synthetic oil or the benefits that accrue from its use. You can almost see the warranty department lawyers, blue pencil in hand, going over the text. Again, US Mobil addresses that head-on with, in effect, 'Follow the handbook but ... once your vehicle is out of warranty ... '

WHAT THE LABEL SAYS – AND DOESN'T SAY: SERVICE CATEGORIES – ENGINE OILS

4/06

'Mobil' you know but the branding is seldom obvious. No manufacturer will say 'This isn't our top grade' or 'This is our cheapest'. Here, **'Mobil 1'** – their best in the UK – is proudly presented as Fully Synthetic. Had it been 'Mobil Super S' it would have been part-synthetic. Or Mobil S a straight mineral – the cheapest and lowest in the hierarchy. A lubricant's base oil should be indicated on the label but seldom is unless it is trumpeted as a full synthetic. 'Blend' usually means part-synthetic but wording like 'Synthetic engineered' on Castrol Magnatec leaves you with the (incorrect) impression of a full synthetic oil. Magnatec is a part-synthetic. 'Conventional' usually means mineral base. Look for the all-important Service Categories (the 'API' and 'ACEA' letters and numbers), usually relegated to the back of the container. Look, of course, for whether it's an **engine oil or a gear oil** – most important. Here's an example of typical packaging and what it means:

SAE (*US Society of Automotive Engineers*) system, accepted world-wide, indicates viscosity – how 'thick' the oil is. 'SAE' should precede the '0W-40' figures here. High numbers mean thick oil, low numbers thin, free-flowing. Two together as here is a multigrade. When cold the **0W-40** behaves like an SAE 0W, when hot like an SAE 40.

API (*American Petroleum Institute*) oil performance standards for spark ignition engines (**S + letter suffix – SL**) or diesels – compression ignition – (**C + letter suffix – CF**). Suffix usually denotes ascending standards: control of deposits, oxidation, wear, corrosion. Table next spread.

ACEA (*Association des Constructeurs Européens d'Automobiles*) oil performance standards – engine type (letter) and number. Beware, ascending numbers can mean different *type* of oil as well as quality. Prefix 'A' applies to petrol engines, 'B' to 'light' diesels, 'E' to 'heavy duty' diesels. See table next spread.

ILSAC (*International Lubricants Standardisation and Approval Committee*) oil performance ratings (not shown here) appear more often in the US in conjunction with API standards and imply ECII fuel economy – see below – (and other) benefits over the standard API rating. Thus ILSAC GF-3 will meet both API SL and the ECII requirements. GF-4 goes with API SM.

Fuel economy – EC (energy conserving) indicates a +1.5% fuel economy over a standard Reference Oil. **EC II** indicates +2.7%. Economy seekers often opt for ACEA A1 or B1 oils (next spread). EC or ECII is sometimes shown on its own but more often implied when an ILSAC category (above) such as GF-3 or GF-4 (both ECII) featured.

Global DHD, DLD etc. Projected new classification system applicable world-wide. Watch this space.

SuperSyn
TECHNOLOGY
Mobil
1
Turbo Diesel
0W-40
Fully Synthetic Motor Oil

Meets / Conforme à / Πληρεί:
API SL/CF; ACEA A3/B3/B4; MB 229.1

Approved / Agréée / Εγκεκριμένο:
Volkswagen VW 502 00/505 00 (1/97);
VW 503 01; MB 229.3; MB 229.5;
Opel GM LL-A-025/LL-B-025; BMW
Longlife 01; Porsche

— This is on the front —

← On the back →

TBN – and sulphur. TBN is not usually shown on the label. Total Base Number indicates an oil's ability to neutralise the corrosive acids and depletion of additives resulting from sulphur in diesel fuels. Most oils have a TBN around 10 – usually adequate – but a high TBN (c.16) is worth going for if you are going to be using less refined, high-sulphur diesel (over 0.5% by weight) on sale in developing countries. To find out your TBN, helplines are: Castrol 01793.45.2222, Mobil/Exxon 01372.222.558 or website data sheets. Note that API Service Category CF (Mobil 1 above) copes with 'over 0.5%' so is worth looking out for. The down side of unnecessarily high TBN can be ash deposits – bad for exhaust after-treatment systems.

'Turbo diesel' – what engine it's for: In this case customer reassurance only since Mobil 1 is the same oil with or without the 'Turbo Diesel' on the can. No real deception since it meets the requisite Service Categories for both petrol *and* diesel engines: eg ACEA A3/B3/B4. Check the letters and numbers.

'0W-40' – viscosity: a description of the oil – like saying a shoe is a size 9. Has little to do with how 'good' it is. It should, strictly, say 'SAE 0W-40 – see opposite for 'SAE'.

'Fully synthetic' – the base oil: Full synthetic is best so it is trumpeted on the label. Only rarely (plaudits for Halfords) will it clearly indicate when it is part-synthetic or straight mineral oil.

How good the oil is – in derisory small print on the back of the can. These are the vital service categories listed against various national or international oil classification systems – **API, ACEA, US MIL, ILSAC**, etc, (see opposite and overleaf) plus some manufacturers own test schedule specifications – eg VW, Mercedes, GM, BMW *et al*. Note these carefully; eg the '00' and '01' VW suffixes denote radically different oils.

Read the label – all of it, not just the viscosity. Wide-band multigrades are best. Be very particular where manufacturers' specifications are concerned. Stick to them.

MOTORCYCLE OILS
Motorcycles are different in that in the majority of cases the gearbox uses the engine's lubricating oil. Most importantly there is also a 'wet' clutch – ie it operates in the engine oil. Excess friction modifiers – as found in oils of API SH category and above would normally give rise to the risk of clutch slip on a motorcycle. Thus only oils specifically for motorcycles API SG (or SH, SJ or SL *but with* JASO MA) should be used.

The assistance provided in the preparation of this and the following spread by Elspeth Barley at BP Castrol , Dr Mike Wharton and Robin Gregory at ExxonMobil is gratefully acknowledged

ENGINE OIL MARKET SNAPSHOT, mid 2006 – ONE MANUFACTURER: MOBIL

Make and brand	Viscosity	Base oil	Service category API	ACEA	TBN	Notes
Mobil 1	0W-40	Synthetic	SJ/SL/SM/CF/EC	A3/B3/B4	11.0	
Super S	10W-40	Semi-synthetic	SJ/SL/CF	A3/B3	7.0	
Super	15W-40	Mineral	SJ/SL/CF	A3/B3	7.0	
Mobil 1 Turbo Diesel	0W-40	Synthetic	SJ/SL/SM/CF/EC	A3/B3/B4	11.0	
Super S Turbo Diesel	10W-40	Semi-synthetic	SJ/SL/CF	A3/B3	7.0	
Delvac 1 SHC	5W-40	Synthetic	– /CE/CF	B2/E4	16.3	
Delvac XHP Extra	10W-40	Synthetic	– /CF	E4/E7	16.3	
Delvac XHP	10W-40	Semi-synthetic	– /CF	B2/E3	16.3	Also 15/40
Delvac MX	15W-40	Mineral	SL/CF/CF-4/CH-4 CI-4/CG-4	A2/B3/B4/E3 E5/E7	10.0	

Notes:
1. Service Category meanings explained opposite. In general the ACEA system is the easier to follow: A = petrol, B = light diesel, E = diesel trucks. B and E tests are different. Dual qualification is valuable in expedition 4x4 context.
2. TBN number indicates ability to neutralise lubricant degradation through acid from high sulphur diesel fuels. Important.
3. See 'Engine oils – what to actually do', next spread.

Service Categories

Owner's manual? Before we go on: page three and three more to go ... what is wrong with just following the driver's handbook? That, certainly, is the place to start but we are considering exceptional conditions here – expeditions, aid work, harsh climates, possibly poor fuels. no dealership to do your oil change and extended oil drain intervals. Keep going! (It could also benefit you in school-run, commuting, visiting-the-folks, trip-to-the-hills, down-home UK, Europe or the US. So, yes, keep going!)

Service Categories. The oils Service Categories (previous spread and opposite) are enormously important and the subject of vast expenditure by the oil companies. Standards rise continuously – also to facilitate compliance with emissions legislation.

Oil Service Categories overlap – API (US system) and ACEA (European) cover the same ground in different ways. ILSAC (US/Japan) is an API add-on

Total mechanical reliability is even more important in remote areas. Use the best lubricants you can. (See also p 4.13 Wrangler JK.)

Oils contribute to particulates emissions and tweaking formulation can address this and protection of exhaust gas after-treatment devices – to say nothing of highly stressed cam-lobes and fuel injection components. As we saw overleaf, there are, confusingly, different and overlapping systems of classifying oil performance into Service Categories:
- API – the US system
- ACEA – the European system
- ILSAC – a kind of Japanese/US add-on to the API system
- Global – a world-wide system homing in on us now.

(Aren't the others world-wide? They're acknowledged pretty much world-wide but individual producers have to be licensed to use them.) Engines turn in huge mileages nowadays, mainly attributable to the tests and quality of lubricants. The utmost reliability is fundamental to any expedition. Do not hazard it by giving your engine anything but the best lubricants.

Manufacturers' Service Categories. Increasingly, manufacturers are laying down their own oil specifications (eg VW 505 01, Mercedes 229.3, BMW LongLife) to accommodate particular technologies. It is essential that these are complied with, however else you fine tune the spec of your oil. Volkswagen fuel injectors, for example need very special lubrication.

API SERVICE CATEGORIES – US System

Gasoline engine oil categories

Prefix 'S' = spark ignition, ie petrol engines. Suffixes run from 'A' to (mid 2006) 'M'. Categories SA to SH are now obsolete (but see SG regarding motorcycles, previous spread). For petrol engines the latest engine oil Service Category includes the performance properties of each earlier category. List starts with the latest.

SM   For all petrol engines currently in use. Category introduced Nov 2004. Improved oxidation resistance, deposit and wear protection and low temperature performance ('stay in grade') over oil's life. May also be teamed with ILSAC GF-4 yielding better economy.

SL   Introduced 2001

SJ   Introduced 1997

Diesel engine oil categories

Prefix 'C' = compression ignition, ie diesel engines. Categories run from 'CA' to (mid 2006) 'CI-4'. CA to CE are now obsolete. Latest categories usually infer emissions-related changes. For diesel engines the latest engine oil Service Category **may not** include the performance properties of each earlier category, eg 'CF' can deal with fuel sulphur content above 0.5% where later categories are cleared 'up to 0.5%'. The '-4' annotation indicates 4-stroke diesel, '-2' a two stroke, sometimes used in US truck engines. Unlike ACEA, note the API system does not, *per se* differentiate between 'light' and 'heavy duty' diesels – but note 'high speed' below implying car, SUV, pick-up engines. List starts with the latest.

CI-4   Introduced 2002 to accommodate emissions regulations involving EGR (exhaust gas recirculation). For high speed, 4-stroke diesels using fuels with sulphur content below 0.5%. Can be used in place of CD, CE, CF-4, CG-4 and CH-4 oils – but note **not** to replace CF.

CH-4   Introduced 1998. For high speed, 4-stroke engines using fuels with sulphur content below 0.5%. Can be used in place of CD, CE, CF-4, CG-4 oils – but **not** to replace CF.

CF-4   1990. High speed, 4-stroke diesels. Can be used in place of CD and CE oils.

CF   1994. An offshoot from the oil spec hierarchy that is still current. Principal benefit being specified for engines using fuels over 0.5% sulphur. Usually, in current (2006) oils, combined with other higher specs indicating the poor fuels aspect is covered too.

CA-CE   Obsolete categories. API warn that CA, CB, and CC 'Not suitable for engines built after (respectively) 1959,1961 and 1990.'

ACEA CATEGORIES – European system

Gasoline <u>and 'light' diesel</u> engine oil categories

Prefix = engine type: 'A' = petrol, 'B' = 'light' diesel. If label shows 'A+number' the oil is for petrol engines, 'B+number' is for diesels. Both (eg 'A3/B3', as in Mobil 1 example on previous spread) means dual qualification. (See '<u>E</u>' = 'heavy duty' diesels below.) Suffix numbers (A2, B3, B4 etc) *usually* (but not always – eg A5/B5) indicate increasing test severity but also a mix of, for example, diesel injection system, drain intervals or economy criteria. Category 'C', late 2004, ('catalyst compatible) includes formulation to enhance the life of exhaust after-treatment devices such as particulate filters for Euro 4 compliant engines. List starts with the lowest suffix number.

A1/B1   Low viscosity, fuel economy oils for moderately stressed engines. May not suit all units.

A3/B3   Stable, 'stay-in-grade' (reduced tendency for thickening by contaminants) for higher performance engines (but indirect injection diesels) and/or longer drain if specified by maker.

A3/B4   As A3/B3 but high performance engines and including direct injection diesels.

A5/B5   In effect a stable, 'stay-in-grade', long-life, version of the low viscosity oils at A1/B1. Due to the low viscosity, may not suit all units.

Catalyst compatibility oils (see note above)

Certain 'good' qualities of lubricating oils – like coping with high-sulphur fuels – generate sulphated ash. Sulphated ash shortens the life of the exhaust after-treatment devices like catalysts and particulate filters. 'Low SAPS' oils (sulphated ash, phosphorous and sulphur) are formulated to be catalyst-friendly. These are very specific categories to be used only in engines cleared for their use. In general the C1, C2, C3 categories so far formulated run along similar lines as the -1 to -3 above, 'must have' low viscosity, 'can use' low viscosity and 'don't use' low viscosity oils.

Oils for 'heavy duty' diesels

E2   General purpose oil for naturally aspirated or turbocharged engines. Medium/heavy duty.

E4   High performance oil for Euro 1 and 2 emissions engines, severe service conditions, extended oil drains. E3, E5 – Deleted.

E6   As E4 for high output Euro 1, 2, 3, 4 diesels, extended drain intervals, with exhaust after-treatment, especially particulate filters.

E7   Similar to E6: high performance oil for Euro 1-4, highly rated engines, long drain intervals. Accent on engine cleanliness, low turbocharger deposits. Manufacturer consultation.

Ascending numbers and letters used to be a 'better oil' guide. But you have to read it carefully now. Global categories (DHD, DLD etc) is an attempt at a common system.

Engine oil – what to actually do

Making your choice. After all this background information and theory, what should you actually do? Check the oil recommended in your handbook and do not use a less well-specified product. Then:

1. Viscosity 1. The handbook recommendation on viscosity may simply be, say, 15W-40 or may be listed as different oils against temperature spans. Select the one covering the widest ambient temperature range that includes your proposed operations. Use this viscosity as your baseline.

2. Viscosity 2. This is tweakable to the benefit of your engine. If the baseline figure is 15W-40, don't go below, or normally above, the right-hand figure but you can beneficially lower the left-hand figure on a fairly modern engine by using a 10W-40 or a 5W-40 or even a 0W-40. As well as extending the span of operating ambients, this will, more importantly, give you better cold-start oil pumping and reduce engine wear.

3. Service category. The detailed Service Categories run-down on the previous spreads gives the broad picture. Ascertain the minimum service category of the required oil as indicated in the handbook. Oil service categories may well have advanced since your handbook was written and using a high spec – an API SM instead of an API SJ – will always benefit your engine in terms of extreme protection. Don't let the label-talk of 'racing' or 'super high performance' cars put you off; such activities will be helped by high spec oils but your 4x4 will also reap enhanced protection. Be careful with API diesel specs, though, re-read the previous page.

4. Base oil. Then refer to non service category items like oil base. Oil service categories lay down performance capability but do not refer to base oils – for example Mobil Super Diesel (mineral base) and Mobil Super S Diesel (semi-synthetic) both meet ACEA B3. A mineral base oil will have additives similar to but not as durable as those available in more expensive oils. A semi- or full synthetic will have much better cold-

Choosing multi-grades, right-hand figure should be manufacturer's advised but left figure can be as low as affordable. Go for highest service category.

pumping attributes and will be much better at reducing engine wear.

5. Aim high. Combining 3 and 4 above, go for the highest service category and cleverest base oil you can – in the example quoted, Mobil 1 Turbo Diesel 0W-40 is a full synthetic meeting a very high category of ACEA A3 (petrol engines) and B3/B4 diesel) and would do exceptionally well in a petrol engine or (since it has CF too) where fairly high sulphur diesel fuels are used. With its '0W-40' SAE it will certainly pump – to every corner of your engine on a cold start-up – more quickly than a 15W-40 mineral-base (the '0W' is what counts here). However, do read the Service Category notes at the lower half of the previous page. Higher ACEA suffix numbers must be put in context – for example a B1 low viscosity fuel economy oil may be the manufacturers' preference. Also, if there is a manufacturer's spec (eg VW or Mercedes) be certain that the oil you choose meets that spec as well.

6. High-sulphur diesel fuel? Truck oils? The classic expedition situation is a vehicle prepared in the UK arriving in an area where local diesel fuel has a high sulphur content – probably over 0.5%. The 'best' oils as determined by service category and base oil (3, 4 and 5 above) are not always formulated to deal with high-sulphur diesel fuels – but truck oils are. ACEA E4 'high performance' and E6 'very high performance' oils will encompass many (but not all) attributes of the best 'light duty diesel' categories. But also, if you choose right, they come in with very high TBN (16 or 17) to counter high-sulphur diesel acidity as well. The 'not all' caution here refers to trucks being low-revving, long-journey engines so for an expedition light 4x4 use a dual-qualified oil – ACEA B3/E4. This will look after higher-stressed fast diesels as well as any sulphur problem, see data previous spread.

7. Drain intervals – may be increased. If you are on ACEA 'E' diesel oils, do not be tempted to emulate truck drain intervals. Trucks do huge distances between drains because they have enormous oil sumps and often have fairly low-stressed engines. The expedition scenario above can also find you, at the 9000 mile oil change point, unable to buy the same super quality oil you started out with. Should you drain and fill with poor local oil or can you hang on? With top-grade synthetic oil you can extend a drain interval to almost double; maybe a 6000 mile increment here – *if on low sulphur fuels.* High sulphur, alas, is different. See next.

8. Drain intervals – should be reduced. There is a need to *reduce* drain intervals if you have a diesel operating on high sulphur fuels and do not have high TBN oils to use. If your oil has a lower than ideal TBN (page 7.23) reduce your engine oil change intervals. The US diesel doyens Cummins have an elegant formula for assessing this (page 7.23) which, reduced to expedition terms on a low TBN oil, amounts to:

• Diesel fuel sulphur content 0.05%-0.50% – reduce drain intervals to 75% of the usual mileage.

• Diesel fuel sulphur content over 0.5% – reduce drain intervals to 50%.

But what if ... ? If you have taken the sensible precaution of filling with high TBN 'E' synthetic before leaving, the increase in permissible oil drain interval mentioned at para 7 above should be reduced by the factor just mentioned. So in the example, a vehicle with a 9000 mile normal drain interval on a full synthetic B3/E3 or E4 oil should, in Turkey, (sulphur 0.7%) not increase the oil change interval beyond 7500 miles.

9. Buying it. Consider engine oil as a part of your spares pack. In other words, on a long expedition take enough for an en route change. If you cannot take a complete change, just taking a 5 litre can of the right stuff topped up with 'local' will help (see next para). Buying the best oils is not cheap. Sometimes the top brands of truck oils are only available in 25 litre drums. Decide what you need; then shop around. Ring the manufacturers, open an account for your project and get supplied at trade rates through manufacturers' local distributors.

10. Topping up – mixing oils en route. People who care about engines sometimes worry about not being able to top up with the same oil they originally filled with. So long as you do not mix mineral or synthetics with a vegetable oil such as a castor-oil based lubricant (virtually non-existent these days anyway), you can mix oils without doing harm though naturally topping up with the original type oil is best. You can top up with a better oil or a less good one – but sticking to the vehicle manufacturers' own spec, where there is one, is essential. If you are still in the running-in period (first 3000 miles) do not put in synthetic.

Never top up an engine with a gear oil – though the other way round, ie topping up a gear box with engine oil) is safe – if not ideal – and preferable to running low on oil.

11. New engine. Run-in very carefully – especially the first few hundred miles – on mineral-base oil, not synthetics. Get to 3000 miles, then change to full-synthetic.

And finally

Ask , to confirm. This spread and the previous ones are relevant and important to know if you are taking a vehicle on an expedition. However, with the advent of very specific requirements for particular engines, and the rate at which new products appear (often, as another red herring, relevant only to Europe to meet European emissions regulations), you would be wise to bounce your conclusions off the oil manufacturers' (not just the vehicles manufacturers') Customer Service departments, in the UK: Castrol 01793.452.222; Exxon/Mobil 01372.222.558.

See p 7.23-25 re high TBN oil for diesels. Keep to or reduce drain intervals; take an oil change if at all possible. Buy at trade rates by opening account with local distributor.

High temperatures, high torque, soft sand on a slope. The engine is working hard. Take enough top quality oil for en route change on a long trip, especially if fuel quality is poor.

7.8 Water

When to carry it and how much

Quick overview. As with the coverage on fuels and oils for the engine, space here permits only an overview of the subject, covered in greater detail in *Vehicle-dependent Expedition Guide*.

Constant need. Even in normal day-to-day business driving, most drivers will be champing for a cup of tea or coffee by the end of three or four hours. Any excursion that could remotely qualify for the term expedition, right down to a half day in the hills, is certainly going to call for water to be included in the planning.

Fluid intake can increase by up to 800% in hot climate, high-workload conditions compared with sedentary use. Plan water requirements carefully and add reserves.

How much. Ranging between sedentary, no work to vigorous work in ambients of 42°C the span of consumption will be 2.5 to 16 litres per day . Much dependent on workload, consumptions will be:

- Temperate climate: 2.5-5.0 litres per head per day.
- Night/day temperatures 5°/35°C: 5-8 litres per head per day.
- Night/day temp 25°/45°C: 10-15 litres per head per day.

Warm climate, moderate workload can be accommodated with a planning figure of about 5-7 litres per day usually. This is a minimum and is to take care of drinking, cooking and very small amounts for personal hygiene. Not surprisingly, overweight people use more; skinny ones use less.

Temperature. Once ambients exceed body temperature (37°C), consumption rises sharply.

Not like home. Our profligate use of water at home has to be abandoned on an expedition where, as already seen, weight is of major importance. You soon get adept at washing in a single mug of water on a long-duration overseas trip. The above are minima and assume constraints on weight which invariably apply on long trips. A day trip or weekend of camping, of course, does not have to be a session of ascetic self-denial.

Reserves. Carry a sensible reserve to

cover possible breakdown on a long trip. In very remote areas with very little traffic this would be two or three days' supply.

Carrying it, dispensing it

Beyond the cup-holders. Supermarket plastic bottles are not the way to carry water for any trip longer than a few hours. Really robust hard-plastic jerry cans, pre-disinfected with a strong bleach solution and then rinsed, are the only practical method of carrying expedition water. Military 20 litre cans have found their way onto the normal market and are ideal. As with fuel cans, padded racks for water can should be arranged.

Robust personal water bottles are a necessity so that each crew member has their own supply and fill-ups can all take place at the same time.

Dispensing it. It is tedious having to unlash the can every time you need to dispense water so a dip-in squeezy pump is a lightweight, simple way to get over the problem. They can usually be found in caravanning and camping shops.

Using it. If you are not pushing the payload limits there is nothing to stop you taking more than minimum drinking needs and, as it were, splashing out. When Honda brought out the CRV in the UK they made a camp shower accessory available, a solidly-made electrical pump that could be dipped into a can. Three litres for a shower is possible – bliss at the end of a long hot day! If you can't spare that and hate dirt in your hair, a hair-wash alone, using a cup and a bucket, catching and re-using the rinse, can be done with .75 - 1.0 litre.

Water for drinking

Know the enemy. Surprisingly, most tap supplies are – after reassurance from locals – safe to drink. Equally surprising is the fact that virtually all streams, no matter how clear and sparkling, are not. Either way it is not worth risking illness on your trip. Knowing what you are up against and what to do is half the battle. Keeping it simple, the main hazard classifications are:

•*Big bugs – protozoa, parasites.* Unpredictable distribution worldwide. Carried in human and animal faeces, resistant to chemicals like chlorine and iodine. See below.

• *Small bugs – bacteria.* Prolific. Main causes of stomach upsets. Can be filtered by the finest filters and killed chemically.

• *Very small bugs – viruses.* Too small to filter except when they clump (and you don't know when they're doing that!). Succumb to chemicals.

The weapons. Whilst smells and tastes can also be removed with activated carbon, for the bugs you can use:
- Filters and purifiers
- Chemicals
- Heat and boiling (see page 7.31)

Even on a demanding trip, well managed reserves can yield an occasional 3-4 litre hoard – enough for a de-luxe shower like this (left)! Military 20-litre hard plastic water can is the best for storage. Plastic squeezy-siphon (here with extended pipe to reach bottom of can) permits filling of water bottles, kettles, with can still lashed in place. Doubles as dip-stick.

'BUG' SIZES AND WHAT YOU CAN DO ABOUT THEM

	Big bugs (parasites, protozoa) eg: giardia, cryptosporidia, schistosoma, amoebic dysentery, worms	Small bugs (bacteria) eg: E Coli, bacillary dysentery, cholera, typhoid, leptospirosis	Very small bugs (viruses) eg: Polio, hepatitis, rotavirus	Tastes and smells eg: Residual iodine, and chlorine, pesticides, 'bad eggs', chemicals
Size: (1 μm is a micron: 1/1000th of one millimetre)	4 - 12 μm ie, well over 1 μm	0.5 - 3.0 μm ie, around 1 μm	0.02 - 0.08 μm ie, less than 1 μm	Dissolved
Can be filtered out by:	Virtually all micro-filters (see over)	The finest microfilters	Too small to filter but may attach to larger impurities	Activated carbon granules or resin
Can be killed by:	Hot / boiling water. Resistant to chemicals (but see page 7.31)	Iodine, chlorine. silver in most cases	Iodine, chlorine. silver in most cases	n/a

Know the bug sizes rather than their names. Know what zaps what. Giardia and crypto are immune to chemicals so micro-filters are needed.

Chemical treatment

Three options. Chemical treatment for water is of three types:

- Chlorine (Puritabs etc). In some developing countries needs to be used at up to five times 'normal' strength with subsequent de-chlorination by other tablets.
- Silver-based (eg, Micropur). Now considered safe for long-term use after doubts in the late '80s. No after-taste.
- Iodine (eg, Potable Aqua). Should not be used for period longer than 3 to 6 months. After-taste.

Note that these chemical treatments leave some parasites virtually untouched.

Selecting your hardware

Three-pronged problem. A slow look around the table on the previous page and the conclusion on expedition water treatment soon becomes clear. Three facts present themselves:

- Parasites like giardia and cryptosporidia are less numerous than bacteria but very bad news (they lay you low and are then difficult to get rid of); they are almost immune to chemical treatment but large enough to filter easily.
- Bacteria are the main risk and respond to chemicals as well as being filterable.
- Chemicals like iodine and chlorine leave a taste – albeit silver does not.

Three-pronged attack on water impurities is best – micro-filtration, chemical attack on smallest bacteria and viruses and a charcoal de-taster. Then relax.

Three-pronged attack. Clearly your water filtration equipment to take care of all of these problems must address each one in turn and will have:

- A micro-filter with a pore size of 1μm (1 micron) or smaller.
- A chemical element to be sure about the bacteria and take out viruses.
- A de-tasting element to remove tastes and smells from the chemical purifiers and any others in the water.

These stages can be arranged separately by the user but filters are available that combine all three. Micro-filter pore size will be quoted in catalogue literature. A favourite way of incorporating chemical disinfection is to incorporate an iodine resin element into the filter. This will have a finite life which you should check on. And finally many filters have an optional activated charcoal final stage to take out tastes and smells from water. Use of silver obviates the need for charcoal de-tasting (see Katadyn opposite).

Go shopping. The above and the table on the previous page will equip you sufficiently to be able to go shopping for a suitable filter for your needs. The only characteristic not mentioned is flow rate which could be relevant to large group expeditions. Flow rates will vary from 0.5 litres per minute for the very small rucsac units weighing under half a kilo, to 4.5 litres/min for stirrup-pump types weighing over 5 kg.

Check filter capacity too which varies from 380 to 7000 litres before a change is due.

Names of manufacturers that jump to mind are Katadyn, First Need, MSR and, for large remote-group use, Pre-Mac (UK).

Getting fuel and water quantities right is bedrock fundamental. Stowage, lashing-down and getting the high-density loads mid-point of the wheel-base is also important. Though strapped down, the set-up here with no can-height bulkhead for the heavy containers to rest against, is less than ideal but shows the principle – see photo p 8.3, Sec 8.1 'Loading'.

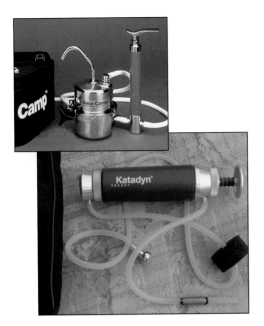

Top: First Need Base Camp filter, at 1.5 litre/ min, large enough for group. Below: Long established Katadyn Pocket ceramic/silver filter/purifier unit: 2μm pore size, process rate of 1.0 litre/min, 50,000 litre capacity, 20 year warranty. Not cheap!

As you might expect, lower temperatures for a relatively long time equals higher temperatures for a short time and the table shows this too.

You will probably have a small digital thermometer with you in the field and if you take the photographic type with a separate probe you can save a lot of time and fuel if you have to purify water using heat. What it all amounts to is:

1. Almost any heat is better than no heat.
2. The real baddies, like giardia and crypto, start to keel over at 55°C.
3. In emergencies, heat to 60-65°C and hold for 10-15 minutes.
4. Just bringing to the boil will kill everything. No need to hold it there.

Heat and boiling is the (fuel-hungry but) reliable fall-back for water purification. Check the table: boiling for 10 minutes is not necessary.

Lethal temperature-x-time combinations:

Worm eggs	50-55°C
Cryptosporidium	45°C x 5-20 min
	55°C x 20 min
	64°C x 2 min
Giardia	60°C x 10 min
Salmonella	65°C x 1 min
Cholera	62°C x 10 min
Viruses	60°C x 20-40 min
	70°C x 1 min
Hepatitis A (waterborne)	98°C x 1 min
	60°C x 19 min

Heat and boiling

The old standby. Tedious, fuel-hungry and productive of warm, flat-tasting water, heat is a good standby method of purifying water. Old standbys often accumulate old wives' tales too and a study of research on the subject carried out over the past 25 years shows that it is not necessary to 'boil for 10 minutes' – or anything like that. The table shows that in fact many bugs begin to lose interest at temperatures as low as 45-50°C.

A test for any purification system! Well water likely to have visible impurities as well as invisible bugs. Allow water to settle, then filter through a fine-fabric bag to preserve your filter element. No filter will improve brackish water.

Section 8

Loading and tyres

8.1. Loading

'King cab' or double cab? The double-cab pickup is an excellent solution to the problem of a mixed load of people and cargo, albeit the high-density load inevitably sits well aft and over – or, worse, behind – the back wheels. (How much does that matter? Check the diagram on the next spread. So surprising you may need to check it twice.) Such vehicles these days are available in working and 'fur lined' versions – with or without rear covers (see p 1.3).

Off-roaders move things

Off-roaders' work. Probably as many off-roaders are bought for their ability to move things as for their ability to go off-road. As already discussed on pages 1.6 and 7.15, a manufacturer will, according to the market, make his vehicle an all-payload workhorse on stiff springs (to take the weight) or a luxurious five-seater with softer springing for a smooth ride and a very much lower payload capability. Neither is 'better' than the other; they are just each made for a specific job.

Same rules apply in loading. To the surprise of some, the same rules apply to loading of both vehicle types and concern:

- Size of load
- Weight distribution
- Packing method
- Securing the load

Capacity – weight and bulk

Never overload. The prime rule in operating any vehicle is not to overload. Despite their toughness, it applies to off-roaders as well. Every engineered object has strength criteria to which it is designed – with margins that are adequate or generous accord-

Margins of durability, strength, handling and braking will be eroded if you overload. Remember also load density. Max GVW may arrive with space still spare.

Typical 'biggest box' – mm (in)

Luxury 4x4 – Range Rover

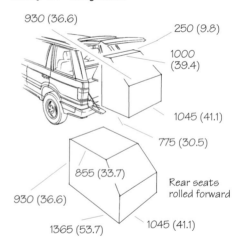

Defender 90

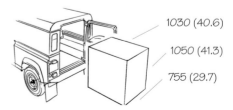

Laid low by the laws of life – or physics (below), this old warrior might have been designed to illustrate the paragraph opposite about the consequences of overloading. Sometimes you get away with it (right). Load density is low but centre of gravity is at tree top level!

ing to design philosophy. Overloading eats into strength and durability margins, adversely affecting handling and performance – as well as safety.

Max payload? EEC kerb weight includes a 75 kg driver and a tank of fuel. 'Payload' is the remaining *weight* you can carry before hitting max GVW – gross vehicle weight. Salesmen and handbooks are equally shy of stating these figures clearly. Knowing them, though, you can come up with some simple guidelines for your useable payload:

- 4 passengers plus xx kilos cargo
- 2 passengers plus xx kilos cargo
- Driver plus xxx kilos ... etc.

Beware load density. A cubic foot of lead vs a cubic foot of compressed straw is an analogy of weight vs bulk that would immediately catch our attention. With high density loads the availability of spare space will obscure the fact that the payload limit has been reached. Equally, with sacks of feathers you'll run out of space before you run out of payload. This kind of problem often sidles up, uninvited, if you are running a vehicle commercially or planning an

overland journey in it.

Margins, off-road weights. If you are coming at the problem from the other direction – What vehicles do I need for this job? – choose a vehicle specification which will comfortably cope with the weight involved rather than be on the limits. This is especially important off-road where you need to give the vehicle the widest margins you can.

Even off-roaders are designed to have a max payload. Know the figure you can add to the driver + fuel-inclusive kerb weight. X people plus Y kg of cargo. Affects handling, safety.

Looking aft in a van-type body: heavy fuel and water cans stowed mid-wheelbase and strapped down against a strong bulkhead.

Weight distribution

What it can take. As the sample axle load table at Section 8.2 shows, all off-roaders are designed, when fully laden, to take a greater load on their springs and axles at the rear because that is the inevitable nature of a normal bonneted design.

Weight distribution would be better termed weight concentration. Keep it low down and at the front of the load bed. Aim for 50/50 front/rear.

Mid-wheelbase, low down. You have seen them; running around, tail-down, headlights pointed skywards ... . Control over weight distribution lies with the operator. On-road, where speeds are higher it is important from a handling point of view; off-road and where conditions are on the limits, especially regarding flotation, the nearer a vehicle can get to a 50/50 fore and aft axle load condition the better it will be. The overloaded end is the end that sinks first in the mud or soft sand. *Keeping the main load ahead of the rear axle* and as low down as possible will enhance both handling and flotation.

Distribution within the load. Thus even within a given load which may get close to your vehicle's maximum GVW it is sensible to place high density items at the front of the load bed and as close to the floor as possible (eg. the fuel cans, photo, previous page).

Check weights for best tyre pressures. Users regularly operating in limiting flotation conditions at less than maximum payload where rear axle load is low, can benefit from a calculated assessment of how low rear tyre pressures can go. Where standard loads or load kits are involved it would pay, as suggested at Section 8.2, to have a vehicle weighed front and rear to determine what axle loads really are.

Eliminate roof racks, external bolt-ons. A natural corollary of this attention to weight distribution is the elimination of roof racks or other external bolt-on paraphernalia. These items increase a vehicle's moment of inertia in pitch and roll and can be a safety hazard when misused. Many expedition vehicles have been grossly overloaded on the roof rack – and some, unsurprisingly, have paid the price by tipping. That is if fatigue cracks have not taken their toll beforehand.

Oh, alright then. There are many operators, however, for whom a roof rack is essential and in these cases remember that the maximum roof load recommended for most vehicles is seldom much above 75 kg. This is enough to accommodate light bulky items such as ladders, small-section timber, canoes and the like.

Whatever you do, and however many times you may have seen pictures of the misguided doing so, do not be tempted to

Grossly overladen roof rack – fuel and water cans – and the result when a surprise dune edge looms. Hard to see with a high sun but good driving and loading could have avoided the roll.

put rows of fuel cans on the roof. It will overstress the vehicle and is a handling-related accident waiting to happen.

Effect of trailers. Remember that a trailer, with its appropriate trailer nose load on the towing hook (see Section 4.1 and 6.4), will, for a given actual nose load, exert a disproportionately high download on the rear axle because the tow hitch is well aft of the axle line. If this sounds unlikely, check the diagram here. This is another reason to keep cargo mass as far forward as possible.

The camel seems to be drawing the owner's attention to a Case B situation in the diagram below. Senior Toyota pickups like this are not designed to bulk-out with high-density cargo, especially with that much rear overhang. (See previous spread.)

Axle load vs load position – 250 kg load

Note how in position B, with the 250 kg 40 inches aft of the axle, the rear axle load increases by more than the added payload. Front axle load is less than at kerb weight.

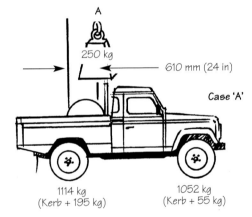

250 kg ⟵ 610 mm (24 in)

Case 'A'

1114 kg
(Kerb + 195 kg)

1052 kg
(Kerb + 55 kg)

Defender 110 HCPU Tdi at kerb weight

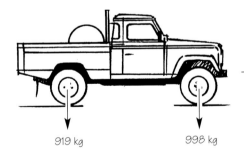

919 kg

998 kg

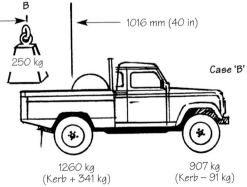

B

250 kg ⟵ 1016 mm (40 in)

Case 'B'

1260 kg
(Kerb + 341 kg)

907 kg
(Kerb − 91 kg)

NB. Danger of exceeding axle weights.
A 638 kg load positioned aft at B would increase rear axle load to the top limit of 1850 kg. Front axle load in this case would be 250 kg lighter than at kerb weight.

Avoid roof rack or anything that will increase vehicle's moment of inertia. Concentrate load mid-wheelbase. If you really do need one, put only light loads on it.

Packing

Serious work. For other than day-to-day errands, regard packing and securing the load in an off-roader as a separate and discrete task. For recreational, commercial or public utility work it is essential:

• *Packing.* Aim for a methodical modular system so that it is easy to load and unload (in a severe bogging say) and so that you know where everything is.

• *Lashing.* Ensure the load is lashed down to prevent it sliding around and causing damage to the vehicle.

Spare fuel. Built-in fuel tanks cannot be off-loaded when a vehicle is badly bogged but do offer compact storage low-down (ie low centre of gravity) when underfloor tanks are fitted. Metal jerry cans for extra fuel can hardly be bettered for safety and ease of handling. For large quantities, 205 litre (45 gallon) steel drums are effective and very robust but the drums themselves are very heavy and, being round, are not space-efficient within a vehicle – more appropriate to carriage of fuel on trucks.

Water. Hard plastic jerry cans (p 7.28) are the best way to carry spare water. Beware the thin flimsy caravan-shop type. Moveable, demountable and easy to lash.

Modular storage. Methodically organised modular storage within the vehicle(s) is essential if you are to keep track of and prevent damage to the equipment you take. Professional expedition organisations such as British Antarctic Survey have for many years used plastic-lidded boxes that locate one above the other without slipping sideways. Storage boxes similar in concept are now available from most DIY superstores.

It is useful to indicate contents on the side and the lid of each box and also keep a written list of everything.

Securing

Tie-downs. Secure your load to avoid damage to the vehicle and the load itself. Not all vehicles have the right number of (or any) tie-downs – cleats to which you can attach straps or ropes – so positioning and

Gravity keeps things tidy but not in a moving 4x4 off-road. Think about, box, stack and strap-down regular loads. Modular boxes for random loads bring order.

Typical generic payload span*	
Ford Explorer	440 kg
Toyota Colorado TF 5-dr	585 kg
Defender 90	654–923 kg
Shogun 2.5TD 3-dr	700 kg
Defender 110	1020–1245 kg

Depending on engine, body type, suspension and transmission.

Typical unit weights	
205 litre (45 Imp gal) barrel, empty	20 kg
205 litre barrel full of petrol, kerosene	185 kg
" " diesel, lube oil	200 kg
" " water	225 kg
20 litre (4.5 Imp gal) steel jerry can, empty	4 kg
20 litre steel jerry can full of petrol, kerosene	20 kg
" " diesel, lube oil	22 kg
" " water	24 kg

Standard 205 litre (45 Imp gal) barrel, jerry can. Dimensions in mm (inches)

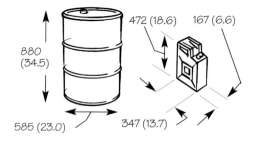

installing these will be part of your modifications programme (See page 7.19.) The driver of a quiet, rattle-free vehicle becomes subject to the 'Rolls-Royce syndrome' and drives more confidently and more smoothly than when his nerves are a-jangle with repetitive internal noise.

Straps and nets. Grip-buckle luggage straps or quick-release tensioning straps are the only reliable ways of securing a load against the provocation of a vehicle ride

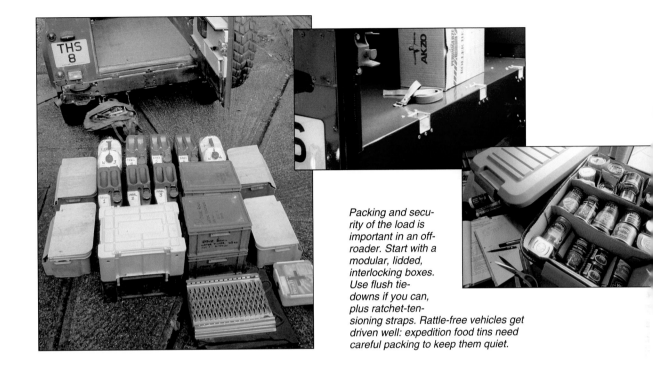

Packing and security of the load is important in an off-roader. Start with a modular, lidded, interlocking boxes. Use flush tie-downs if you can, plus ratchet-tensioning straps. Rattle-free vehicles get driven well: expedition food tins need careful packing to keep them quiet.

over a bad track. You will learn too that often the use of a soft item between the box and the strap will enable it to be cinched tighter. Storage boxes are strapped-down in ones and twos but when soft baggage such as personal kit is then put on top, that too has to be secured, especially in a soft-top vehicle. In this case a groundsheet or other dustproof fabric sheet should be used first with a cargo net on top – it has the additional advantage of denying to thieves a view of the vehicle contents. Grip-buckle and tensioner straps are usually available in DIY stores and outdoor shops. Ratchet-tensioner strapping can often be bought in motorcycle outlets – they are used for securing bikes to trailers.

Install internal lashing cleats to suit your most-used cargo format and for special heavy items that slide about on corners. Well worth the trouble – and essential off-road.

Typical working vehicle load criteria – Defender 110 HCPU example

5 x 205 litre drums diesel – 1000 kg
5 x 205 litre drums water – 1125 kg
(NB Space for 6 drums)

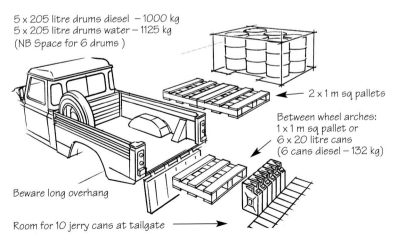

2 x 1 m sq pallets

Between wheel arches:
1 x 1 m sq pallet or
6 x 20 litre cans
(6 cans diesel – 132 kg)

Beware long overhang

Room for 10 jerry cans at tailgate

8.2 Tyres

Tyre types

Specialisation vs compromise. It's a swings-and-roundabouts world full of conflicting alternatives and nowhere more so than when equipping off-roaders with tyres. The diagram, devised by a leading manufacturer, right, says it neatly. There's a special tyre for every condition and the converse is true: whatever tyres you have fitted will have disadvantages in conditions other than those for which they were designed. This is a simple fact of life – and the laws of physics. Any attempt to produce a multi-purpose, compromise tyre results in exactly that – a compromise. Tyre 'A' above is optimised for off-road conditions so is probably noisy and jolty on highways. Tyre 'B' tries to encompass it all, grips well on wet tarmac, is quiet but doesn't do so well off-road as 'A'. Having said that, there are now some very impressive 'all-terrain' tyres.

Tyres – what to look for. The table opposite gives more detail. Seek:

1. Tread suitable to your main terrain type without too much sacrifice on others you will encounter – see table.

2. Flexible sidewalls to permit lower inflation pressures where needed. A higher-than-needed load index (p 8.17) means thicker, stiffer sidewalls – albeit they may better resist rock damage.

3. Speed rating appropriate to your vehicle – table page 8.17.

4. Low-inflation capability appropriate to emergency conditions you may encounter – especially soft sand.

Specialist tyres exist for every use. The converse of that is that for any variation in vehicle use all tyres are a compromise.

Tyres – either/or options

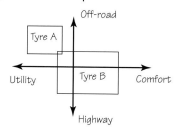

5. Remember the on-road case is also a special case. Most off-road-biased tyres are noisy on-road and may have poor – or bad – wet-tarmac grip.

Makers know best. Know what you want but listen to the tyre makers too. Many will have worked closely with the vehicle manufacturers and will give a technically informed final OK to your choice.

Choosing your tyre. Because an even-handed multi-brand appraisal would take volumes, the well-deserved reputation of Michelin and affiliate BFGoodrich have been singled-out as examples here for their wide range and especially their combined skills with on- and off-road tyres.

Tyres – wider, thinner, less functional

Visual extravagance, cornering and ... ?. If the sidewall of your tyre has '265/30R22' written on it, the '30' means the distance between the rim seat and the tread is only 30% of the tyre width of 265 mm – very thin indeed. The 30 is the aspect ratio. On most sensible tyres it is around 75-85%. Such low profile tyres, invariably purchased with large diameter alloy wheels (22" here) keep stylists and accountants happy and many owners regard them as 'cool'. They usually offer extra cornering grip, high speed capability and poor ride on any but the smoothest roads – minimalist sidewalls don't allow much flex. They are generally quite inappropriate for any off-tarmac use.

Lo-pro – limited choice. With the hitherto virtually standard 15- and 16-inch rims for 4x4s, tyre makers offered tyres for a wide range of needs on these rims – road,

Support ring (high strength steel)

Flexible support (rubber)

The shape of things to come. Bridgestone run-flat as fitted to T180 Toyota RAV4. Like Michelin's Pax, conventional sidewalls permit normal ride and handling. 100 miles at 50 mph deflated. Just as well; specialist fitting needed.

TABLE 1 – TYRE TYPES FOR 4x4s

Road oriented A car tyre only bigger.	Optimised for tarmac. Close tread, relatively smooth, often with sipes ('knife cuts') for wet-tarmac grip. Michelin Diamaris shown.	**For:** Fairly hard 'summer' compound gives long life, quiet, smooth running, good braking. **Against:** Close tread susceptible to quickly filling in mud off-tarmac, reducing traction. Pretty useless off-road in wet conditions.	
Winter tyre Optimised for conditions of rain, snow or ice below 7°C.	New generation 'softer', high silica rubber, quantifiably better at low temperatures. Close, small bold tread. Multiple sipes help wet grip and tarmac cornering. Michelin Alpin 2 shown	**For:** Reduced braking distances, better cornering grip on snow and ice or even at low temperatures in the wet. **Against:** Faster wear in summer conditions. Close tread susceptible to filling in mud, reducing traction.	
Mud tyre General purpose off-road, mud and stony tracks tyre.	Bold, open tread pattern, sharp right-angle edges. Quite narrow, some have 'swept-back' tread pattern designed for particular direction of rotation. The larger the blocks and bigger the spaces between them (voids) the better the mud performance – and the worse the noise and, on wet tarmac, grip. BFGoodrich Mud Terrain (top) – well respected. Below is Michelin 4x4.O/R, chunkier, noisier.	**For:** Very good in all types of mud and clay. **Against:** Grip on wet tarmac not as good as road tyres or 'all-terrains' (below). Some 'heel and toe' wear on large tread blocks shortens life. May be noisy or have limited speed rating. (Note: This is the worst tyre for dry unbroken 'piecrust' sand – dunes – though where sand is already churned and the crust broken, mud tyres can be surprisingly effective.)	
Multi purpose Usually called 'all terrain'	Milder tread than mud tyre. BFGoodrich All Terrain here – an established classic. Very good in sand/rock desert. Accepts low pressures (at low speeds). Sipes enhance wet road grip.	**For:** Excellent compromise for frequent on/off road use, eg farming. Very good at handling the demands of mixed sand/stone desert terrain. Grip on wet tarmac better than mud tyres. **Against:** Outclassed in bad mud by the above.	
Sand tyres Michelin XS shown is benchmark for sand. Tread design brazenly pirated.	XS has subtle tread with shouldered blocks to compress sand in inverted 'cups' (enhancing flotation and traction) rather than cutting through it. Circumferentially grooved tyres look good but are ineffective in sand.	**For:** XS excels in all types of sand. Robust enough for all desert terrain. **Against:** Very poor grip on wet tarmac. 'Heel and toe' wear on tread blocks, noisy. Takes ultra low pressures but sidewall bulge vulnerable to damage on rock; take care. (Note: In mud, good flotation, poor traction.)	

Every optimised tyre has its pros and cons; best off-road performance is usually at cost of on-road grip in wet conditions. Best sand and best mud tyres are opposites.

heavy mud, snow, sand, 'all-terrain'. With low-profile tyres , choice is usually limited to road treads only.

Deflation pressures? The off-road scenario for low profile tyres is not good since a softer tyre here puts the rim even closer to the ground risking rim and tyre damage. But Michelin OK off-road deflation to 80% of road pressures for tracks (but not below 1.5 bar, max speed 40 mph) and 70% for mud and sand (1.5 bar min, 12 mph max).

Many are besotted by the cosmetics of wheels and tyres such as this 325/30R21W on 11" 'cotton reel' rims (the W = 168 mph max which should liven up the school run.) With a reputation for tramlining and poor ride, though, these tyres cannot be recommended for an all-round 4x4.

Axle loads and tyre pressures off-road

Off-road tyre pressures – relevance of axle loads. For 'best' off-road tyre pressures you need to know axle load. The sequence:

- Know front/rear axle load – samples at Table 2 below. Go to a weighbridge – photo next page.
- From this determine tyre pressure for a chosen maximum speed – Table 3. (Ask for a similar table for your tyres.)

The figures in your vehicle handbook assume maximum load and a vehicle free to go to its maximum speed; in other words, foolproof day-to-day on-road conditions.

Tyre pressures and axle loads are interdependent – both affect sidewall deflection, a critical criterion.

There are also handling considerations. Off-road you'll sometimes get better performance – flotation and traction – with tyres at lower pressures. Going too low – or too fast at these low pressures – can damage the tyres (or produce handling problems) so you have to do some checks.

Simple checking first. Tyres give their optimum performance – the best combination of grip, handling response, operating temperature (important for structural reasons) and a degree of shock absorption – when their elements (tread, beads and sidewalls) are optimally disposed to one anoth-

---

TABLE 2 – SAMPLE VEHICLES: ACTUAL FRONT / REAR AXLE LOADS					
Vehicle type *Maximum weights:* GVW and maximum individual axle loads. See notes 1 and 2. GVW / front / rear max	Body type and/or man- ual/auto	Axle loads at *kerb weight –* 2.5 petrol engine Front/rear Kg	Axle loads at *kerb weight –* V8 petrol engine Front/rear Kg	Axle loads at *kerb weight –* 2.5D or VM engine Front/rear Kg	Axle loads at *kerb weight –* Tdi engine Front/rear Kg
Defender 90 Std: 2400/1200/1380 Hi-load suspension: 2550/1200/1500	Soft top Pick up Hard top Station wagon	922/714 919/717 916/767 911/790	908/719 905/722 902/770 897/793	946/710 943/722 940/763 935/786	971/724 967/727 960/786 959/834
New Range Rover All versions: 2780/1320/1840	manual auto		*4.0 V8* 1171/1081 1176/1086	*4.6 V8* 1171/1081 1176/1086	*2.5 diesel* 1187/1072 -

NOTE 1 – Using the figures. *Example, ringed above:*

> **Defender 90**
> Std: 2400/1200/1380

This means the Defender with standard suspension (ie not fitted with the hi-load heavy duty springs) has a maximum loaded weight of 2400 kg. *Individual* axles can take a max of up to 1200 kg at front, 1380 kg at rear – but not at the same time (since 1200 +1380 = 2580 would exceed the 2400 kg GVW maximum for standard suspension).

NOTE 2 – Using the figures. *Example, ringed above:*

> **Defender 90.** Station wagon, Tdi engine, axle loads at kerb weight: 959/834

This means an *empty* Tdi Defender 90 Station Wagon has axle loads of 959 kg front and 834 kg rear. If you aim to carry a 300 kg payload in the rear (assume exactly over the rear axle), the rear axle load will be 1134 kg. So 959/1134 are the figures you would enter into the tyre pressures table on the next page.

NOTE 3: Gross vehicle weight (GVW), ie weight fully laden, is the maximum weight for which the suspension was designed so is constant for a given vehicle type. Only where the suspension itself has an alternative specification, as in the Defender 90 , or where heavier diesel engines are fitted, are different GVWs or GVW axle loads shown.

NOTE 4: Because it is not always easy to get weight distribution front/rear precisely correct, individual axles may be loaded to the 'max' figures shown so long as the *overall* GVW is not exceeded. Note that in most cases the sum of the front and rear 'max' figures would exceed the GVW so do not load <u>both</u> axles to max. The Defender 110 has max and actual axle loads at GVW that are the same.

NOTE 5: Kerb weight (sometimes 'EEC kerb'), is defined as unladen weight plus full fuel plus a 75 kg driver.

er. The main criterion in determining this is sidewall deflection and this is established by the load on the tyre and its internal pressure. There is thus a theoretically optimum tyre pressure for every change in axle load or payload within the vehicle – and then for every speed. This is why front and rear tyre pressures are different. In practice, and to ensure you do not spend your whole life changing tyre pressures, there is some latitude and usually two sets of pressures (ie front and rear) are quoted for vehicles – one for the unladen and one for the fully laden condition. These, of course, are based on

individual front and rear axle loads – the weight each axle carries – and they assume freedom to use all the performance the vehicle offers in terms of speed.

Desperate for traction and flotation?
But you can get more from your tyres if you *know the loads and can stick to strict speed limits*. Michelin are mature enough to quote these for the sensible user. Examples of axle loads, and an indication of what affects them, are given in Table 2 opposite. If you apply these to Table 3 below – use the Note – you will get the *minimum* pressures that you may use for a given load and speed. If all this seems a bit academic sitting reading this book, in practice you will find it a pillar of common sense and harmony between tyre makers who know their stuff and an off-road operator who needs all the help he or she can get in difficult conditions.

If this sounds as if it is written from the heart, it is! Sometimes off-road flotation is very poor indeed. You don't want to run your tyres so soft as to risk damaging them but you do need to know the most deflation you can safely use, accept the associated speed and load limits – and keep moving.

If you want the best tyre performance or want to save the time wasted in recovery in your fleet, check axle loads and tyre pressures.

NOTE – Using the figures. *Example:* Take the Tdi Defender 90 Station Wagon on the previous page (Note 2) with front/rear axle loads of 959 and 1134 kg.
• **On-road.** Reading from the axle load column below, for a 120 kph road speed (interpolating or using next highest pressure), the vehicle should run at 1.5 bar front and 1.9 bar rear *minimum*.
• **Off-road.** Similarly the off-road figures that may be used, where you want the lowest pressures for reasons of flotation or ride, are 1.0 bar front and 1.3 bar rear *on tracks* at a *speed not exceeding 65 kph.* If you got bogged in soft sand, the emergency soft would be 0.6 bar front and rear *at a speed not over 20 kph (12 mph).* (NB Here, for handling reasons, 0.6 bar not recommended; see Table 4.)

TABLE 3 – EXAMPLE: 7.50x16 MICHELIN XS – PRESSURES vs WHEEL LOAD/ SPEED

Axle load	Wheel load	On-road tyre pressures – bar										Off-road pressures – bar	
kg	kg				Speed km/hr							Track	Sand/ mud
		120	110	100	90	80	65	50	40	30	20	65 kph	20 kph
2000	1000	3.75	3.8	3.8	3.5	3.4	3.4	3.4	3.3	3.3	3.1	2.6	1.3
1880	940	3.5	3.4	3.3	3.2	3.2	3.1	3.1	3.1	3.0	2.8	2.4	1.2
1800	900	3.3	3.2	3.1	3.0	3.0	3.0	3.0	2.9	2.8.	2.7	2.2	1.1
1600	800	2.8	2.7	2.7	2.6	2.6	2.6	2.5	2.5	2.4	2.3	1.9	0.9
1400	700	2.4	2.3	2.3	2.2	2.2	2.2	2.1	2.1	2.1	1.9	1.6	0.7
1200	600	1.9	1.9	1.8	1.8	1.8	1.8	1.7	1.7	1.7	1.6	1.3	0.6
1000	500	1.5	1.5	1.5	1.4	1.4	1.4	1.4	1.3	1.3	1.2	1.0	0.6
800	400	1.1	1.1	1.1	1.0	1.0	1.0	1.0	1.0	0.9	0.9	0.8	0.6

It may well be that your handbook does not give the individual axle load detail shown in Table 2 on the previous spread. Use a public weighbridge to get your own, weighing each axle in turn then the whole vehicle as a double check.

So axle loads really matter? If you are wondering how you got by all these years without knowing axle loads to work out tyre pressures, it is because vehicle manufacturers usually quote catch-all figures that assume max payload, on-road driving up to max speed and play safe. The axle load calculations apply when, off-road, you are trying for the lowest a tyre pressure you can safely use to get best flotation and traction.

The span of the figures is surprising. An unladen Defender 90 rear axle carries only 38% of the load that the rear axle of a laden Defender 110 does. Axle load is greatly (and even more surprisingly) affected by load distribution – that diagram on page 8.5 gives the well-I'll-be-darned facts.

What to actually do. Having chosen your tyre type from Table 1, and ascertained your axle load from Table 2 (or from a weighbridge – left) you would apply it to a manufacturer's data sheet like Table 3 to get the operating pressures on- and off-road.

NOTE – Table 4

Michelin off-road tyres. Although low speeds are involved, using the example in Table 5, Land Rover have imposed their own lower limits of tyre pressures for handling reasons and to reduce the possibility of dislodging a tyre.

If you are using non-original-equipment (OEM) tyres the manufacturer or dealer should have a table like Table 3. Don't take no for an answer. Customer service should help.

Certain of Michelin's off-road tyres are, however, cleared by Michelin structurally and operationally to function at and benefit from exceptionally low pressures – down to 0.60 bar (9 psi) – where the absolute limit of flotation must be combined with the tyres' other unique features. Michelin stipulate only that 'track' and 'emergency flotation' speed limits (right-hand columns, Table 4) are observed and that, in sand, tubes should be used in case sand gets between bead and seat.

These tyres will perform magnificently but you must still treat them with care; beware of damaging sidewalls, beware of lateral stress like sharp steering inputs that could roll them off the rims. Observe the speed limits scrupulously, re-inflate when clear. Pressures, listed against axle load, for the various tyres are shown right. Sample axle loads are show at Table 2 (page 8.10). If not available, check yours on a weighbridge.

Other manufacturers. If you use another brand of tyres, information like this should be available. Don't go down to these kinds of pressures without specific clearance from the manufacturer's Technical Department.

TABLE 4 – MICHELIN OFF-ROAD TYRES			
Tyre type/size	Axle load kg	Tracks 40 mph max	Sand/mud 12 mph max
7.00 R16 XCL	1000	1.20	0.60
	1400	1.90	1.00
	1600	2.30	1.20
	1800	2.70	1.40
7.00 R16 XZL	1200	1.30	0.60
	1400	1.50	0.80
	1600	1.80	0.90
	1800	2.70	1.30
7.50 R16 XCL	1000	1.10	0.70
	1400	1.80	0.90
	1600	2.20	1.10
	1800	2.50	1.30
	2240	3.30	1.80
7.50 R16 XS	1200	1.30	0.60
	1600	1.90	0.90
	1800	2.20	1.10
	2000	2.60	1.30
7.50 R16 XZL (Also known as '4x4 O/R')	1200	1.40	0.70
	1400	1.70	0.90
	1600	2.00	1.10
	1800	2.40	1.30
	2240	3.10	1.80

Tyre pressures – three conditions

Optimum pressures. So partly to recap and partly to re-establish perspective on a subject you may not have considered quantitatively before, to get the best out of your tyres and vehicle on:

• roads
• on tracks and poor roads and
• emergency flotation conditions

you need three sets of tyre pressures. As we have seen (Sections 4.7, 4.8 and in the diagram here), lowering tyre pressures increases the size of the tyre 'footprint' and thus lowers the pressure per unit area on the ground. The ground is thus less stressed and will yield better traction and flotation, so assisting a vehicle in traversing difficult terrain or in self-recovery if it is stuck.

The on-road constraints. Having the best soft sand flotation in the world isn't much use to you if are hustling down a winding tarmac road late for an appointment. The on-road handling requirements of the vehicle have to override possible off-road demands when the vehicle is in everyday use. Off-road low pressures would bring the following problems on-road:

• Overheating of the tyres
• Danger of rolling the tyre off the rim
• Sluggish, soggy steering response.

What deflation does

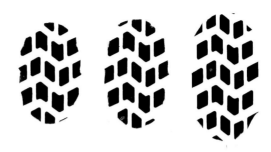

Tyre footprint of Michelin XS at (left to right) road pressures, track pressure and emergency flotation pressure. Percentage increases in area are considerable.

These are symptoms that range from the inconvenient to the downright dangerous. Hence there are optimum pressures and concomitant speed limits – *which must be observed* – for roads, tracks and emergency flotation conditions.

What you finish up with. What you need, as a result of all these deliberations, then, is a table like the one below. Do it on a piece of card, laminate it and keep it in the vehicle with your inflator and pressure gauges – see overleaf.

Different tyre pressures for different conditions. ESSENTIAL to keep within speed and load limitations and re-inflate tyres when back on easier ground.

TABLE 5 – SAMPLE VEHICLE – DEFENDER 90: MANUFACTURER'S TYRE PRESSURES

(Single, all-loads, all-speeds handbook pressures underlined. Track/emergency pressures are higher than those at Table 4 for handling reasons. Drive very carefully and Table 4's lower figures could be used.

Tyre no	Tyre name and size	Load index / speed symbol (See table on page 8.17)	Vehicle weight	Hard-road pressures (to max speed) Front / rear	Tracks and poor roads. 40 mph max Front / rear	Off-road emergency flotation. 12 mph max Front / rear
1.	Michelin 205 R 16 X M+S	99Q	Kerb	1.9 / 2.1	1.6 / 1.9	1.2 / 1.2
			GVW	<u>1.9 / 2.4</u>	1.7 / 2.1	1.2 / 1.4
2.	Michelin 7.50 R 16 X 4x4	108N	Kerb	1.8 / 2.0	1.4 / 1.6	1.1 / 1.2
	Michelin 7.50 R 16 X-CL	112L	GVW	<u>1.9 / 2.9</u>	1.5 / 2.2	1.1 / 1.7
	Michelin 7.50 R 16 XS	108N				
	Michelin 7.50 R 16 XZL	108N				
3.	Goodyear 7.50 R 16 G90	116N	Kerb	1.8 / 2.0	1.4 / 1.6	1.1 / 1.2
			GVW	<u>1.9 / 2.9</u>	1.5 / 2.2	1.1 / 1.7
4.	BFGoodrich 265/75R16 MudTerrain	120Q	Kerb	1.7 / 1.9	1.4 / 1.4	0.8 / 0.8
and....	BFGoodrich 265/75R16 AllTerrain	120Q	GVW	<u>1.9 / 2.4</u>	1.4 / 1.6	1.0 / 1.4

Inflation, pressures, tubeless, repairs

Tyre pressures – speed warning. It is important to emphasise, again, the speed limitations when driving with tyres at reduced off-road pressures shown in the columns on the previous spread. Never exceed the speed limits shown there. Driving too fast on under-inflated tyres will cause structural damage to your tyres through overheating and possible delamination of the carcass. It will usually produce unacceptable handling and the possibility of rolling the tyres off the rims on corners. Be sure always to *be equipped with an accurate tyre pressure gauge and a re-inflation pump* if you are going off-roading.

Pressure gauges. Care of tyres can be set at nought by that weakest of weak links the tyre pressure gauge. The pen-type gauge is often inaccurate and some dial gauges are not necessarily much of an improvement. Even the good ones should still be checked against one or more air hoses at service stations which in the UK have to be checked by law. Alas these too cannot always be trusted. Keep your proven tyre gauge in a dust-proof plastic bag in the vehicle at all times.

WARNING. A repeat warning about not exceeding speed and load limitations on tyres at reduced pressures. Get, and take care of, an accurate tyre pressure gauge.

Re-inflation. After pressure reduction for off-road work tyres *must* be re-inflated before road speeds are resumed. A half-hearted resolve to 're-inflate at the next garage' is not good enough and is dangerous. Re-inflation is best done by an electric pump carried with you. That way it can be done as and when needed. Again you should be circumspect about the standard of unit you buy. Tyres fitted to off-roaders need a lot of air compared to car tyres so get a pump that is large, robust and can stand up to long periods of use without overheating. Those available in UK consumer motoring outlets are rarely up to this standard.

Tubeless tyres – no. When prolonged severe off-road conditions are likely – an expedition or an aid project, for example – it is in most cases sensible to fit tubes in your tyres. In extreme conditions when inflation has been reduced to emergency soft, unseating of a tubeless tyre from the rim and total loss of pressure could occur. Secondly, changing or repairing a tyre by hand in the field is possible with a tubed tyre: the same thing would not normally be possible with a tubeless tyre. For those you need a lot of air at a high pressure – but see below.

Tubeless tyres – yes? An on-board compressor and air reservoir, however, would make re-mounting tubeless tyres in the field feasible. It would provide a large volume of fast-moving air to blow a tubeless tyre back onto its rim. BOAB, originating in ever-practical Australia, (www.boab.biz) have devised exactly that – amongst other sensible, down-to-earth equipment for tyre related problems in the outback such as bead-breakers, and a repair kit for properly fixing punctures and damage to outer covers.

New wheels? Wheels designed with an internal AH rim (asymmetric hump) profile to enhance bead retention of tubeless tyres at very low pressures are, by some, not recommended for use with tubes. Low pressure flexing of the tyre is said to cause chafing of the tubes on the internal rim humps. This is seldom the case in fact but check with your tyre manufacturer when fitting tubes to tubeless tyres.

TruckAir, fan-cooled 12v inflator is designed for prolonged use on 4x4s and raises a 7.50x16 from 1 to 2 bar in under 4 min. Excellent Michelin gauge (lower rt) holds a reading until zeroed. (www.demon-tweeks.co.uk).

Component display (left) of BOAB tubeless tyre kit. Compressor fills reservoir; released air re-seats tyre. Useful equipment for small expedition or aid group of vehicles. BOAB stow-and-forget, all-types kit (top right) includes subtly-shaped tyre levers and ingenious 'Tyre-plier' for shifting tyre beads (middle right). Repair kit box (right) is comprehensive and includes all-important step-by-step booklet to refresh your memory in the stress of the moment. Needs only paintbrush and jar of tyre lubricant – makes a big difference..

'Cold' tyre pressures. Tyre pressure should always be checked 'cold', ie after the vehicle has been standing for an hour or more, nominal 17°C. Pressures should be varied (up or down) by 5% for every 10°C. So a 'book' figure of 2.0 bar at 17°C should be set at 2.2 on a cool vehicle at an ambient of 37°C. Never 'bleed' pressure from a warmed-up tyre.

Tyre repairs in the field. For prolonged operation in the field in remote areas you should acquire the ability to remove and repair tyres and tubes. It will take time but is surprisingly easy to do once you have had a demonstration from your local tyre-fitting establishment. Be sure they show you the all-manual way, not using a rotary bead

breaker. Long tyre levers, tyre lubricant and technique are the ingredients. And exclusion of grit or sand from the tyre during the process; use a clean ground sheet. Your driving should preclude the possibility of serious damage to the tyre carcase so there is no need for the carriage of heavy extra spare wheels. If you do not have the 'Tyre-plier' shown here, placing the wheel under the chassis and jacking between the chassis and the tyre will shift the reluctant bead.

Data on load and speed ratings, tyre construction and build are inscribed on the sidewall – see diagram opposite for full data and tables below right for decoding load index and speed symbol. Thus the Michelin X M+S 244 in the photographs, having a 99T load/speed rating is cleared to a maximum load per tyre of 775 kg up to 118 mph (at appropriate pressures).

Tyre nomenclature

If you have to buy an unfamiliar tyre, everything you need to know about it will be written on the sidewall. If it isn't, don't buy it.

The small print. A considerable amount of information is inscribed on the sidewall (and tread) of tyres, all of which is relevant to its specification – despite the assurances of those who would try to sell you tyres that are 'the same' as the one you specifically seek. The principal dimensions of a tyre are its width (not the depth between tread and bead) and the wheel diameter to which it is fitted. Thus a '7.50 x 16' is a tyre designed for a 16 inch diameter wheel and having a normal inflated width (ie the external nominal width of the inflated, unladen tyre) of 7.50 inches; it is not necessarily the width of the tread itself. This width data can also be shown in millimetres (still allied to a rim size in inches) as in the 205 x 16. Other criteria, some of which are shown in the diagram opposite, are:

Manufacturer's generic name such as MIchelin 'X'

Manufacturer's type number or name, eg XCL, Rangemaster, Wrangler

Nominal section width in mm, eg 205, 235 (ie, max width of tyre, not tread, on normal rim)

Aspect ratio (cross section height:width ratio percentage)

    – follows metric width when shown (so a 235/70 would be nominally 235 mm wide
    with a tyre sidewall height approx 70% of the size of the width, ie 164.5 mm)

'R' for radial

Overall tyre diameter (usually given in the US)

Load index/speed symbol – see tables opposite

Maximum load and pressure – in lb and psi in addition to load index (US requirement)

Sidewall and tread construction – plies and material, eg steel, rayon (US requirement)

Ply rating – (equivalent) sidewall plies in a cross-ply tyre

Wear indicators

Country of manufacture

Direction of rotation – sometimes shown when relevant

ECE and US Dept of Transport type approval mark

Tyre sidewall markings

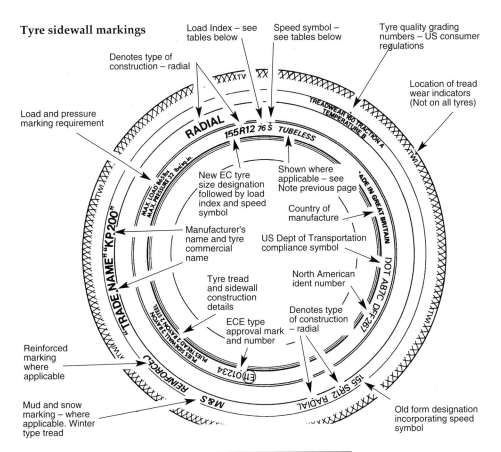

Tyre load index			
(NB Max load *per tyre* at full road pressures at speed shown by accompanying speed symbol)			
Index	kg	Index	kg
97	730	111	1090
98	750	112	1120
99	775	113	1150
100	800	114	1180
101	825	115	1215
102	850	116	1250
103	875	117	1285
104	900	118	1320
105	925	119	1360
106	950	120	1400
107	975	121	1450
108	1000	122	1500
109	1030	123	1550
110	1060	124	1600

Tyre speed symbol		
(NB Max speed at full road pressures at per-tyre load shown by load index		
Symbol	kph	mph
J	100	62
K	110	68
L	120	75
M	130	81
N	140	87
P	150	93
Q	160	100
R	170	105
S	180	113
T	190	118
U	200	124
H	210	130
V	240	149
VR	>210	>130
W	270	168
Y	300	186
ZR	>240	>149

Tyre pressures – bars to (nearest whole) psi			
Bars	psi	Bars	psi
1.1	16	2.7	39
1.2	17	2.8	41
1.3	19	2.9	42
1.4	20	3.0	44
1.5	22	3.1	45
1.6	23	3.2	46
1.7	25	3.3	48
1.8	26	3.4	49
1.9	28	3.5	51
2.0	29	3.6	52
2.1	30		
2.2	32	4.3	62
2.3	33	4.4	64
2.4	35	4.5	65
2.5	36	4.6	67
2.6	38	4.7	68

Using the figures: A load/speed index of 108N defines ultimate capability: max load of 1000 kg per tyre; max speed 87 mph. Having selected your tyre, then apply tyre pressures according to actual loads and speeds in tables 1-5.

Section 9

Reference

9.1 Glossary

Separate body and box-section chassis. Very strong construction method permitting many body styles to be used on same running gear. Puts weight down low giving low centre of gravity. If single body-style permits it, modern approach is to go for unitary body-chassis. Overall result structurally efficient, stiffer torsionally, just as strong if not stronger, usually lighter, sometimes lower.

Anatomy. Diagram shows anatomy and concept of assembly exemplified by an early Discovery. Start is with a box section chassis lowered onto axle / suspension sub-assemblies. Engine, gearbox and transfer gearbox – as a single unit – is then lowered onto chassis to pick up on four mounts, two aft and two at mid-point of engine. Body shell – wired, trimmed, furnished on another line – is then lowered (the 'body-drop') onto engine-chassis unit to pick up on ten rubber body mounts (six of which highlighted here with arrows). Separate body and chassis is very robust. Has pros and (mainly) cons – see comments at far left.

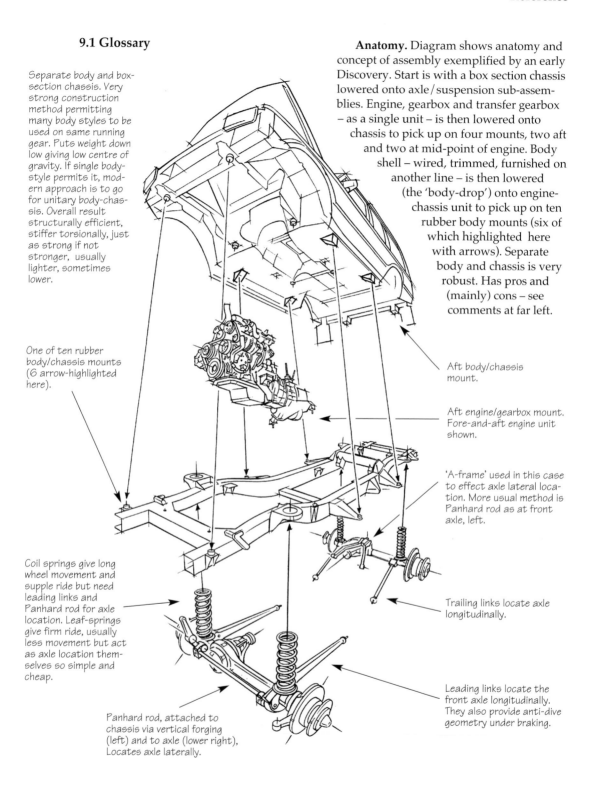

One of ten rubber body/chassis mounts (6 arrow-highlighted here).

Aft body/chassis mount.

Aft engine/gearbox mount. Fore-and-aft engine unit shown.

'A-frame' used in this case to effect axle lateral location. More usual method is Panhard rod as at front axle, left.

Coil springs give long wheel movement and supple ride but need leading links and Panhard rod for axle location. Leaf-springs give firm ride, usually less movement but act as axle location themselves so simple and cheap.

Trailing links locate axle longitudinally.

Leading links locate the front axle longitudinally. They also provide anti-dive geometry under braking.

Panhard rod, attached to chassis via vertical forging (left) and to axle (lower right), Locates axle laterally.

ABS. Anti-lock braking system; prevents wheels locking under maximum braking. Works on the principle of braking a wheel until it just begins to skid (this is the point where braking efficiency would drop off dramatically) and then releasing the brake pressure and re-applying the brakes. Wheel speed sensors identify the skid point and trigger a release in brake pressure. The cycle is repeated many times a second – with appropriate 'cobblestone' feedback on the brake pedal to indicate you are in ABS mode. See also Cadence braking.

A-frame. Means of effecting lateral location of the rear axle in some vehicles. Also controls axle rotation. See diagram left. More usual method is use of Panhard rod.

Air suspension. Rear (and sometimes front and rear) springing effected by inflatable airbags as in buses and commercial vehicles. Supple ride. Easy to engineer self-levelling and variable suspension heights into the system. Used by Land Rover, Porsche, Volkswagen and Toyota 4x4s.

Anti-lock brakes. See ABS above.

Anti-roll bar (ARB). A U-shaped bar of steel (about 25 mm diameter) anchored at the bottom of the U to each side of the chassis in pivoting rubber mounts. The free ends of the U are attached to each end of a front and/or rear axle to limit roll of the body relative to that axle. If the chassis/body is called on to move up and down parallel to the axle the ARB offers no interference; if, however body roll forces are induced by cornering, the twisting moments on the ARB tend to inhibit roll. In an off-road vehicle an ARB must be carefully designed not to limit axle articulation excessively and thus affect off-road performance. There are ways round this; see panel, page 2.6.

Approach angle. In side-view, the angle between the ground and a line, ahead of the vehicle, joining the periphery of the front wheel and (typically) the front bumper or other low component. It represents the size

or steepness of a slope or obstacle that can be approached or climbed without striking bodywork. See page 3.6.

Articulation. The ability of one axle to move – left wheel up, right wheel down or vice versa – relative to the chassis or its fellow axle. It is a measure of the ease with which wheels can stay in contact with the ground – and thus retain traction – on very 'twisty' off-road terrain. See page 3.8 and 5.4.

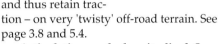

Articulation angle, longitudinal. See Longitudinal articulation angle.

Assembly. See opposite.

Axle location. Axles and wheels move vertically relative to a chassis/body but must be located accurately longitudinally and laterally. Semi-elliptic leaf-springs fulfilled the suspension and location function in the old days and many current pickups. Diagram facing page shows how the function is achieved with coil springs favoured for better ride and longer wheel movement.

Axles, live, one-piece. Also referred to as rigid or (incorrectly as) beam axles, in which the drive shafts to the wheels run within rigid casings as in the diagram above. Live axles permit large wheel movement and give better ground clearance for a given wheel diameter compared with independent suspension (see p 3.7) but unsprung weight is higher so ride quality can suffer. Toyota Landcruiser was available with live axle or independent front suspension for different markets.

Battery designation. Three figures define battery designation by encapsulating performance in relation to standard criteria. A '380/120/90' battery thus has a maximum rapid-discharge current at -18°C of 380 amp; it can maintain a discharge of 25 amp at 25°C for 120 minutes before reaching a terminal voltage of 10.2 volts. Its rate of voltage drop at the max rapid-discharge of 380 amp (at minus 18°C) will be such that 5-7 seconds after commencement of discharge, voltage will have dropped to 9.0 volts. This is multiplied by 10 to give <u>90</u>.

Bridle. A rope or cable attached to two points – typically the right and left chassis members – of a vehicle and converging to a point of tow rope attachment (see p 5.6).

Cadence braking. A method of manual braking with the foot brake to simulate the action of ABS brakes – see above. Very effective in slippery conditions where brake locking has occurred or might otherwise occur. The driver applies the footbrake in a series of very rapid jabs at the pedal taking the wheels up to the point of brake locking and then releasing them before the inevitable fall-off in braking efficiency takes place. Effects improved braking in any extremely slippery conditions such as ice, snow, wet mud, or rain. See Sec 3.2, 4.11.

Camber. The angle at which, when viewed from the front, the front wheels of a vehicle splay out (positive camber) from the vertical – as shown in diagram. In some layouts it varies with position of suspension. Camber affects lateral control and ideally should be zero at all times. On an off-roader with live ('beam') axles, camber angle is always zero.

Front axle

Camber angle

Capstan winch. A winch, generally mounted on or just behind the front bumper, usually run from an engagable extension to the engine crankshaft. The active component is usually a slowly revolving drum, about 15 cm in diameter, round which a rope may be wound to effect a winching operation. Has the advantage of being powered by the engine at idling speed and being a very low-stress unit that may be used all day without overheating or high (any) electrical load. See Sec 5.4.

Castor (or caster) angle. When the front wheels are moved right or left to steer the vehicle they each move about a steering axis. The aft inclination of this steering axis from the vertical (when viewed from the side) – about 3° in the case of some off-roaders – is the castor angle. Like castors on a tea trolley or office chair, this puts the ground contact point of the wheels behind the

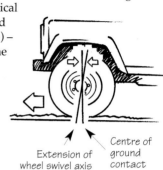

Extension of
wheel swivel axis

Centre of
ground
contact

Distance between the two is
'trail'. Angle between the two
lines is castor angle.

pivot axis and the result is a self-centring action tending to keep the front wheels pointing forward when in forward motion. Note that in deep sand, with a 'bow-wave' build-up of sand ahead of the wheels, the effective ground contact point moves ahead of the steering axis and can give the effect of negative castor with 'runaway' steering. The same thing happens when vehicle is travelling in reverse – the ground contact point being 'ahead' of the steering axis and again tending to make the front wheels 'runaway' to full lock – see Sec 4.4, (failed climbing of steep off-road inclines). Also see Steering feel, page 9.11.

Centre differential. A differential gear device – diagram page 2.4 – between front and rear propeller shafts, installed at the point where the transfer box splits engine power between the front and rear propshafts. Working in the same way as the conventional rear axle differential on a two-wheel drive car, it allows differential rotation of front and rear shafts to accommodate the small rotational differences encountered in normal running, going round sharp corners etc. Such a device is essential in a vehicle having full-time or permanent 4x4.

Vehicles with part-time or selectable 4x4 are not fitted with centre differentials and thus cannot be used in four wheel drive on hard roads. See pages 1.7, 2.2, 2.4, and 2.16.

Chott. Local name for salt flat or sebkha in Tunisia, Algeria and Morocco.

Constant velocity (CV) joints. Another battleground for the accountants vs the engineers. It's CV joints vs Hooke's joints; the latter being the well-known type found as universal joints on prop shafts – cheaper but less able to cope with large angles between input and output shafts. With Hooke's joints at high angles the output drive is jerky – variable velocity rather than constant velocity. For front-wheel drive cars or 4x4s with permanent four-wheel drive, CV joints at the ends of the front axle are virtually essential. (This is between the front drive shafts and the stub axles that the front wheels are mounted on). Without CV joints there is driveline vibration and unacceptable steering feedback on full lock – the steering wheel tending to jerk one way then the other as you go round a steady full-lock turn. Quite a few selectable-4x4 vehicles have Hooke's joints at the front stub axles. Even one or two permanent 4x4 vehicles (see pp 2.2-5) have appeared in this format where bought-in axles were involved. The salesman will almost certainly not know, but it is worth checking you have CV joints at the front when you buy a vehicle.

Continuous rolling contact. Description of a wheel in steady rolling contact with the ground without slip, wheelspin or slide (as with locked brakes). Should be the aim at all times both on- and off-road under drive or braking conditions. See Sec 3.2. Also see Discontinuity of rolling contact, below.

Co-ordinated tow. When recovering a stuck vehicle, the process by which the engine power of both the tug and the stuck vehicle are co-ordinated – usually by a signal from an external marshaller – and the clutches of both vehicles are engaged at the same time. See pp 5.7, 5.8.

Corrugations. Deformation of an unsurfaced track taking the form of transverse, close-pitch undulations at right angles to the direction of the track. Often referred to as 'washboard'. See page 4.34.

Coupled brakes. Brake system installed with certain large trailers whereby the trailer brakes get to be applied at the same time as the brakes of the towing vehicle. Vehicles must be specifically modified to operate this system – with appropriate trailers. See page 4.8.

Cross-axled. See Diagonal suspension.

Cross-ply tyre. Old-design tyre in which the sidewall reinforcement plies run diagonally from the bead towards the tread – each layer of textile at a different angle to its adjacent layer (left). Generally super-

seded by radial-ply tyres (right) whose thinner, more flexible sidewalls and braced tread yield better grip and lower rolling resistance. Cross-ply tyres have thicker, multi-ply sidewalls, not so flexible as radials', hence yield less surface grip on tarmac and return slightly higher fuel consumption. More tolerant of sidewall damage than radials and – see page 4.33 – can have low-cost applications when operating continuously on rock. They are intolerant of reduced pressures in soft going which due to the thick sidewalls, causes overheating and possibly delamination of the tyre.

DAC – Downhill Assist Control. Toyota's version of Land Rover's Hill Descent Control enabling slow, controlled descents to be made on very steep slippery off-road hills. See p.6.8, also HDC.

Departure angle. In side view, the angle between the ground and a line, aft of the vehicle, joining the periphery of the rear wheel and (typically) the rear chassis member or other low component. It represents the size or steepness of a slope or

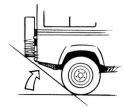

obstacle that can be approached or climbed in reverse without striking bodywork. See page 3.7.

Diagonal suspension. A manifestation occurring off-road when a vehicle is, for example, diagonally crossing a small but well-defined ridge. When the ridge is so severe that, say, the right front wheel and the rear left wheels are on full 'bump' (ie fully up in the wheel arches) and the other wheels are hanging down to the full extent of wheel travel, the

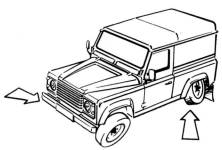

vehicle may be described as being diagonally suspended or on diagonal suspension. Some also refer to this state as being 'cross-axled'. The hanging wheels are usually spinning unless a cross-axle diff-lock is in use. What to do is dealt with at Sec 4.3.

Diagonal wheelspin. The wheelspin that can take place on the fully extended (or off-loaded) wheels in a condition of diagonal suspension as described on the previous paragraph. Can occur crossing ditches or ridges diagonally (see Sec 4.3) but, in the presence of weak ground under these wheels is usually the basis of every lost-traction situation – hence the importance of cross-axle diff-locks (box, page 2.4).

Diff-lock. See first 'Centre differential' above, the box on page 2.4 and, for a light summary, the 'Leonardo' system, Phase 3, page 1.7. Differentials permit power delivered to an axle or pair of prop shafts to be split in any ratio from 100% to 0%, usually self-adjusting according to the load that is at each wheel. Off-load one wheel completely (eg let it spin on ice) and it will spin happily while its companion wheel stays still. To

prevent this, a differential lock is provided – for the centre diff almost invariably, less often for the axles.

The diff-lock locks the centre differential, thus locking front and rear prop shafts together (or, in the case of an axle, the left and right half-shafts). This ensures they revolve at the same speed and traction is regained. Diff-lock is usually engaged for difficult off-road conditions but should never remain engaged on hard grippy roads. See Section 2.

Differential casing. Not to be confused with the centre differential. Each axle, of course, has a normal cross-axle differential at the point where the propeller shaft from the transfer gearbox meets the axle. The size of the crown wheel and pinion plus differential demands a bulge in the axle casing – referred to as the diff casing. It has special significance in off-road vehicles because it is the lowest point of the axle and thus the point of least ground clearance – diagram, page 3.7.

Direct injection. See Indirect injection!

Discontinuity of rolling contact. Generic term for wheelspin and wheel slide – as on locked brakes. See Sec 3.2 and Continuous rolling contact, above.

Divergent. A dynamic condition that 'gets worse of its own accord' – eg an oscillation of ever-increasing amplitude or a turn that, once initiated, tightens up on its own. See also Oversteer, divergent.

Electric parkbrake. Electrically actuated parking brakes found on some recent 4x4s – see p.2.19.

Electric range change. Method of shifting transfer gears by pressing a button or turning a switch instead of by manual lever. See page 2.13.

ETC – Electronic traction control. See 'Traction control'.

Emergency flotation (tyre pressure). Very low tyre pressure (50-60% of normal road pressures), always associated with a low maximum permitted speed (20 kph or 12 mph) used for traversing or recovery from very soft ground. Such low pressures cause extreme tyre sidewall flexing, hence the speed limitation. See page 4.26 and pages 8.10-13.

Emergency soft. Another name for emergency flotation tyre pressure – above.

Engine braking. Vehicle retardation derived from engaging a low gear and taking your foot off the throttle. See also Sec 4.5, 6.4.

Fesh-fesh. Desert terrain: a thin crust of fine gravel or windblown sand laid over deep very fine dust of powder consistency – usually gypsum – often found in hollows around chalky outcrops.. Can be bad enough to bog a vehicle. Hard to spot due to overlay of normal-looking sand. See p.4.31.

Flotation. Characteristic of a vehicle, by reason of large softly inflated tyres, not to sink on soft going such as mud or sand. See Sec 4.7 and Sec 8.2 at page 8.13.

Four-wheel drive (4x4). Vehicle transmission system in which engine power is applied to all four wheels. The term '4x4' (four by four) has the specific connotation that it is a four (wheeled vehicle driven) by four (wheels). See Sec 1.3.

Full-time 4x4. A transmission system on a four-wheeled vehicle in which all four wheels are driven by the engine all the time. (As opposed to a vehicle that is normally in two-wheel drive with four-wheel drive selected by a separate lever or button when required.) See Sections 1.3, 2.1.

Gerotor. Hydraulically engaged multiplate clutch used in diff locks in Jeep's earlier versions of Quadra-Drive 2. See also Haldex limited slip coupling, p 2.5.

Geometric limitations. A term coined for this book to describe the limitations and extent of approach and departure angles, ramp angle, steering lock, articulation and – an even newer term – longitudinal articulation angle. See Sec 3.3.

GDI. See Indirect injection, next page.

Ground clearance. Space between the ground and a given mechanical part of the vehicle. Usually, when quoted for a vehicle, taken as the least for any component on the vehicle – the space under the differential casing. But note difference between under-axle and under-belly clearance – see diagram page 3.7.

Ground offset. Sometimes also called 'steering offset' and concerns what is happening at the point the front tyres touch the ground. Ground offset is the lateral distance, when viewed from the front, between the centre line of the front wheel at ground level and the point where the extension of the steering swivel pin (or king pin) axis touches the ground. Ground offset influences the amount of 'drag' present at each front wheel. When other than zero, these cancel out, side-to-side, in normal straight, hard-road driving. But if, say, the left wheel hits a bump the offset drag on that wheel can cause the steering to also pull to the left. Off-road, the condition is greatly magnified. If one wheel goes through thick 'draggy' mud off-road, or hits a large bump, steering feel and the feedback of shock is considerable, hence the need for a steering damper.

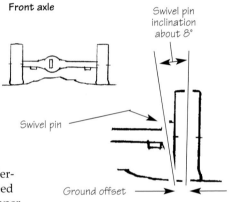

Front axle

Swivel pin inclination about 8°

Swivel pin

Ground offset

Zero offset is the ideal but very hard to achieve with the complexities of all-wheel drive and brakes to cram into the relatively small space of a front wheel. Designers are getting better at it. Land Rover products used to have ground offset approaching three inches but the 'P38' Range Rover has reduced ground offset to 17 mm, enabling use of recirculating ball steering system instead of the feedback-absorbing worm and roller of yesteryear. Some light 4x4s with very small ground offset use high-feedback rack and pinion steering.

Ground stress. Term coined for this book to indicate how much strength is being asked of a particular piece of ground in terms of flotation or lateral shear to accommodate traction, braking or acceleration. See Sections 1.4 and 4.7.

GVW. Gross Vehicle Weight – the maximum permitted laden weight of a vehicle including payload, fuel and driver. This is the figure for which the entire vehicle is designed and stressed. To exceed it is to endanger its durability and safety.

HDC – Hill Descent Control. A method, pioneered by Land Rover, using ABS and throttle control, for keeping a vehicle at or below a target speed enabling slow, controlled descents to be made on very steep slippery off-road hills.

Half-shaft. The shafts taking drive from the axle differential to each wheel.

Handbrake. What it sounds like, usually implemented by small drum brakes on the rear wheels, even if disc brakes are standard. See also Transmission brake, page 9.13. See also 'Electric parkbrake', p.2.19.

Harmonics. Here taken as relating to the natural frequency of a vehicle's suspension system that can influence the formation of transverse surface corrugations on unsurfaced tracks. See Sec 4.9.

Heel and toe wear. Jargon for the uneven front to rear wear on individual blocks of a chunky off-road tyre tread when used for extended periods on roads. Affects on-road grip; see page 8.9, 'Mud tyre' and 'Sand tyre'.

Hi-lift jack. Versatile lever-operated mechanical bumper jack capable of a lift of about a metre. See page 5.5.

Hi-lo lever. Term sometimes used to describe the transfer gearbox range change lever. See Section 1.4.

High box. Transmission status when the two-speed transfer gearbox lever is in the high ratio position – for normal, on-road, day-to-day use. See Sec 1.4.

High load suspension. An option on some vehicles (stronger, dual-rate rear springs) enabling GVW and payload to be raised.

High ratio, high range. Term to describe the transmission when the transfer gearbox lever is in the high position – high box above.

Hydraulic tappets. Method of operating the engine cylinder valves incorporating what is in effect an oil-filled section of the operating rod. Method is 'self-adjusting', eliminates need for and noise emanating from 'valve clearances' associated with normal actuation method.

Hydraulic winch. Winch with rotational function actuated by a hydraulic motor. Power source is hydraulic pump mounted on power take off at rear of gearbox. See Sec 5.4. Some add-on winches work using the vehicle's own power-steering pump.

Independent suspension. Suspension system in which each wheel is separately sprung rather than being attached to a common beam axle. See page 1.4 and diagram p.3.7..

Indirect injection. Diesel fuel injection system in which fuel is injected into a pre-combustion chamber separate from the cylinder. With *direct injection*, the fuel is sprayed directly into the top of the cylinder – more power, more economical, noisier. GDI – gasoline direct injection – has now come to petrol engines offering very lean burn, good economy.

Kerb weight. As defined by EEC, empty vehicle plus full fuel plus 75 kg driver.

King pin. See Swivel pin.

Leading link. Axle locating component. See Trailing/leading link.

Leaf-springs. Suspension system that combines a springing medium with axle location both longitudinally and laterally. Semi-elliptic 'cart springs' anchored at the front, attached to a swivelling link at the rear end. Usually used as rear suspension (front too, sometimes) in pickups and a number of US 4x4s. See Table, page 7.17.

Levelled suspension. A means of eliminating the squat of the rear suspension under load using a hydraulic self-levelling unit or air in air suspension. In the latter case, some vehicles offer extreme high position for off-road use, or squat to ease the attachment of a caravan for towing.

Longitudinal articulation angle. A single number, coined for this book, taking account of both wheel movement and wheelbase, that conveys the off-road, 'twisty ground' potential of an off-road vehicle. It is the angle between the ground and a line joining the front and rear hubs (or tyre periphery) when one wheel is on full bump and the other fully extended. A given maximum wheel movement enhances this capability more on a short wheelbase than on a long wheelbase vehicle. Higher values mean better articulation; small differences in articulation angle make quite large differences to performance. See diagram page 3.8.

Low box. Low range; when the transfer gearbox lever is in the low position – used for difficult off-road conditions demanding greater traction or low speed control. See Sec 1.4.

Low ratio, low range. Term to describe the transmission when transfer gearbox lever is in the low position. See Low box above.

M+S tyres. 'Mud and snow' tyres. A generic term for 4x4 tyres with a road-oriented, not especially bold, tread pattern suitable for mild snow and mud conditions. Now rather superseded by the 'All terrain' description. See Sec 8.2, Tyres.

Marshalling. ('Marshaller' derived from ground-crew who marshal aircraft at airports.) In the context of off-road operations, the detailed direction of a vehicle by a marshaller outside the vehicle who is able to see all four wheels and also the difficult ground being traversed. Marshalling should be undertaken when there is the danger of damaging tyre sidewalls or the underside of the vehicle on rocks or other obstacles. See Look before you leap, Section 3.4.

Mechanical sympathy. In the context of this book, concern for and empathy with the structural stress, durability of, and possible damage to mechanical components of your vehicle. In a phrase, caring about your 4x4. See Mind-set, page 3.2.

Mud tyres. Bold, open-tread tyres optimised for mud with noise and grip disadvantages on hard roads. See page 8.9, Tyres.

Multigrade oil. Lubricating oil exhibiting characteristics of a thin oil at low temperatures and a thick oil at high temperatures. See pages 7.24-27.

NATO towing hook. Large, robust, four-bolt attachment, towing pintle with top-closure originally specified for NATO 7.5 tonne military vehicles. Suitable for off-road towing ; noisy, due to trailer towing eye not being a close fit over the hook. See Sections 4.1 and 6.5.

Nose load. Trailers should be nose heavy in order to avoid weaving instability; the nose load is the amount of nose-heaviness measured at the tow-hitch and must be considered part of the towing vehicle's payload. See Sec 4.1.

NVH. Abbreviation for 'noise, vibration and harshness', an affliction the engineers try very hard to eliminate by the likes of carefully tuned power train mounts, suspension isolation pads, air suspension etc.

OEM or OE. Abbreviation for 'original equipment manufacturer', usually referring to tyres as supplied on a vehicle when bought from the factory.

On-foot recce. Inspecting a difficult off-road obstacle on foot before committing your vehicle to it. See Sec 3.4.

Overrun brakes. Trailer brakes activated by the tendency of the trailer to overtake – or overrun – the towing vehicle when the vehicle brakes or slows down. See Sec 4.1.

Oversteer, divergent. Tendency for an initiated steering command to 'run away' toward full lock or (Sec 4.1) for an extremely nose-heavy trailer to cause this condition on a fast, sharp bend. See Steering feel.

Over-torque. Used in this book to convey the concept of applying too much torque (or power) to the wheels so that they break their grip with the ground and spin.

Panhard rod. A suspension component, a rod of the order of 30 mm diameter and about a metre long, that laterally locates a front or rear axle relative to the chassis. One end is attached and pivoted to the (say, right hand) chassis member and the other end to the (in this case, left hand) end of the axle. The arrangement permits vertical movement of the axle, and articulation, whilst constraining lateral movement relative to the chassis. See 'Anatomy', page 9.2.

Part-time 4x4. See Selectable four-wheel drive, facing page and page 2.2 et seq.

Permanent four-wheel drive. See Full-time 4x4, above and page 2.2 et seq.

Power take-off. Attachment to rear of gearbox for running accessories such as hydraulic pumps or shaft drives to winches and saws.

PTO. See Power take-off above.

Radial ply tyre. A type of tyre construction originated by Michelin in the 1950's and now almost universally adopted by all makers, in which sidewall structural plies run radially out towards the tread instead of criss-cross diagonally. With their thinner, more flexible sidewalls, radial tyres have lower rolling resistance than cross-ply tyres (yielding better fuel consumption) as well as giving longer tread life. They can accommodate the use of low inflation pressures off-road without overheating, due to their flexible sidewalls, but are sometimes more prone to sidewall damage when operating in rocky or stony conditions. Because radial tyres invariably also have a braced tread area of great dimensional stability, they 'track-lay' the tread (like a tank), do not suffer from 'tread shuffle' and so achieve more traction in limiting off-road conditions. See also Cross-ply tyres and diagram, page 9.5.

Ramp angle. A measure of vehicle under-belly clearance or the ability to drive over a sharp ridge or ramp without touching the underside of the vehicle on the obstacle. A short wheelbase vehicle with large wheels will have the smallest ramp angle and best under-belly clearance. See diagram and text page 3.6.

Ramp breakover angle. The fuller title of Ramp angle, above.

Range change. Term sometimes used for the transfer gearbox lever. See Sec 2.3.

Rolling contact – see Continuous rolling contact.

Salt flat. Salt marsh (also known as 'chott' or 'sebkha') of very unreliable consistency and bearing strength found in desert regions and characterised by a top crust of varying thickness and strength with soft salt mud of great depth beneath it. See Sec 4.8.

Sand ladders. A pair of aluminium ladders, about 170 cm long, specially made with rungs closer than normal, to lay beneath the vehicle wheels in soft sand to give grip and flotation. See Sec 5.1.

Sand tracks, sand channels. Generic name often given to any item fulfiling the role of a sand ladder, eg PSP (pierced steel planking), articulated grips. See page 5.3.

Sand tyres. Term often used to mean *desert* tyre – which implies an ability to cope with desert rock and stones as well as sand. These tyres are characterised by tread blocks of a gentle, shouldered profile with no bold, right-angled edges such as a mud tyre would have. Radial construction is far more suited to the low inflation pressures sometimes used in sand. Despite their appearance, smooth 'balloon' or 'aircraft' tyres with circumferential groove treads are far less effective in sand than a radial such as the Michelin XS. See Sec 4.8 and Sec 8.2, Tyres.

Sebkha. See Salt flat above.

Selectable four-wheel drive. Also known as 'part-time 4x4', a four-wheeled vehicle which proceeds normally in two-wheel drive but on which, by means of a lever or button control, four-wheel drive may be selected. It is important to remember that such vehicles in four-wheel drive seldom have the benefit of a centre differential so should not be used on hard roads or firm grippy surfaces in this mode. See Sec 2,1.

Self-centring. The characteristic of steered wheels to resume the straight-ahead position due to castor angle (see Castor angle, page 9.4) when the steering wheel is released. This characteristic can be utilised to enhance safety when driving in deep wheel ruts on slippery ground. See page 4.10 and Steering feel, this page.

Self-levelling suspension. See Levelled suspension.

Sidewall. The external 'walls' of a tyre between the tread and the bead or wheel rim. This area is particularly vulnerable on radial ply tyres to damage in off-road operations from side-swiping sharp rocks. Driver awareness essential. See page 4.34..

Sidewall deflection. Outward movement of the tyre sidewall in the region of the ground contact patch. This is a normal phenomenon but can also be caused by low inflation pressures or hitting a sharp bump with excess speed. It is fundamentally important not to run tyres at less than rec-

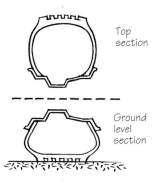

Top section

Ground level section

ommended inflation pressures for given maximum speeds and loads (see Sec 8.2 Tyres). If these limitations are not observed you will exceed the manufacturer's specified limits for sidewall deflection and thus cause overheating and serious damage to the tyre.

Shock loading. In the context of this book, taken to mean the arrest of mechanical motion in an excessively abrupt way or the application of sharp load reversals in such a way as to risk structural failure. For example, the application of a transmission handbrake whilst the vehicle is in motion, the sharp arrest of a spinning wheel on a rock or the forced engagement of low ratio transfer gears can cause unacceptable shock loading of the axle half-shafts. (See Transmission brake, next page.) Engaging diff lock whilst one or more wheel is spinning could also result in severe and damaging shock load to the transmission (See also Mechanical sympathy, page 9.9.)

Small gear lever. Don't be embarrassed if you can't remember the name for the transfer gear lever..!

Snatch tow. A method of recovering a stuck vehicle in which the towing vehicle is in motion before taking up the slack in the tow rope. A potentially very dangerous and extremely specialised procedure demanding special-purpose stretch ropes and precise methods. The chief, and likely, hazards derive from broken ropes or attachments breaking away from the vehicle to hazard bystanders or the vehicles involved. See Recovery – snatch towing, Section 5.3.

'Soft-roader'. Common usage term to describe a 4x4 vehicle not designed for ardu-ous off-road use and thus not equipped with a two-speed transfer gearbox providing low-range gears - see 'Transfer gearbox', next spread. 'Soft roaders' are also usually equipped with auto-engaged 4x4 systems – see page 2.2.

Steering feel. Steering feel is a vital and safety-relevant ingredient of the feedback between vehicle and driver. The communication is achieved almost entirely by assimilating the amount of self-centring or castor action present and how it compares with normal on-road conditions. (See first Castor action and Castor angle above – page 9.4.) It is important for drivers always to be alert to variations in steering feel and to know what may cause them. A very brief summary follows:

1. *Power steering.* On most off-roaders this is power *assisted* steering so feel is retained at all times. In most Land Rovers, for instance, the centre 6°, ie 3° either side of straight ahead, is not power assisted and this aids straight-ahead feel. Be alert to the possibility of inexperienced mechanics having adjusted this out.

2. *In slippery ruts* accurate feel – the correlation between steering command, resistance at the wheel and the behaviour of the vehicle – will be lost because the wheels will not grip the sides of the ruts. Because of this you will find it hard to know exactly which way your wheels are pointing. It is essential to check visually until back on normal ground – see photos page 4.11.

3. *In soft sand*, as noted above, the effective ground contact point may well be *ahead* of the swivel pin axis (see diagram page 9.4) and this can give 'negative castor action' effect – ie a tendency for the wheels to run away to full lock. This will be particularly – and dangerously – apparent when descending the slip face of a sand dune. Grip the steering wheel firmly with both hands and, down a sand-fall, have a marshaller guide you: and watch the marshaller – he is the only one who can tell which way your front wheels are pointing.

4. *Rock or rough ground.* Whilst the steering design and power assistance of most

4x4s is optimised for on- and off-road driving, be aware of the potential for serious kickback when traversing rough ground, rocks and boulders. If the vehicle's steering geometry includes large ground offset (see Ground offset, page 9.7), one wheel sidewalling an obstructive rock will cause excessive sharp kickback to that side. Grip the steering wheel firmly and keep your thumbs outside the rim so that sudden, unexpected kickback does not cause injury.

    5. *Ice, snow, slippery conditions* – on road. This will be well-enough known to experienced 4x2 drivers but is still worth mentioning here since the same laws of physics apply to 4x4s. When grip is at a premium obviously the self-centring of the front wheels will be dramatically diminished – ie castor action will be all but absent – and that heart-sinking 'lightness' of the steering wheel will be experienced. As in a surprising number of off-road situations, really delicate 'finger-tip' steering and 'the midwife's touch' are the order of the day. Plug in the sensory amplifiers.

    Steering lock. Extent to which the steering wheel may be moved to the right or left. 'Full lock' implies movement of the steering wheel as far as it will go, right or left.

    Steering offset. See Ground offset, on page 9.7.

    Survey on foot. Inspect before you drive. See On-foot recce, above and Sec 3.4.

    Swivel pin. Sometimes known as king pin. The axis about which a front wheel pivots in order to effect steering. Swivel pin axes are invariably inclined aft to achieve a castor angle or trail thus providing self-centring – see page 9.4, Castor angle. When viewed from the front, the swivel pin lower end is further outboard than the top end. This inclination helps reduce ground offset and improves steering in other respects. See diagram at page 9.7, Ground offset.

    Swivel pin inclination. See above.

    Synthetic lubricant. Advanced lubricating oils for engines and transmissions demonstrating exceptional stability and film strength. Engines should not be run-in using these oils but once carefully bedded-in

(2000-3000 miles) on mineral oils, wear will be dramatically reduced by use of synthetics. Often blended with mineral or special oils and sold as 'Semi-synthetic'.

    TBN. (Total base number). A characteristic of engine lubricants indicative of the its ability to neutralise the corrosive acid contamination of that oil by high-sulphur diesel fuels encountered overseas. For an indirect-injection diesel aim for 20x the sulphur content, for a direct-injection, 10x. For example, a high sulphur fuel (Turkey, say) at 0.70% demands a TBN of 20x0.7 = 14 for an indirect-injection engine. See pages 7.23 and 7.26 re fuels and the TBN of typical oils.

    'Terrain Response'. A trade name and concept, peculiar to Land Rover vehicles, for tuning automatic transmission change points, throttle response and diff lock settings according to the off-road terrain being negotiated – eg ice and snow, mud and ruts, sand, rocks. Terrain response mode is selectable on a rotary switch. See page 2.22.

    Toe-in / toe-out. Amount by which front wheels, in plan view, are not parallel to each other. This is a designed-in feature that affects handling and steering feel and there are defined limits for each vehicle.

    Traction. In the context of this book the concept of achieving grip between the wheels and the ground without slip, skid or sinkage. See Sections 1.4, 3.2.

    Traction control. This inhibits wheelspin by applying brake to a spinning front or rear wheel and thus enhances traction on ice, snow or in severe off-road conditions. It is usually an automatic function though may be switchable. It utilises ABS sensors for wheel speed determination and brakes the spinning wheel and thus applies, through the axle differential, torque to the stationary wheel. Like ABS, it is especially effective in maintaining control when one side of the vehicle is on a more slippery surface than the other – a so-called 'split-μ' surface (pron: 'split-mu'). Often a dashboard light illuminates when the system is operating. The function is usually inhibited above a certain speed to preclude overheating Can be a good day-to-day aid to off-road traction if the cut-in time is not too extended but in serious, continuous, on-the-limit off-road driving a solid mechanical – and mechanically engaged – diff-lock is better. See pages 2.6 and 3.4.

Tractive effort. The amount of 'pull' exerted by a vehicle as a result of traction.

Trailer nose load. See Nose load, page 9.9 above.

Trailer preponderance. Term sometimes used to denote down-load on the vehicle towing hitch – see Nose load, page 9.9 above and Towing – on-road, Sec 4.1.

Trailing link / leading link. These are suspension components (see large diagram, page 9.2) that locate a coil- or air-sprung axle fore and aft relative to the chassis, allowing it to rise and fall as required whilst also transmitting braking loads and thrust from the wheels. Used in conjunction with a laterally locating Panhard rod (or an A-frame) to locate an axle totally and associated with what is often termed 'five-link' suspension.

Transfer gear lever. The 'small gear lever', in the cab next to the main gear lever. It controls whether the transmission is in 'high range' or 'low range' in the transfer box – and in selectable 4x4 vehicles, whether 4x2 or 4x4 is in use. The same lever often controls the engagement of the centre diff lock. Many 4x4s now have an electrically operated, switch-controlled range change

Transfer gearbox. Originally the name implied the transfer of power from the main gearbox to the front axle as well as the rear axle on a four-wheel drive vehicle. In many off-roaders a two-speed transfer box is fitted, thus providing low range gears as well as high range. Here the transfer gearbox has the additional role of permitting power from the main gearbox to go to the axles at normal 1:1 gearing (high range) or geared down, usually by around 2:1 (low range). So-called 'soft-roaders' usually do not have a two-speed transfer gearbox. See diagram, page 1.10.

Transmission brake. The handbrake on Land Rover Defenders and other early models, traditionally, operates through a single large brake drum on the rear propeller shaft at the point where it leaves the transfer gearbox and is thus called a transmission brake. By doing this, when the vehicle is in four-wheel drive (current Land Rover products have permanent 4x4, but early models did not) it was in effect a handbrake on all four wheels, To be safe using the transmission brake on a slope off-road, the centre diff lock should be engaged. Even then, there are conditions of near-limits articulation where the axle differentials will permit the handbrake to fail in its primary function; *be sure all four wheels are firmly on the ground*. The same transmission brake principle is used on 4x4 Bedford trucks. On any vehicle it should be used as a parking brake only and should *never be operated whilst the vehicle is in motion* except in emergency.

Transmission wind-up. Read first 'Centre differential', page 9.4. A 4x4 with no centre differential (ie a 'Type 1', selectable 4x4 – see page 2.2) or one driven with the centre diff locked (ie in both cases the front and rear propeller shafts locked together) is unable to accommodate the small differences in distance normally travelled by the front wheels compared to the rear wheels. The diff-lock ensures both propeller shafts rotate exactly the same amount despite the small differences in distance actually travelled. This results in some wheel slip and scuff which, on loose ground, can take place without any harm. On hard roads, however, the superior wheel grip makes it difficult for the wheels to slip much and in the process of trying to do so considerable torsional stress builds up in the transmission. This is known as transmission wind-up and can sometimes exert so much stress that the diff-lock gears (or the selectors for engaging 4x4 from 4x2) will not disengage when so selected. You will also sense very heavy steering. If this occurs due to your forgetting to de-select diff-lock (or four-wheel drive) on hard ground and the diff lock or 4x4 lever will not disengage, the solution is to reverse the vehicle some distance until the selectors are free (depress the clutch and give the lever a sharp thump) and/or the diff-lock warning light extinguishes. (Note, despite there being no centre diff there either, none of this applies to a 'Type 2' (p 2.2 diagram) auto-engage, 'soft roader' since the front-rear prop shafts can accommodate some slip.)

Tyre sidewall markings. Details of all information inscribed on the sidewalls of tyres is contained on page 8.17.

Unladen. Vehicle carrying full fuel tank, driver but no payload or other load – see Kerb weight, page 9.8.

Viscous coupling unit (VCU). Imagine two shafts facing each other end-to end. On the end of one shaft is, conceptually, a jam jar, internally splined – which overlaps the second shaft so that one shaft (externally splined) is inside the hollow end of the other. A classic viscous coupling (VC) between two shafts consists of interleaved vanes, alternate vanes being splined to each shaft. So vane 1 is splined to the 'jam jar'; and vane 2 is splined to the shaft inside the 'jam jar'. Special silicone fluid takes up the space between the vanes. A VC has the paradoxical characteristic that when one shaft moves at a markedly different speed to its neighbour, the viscous fluid is 'stirred' and very soon locks the vanes together, inhibiting relative movement and causing both shafts to move as one. A typical application for a VC is to engage 4x4 on a front-wheel drive vehicle when the front wheels spin due to poor traction conditions. The difference in rotational speed between front prop shaft and the rear prop shaft causes the VC to lock-up and transfer drive to the rear axle as well. The lock is not 100%.

Viscous coupling pre-load. In Land Rover's first generation Freelanders (and Fiat's Ducato van before that) with a VC between front and rear prop shaft, slightly different front and rear axle ratios caused the prop shafts to turn at slightly different speeds even without obvious front wheel spin so the VC is in a part-locked condition all the time and transferring some power – about 10% – to the rear axle. Neat.

Wading plugs. Applicable to older Land Rovers. See page 4.36.

Wheel movement. Phrase generally used in the context of maximum available vertical suspension movement at each wheel. This is of major importance to an off-roader in the pursuit of maximum axle articulation (see Articulation, page 9.3 *et al*). Long-travel coil springs are the classic solution to this pioneered by early Range Rovers but associated body roll displeased mainly on-road users and roll-inhibiting devices like anti-roll bars are now limiting axle movement relative to the body. Manufacturers are using traction control in the off-road case to deal with any wheelspin resulting from more limited wheel movement on very uneven ground – see panel, page 2.6 'Solutions to roll control', and also page .2.7.

Wheel-slide. See above Discontinuity of rolling contact, page 9.6 and diagram, page 3.4. A condition in which one or more wheels slide over a slippery surface rather than rolling over it; can be provoked by brake lock-up or excessive engine braking – for which also see Sec 6.4.

Wheelspin. See Discontinuity of rolling contact, page 9.6 and diagram, page 3.4. A condition in which a stationary or moving vehicle has power applied to the transmission in conditions of poor grip and one or more wheels spins without associated forward motion (or rearward if in reverse). See Gentle right foot, Sec 3.2 dealing with control of throttle and brake.

Zero offset. Refers to steering geometry – see 'Ground offset' p 9.7 diagram.

9.2 Index

Ingredients of this picture:
1. Astronomical data: moonrise time and azimuth.
2. Camera, film, tripod.
3. Reliable 4x4 positioned at 24°27'N, 04°24'E.